The
Pressure Cooker
Gourmet

The
Pressure Cooker
Gourmet

225 Recipes for Great-Tasting,

Long-Simmered Flavors

in Just Minutes

Victoria Wise

The Harvard Common Press
Boston, Massachusetts

The Harvard Common Press
535 Albany Street
Boston, Massachusetts 02118
www.harvardcommonpress.com

Printed in the United States of America

Printed on acid-free paper

The Library of Congress has cataloged the hardcover edition as follows:

Wise, Victoria.
    The pressure cooker gourmet : 225 recipes for great-tasting,
  long-simmered flavors in just minutes / Victoria Wise.
       p.   cm.
    Includes index.
    ISBN 1-55832-200-0 (cl : alk. paper)
      1. Pressure cookery.   I. Title.
  TX840.P7.W57 2003
  641.5'87–dc21

                                   2002007422

ISBN-13: 978-1-55832-201-1
ISBN-10: 1-55832-201-9

Special bulk-order discounts are available on this and other Harvard
Common Press books. Companies and organizations may purchase books
for premiums or resale, or may arrange a custom edition, by contacting the
Marketing Director at the address above.

10 9 8

Cover design by Night & Day Design
Cover photograph by Alexandra Grablewski
Interior design by rlf design

for Martha Casselman

dear friend, super agent, and lovely lady

Contents

Acknowledgments

There's no way I could ever close a book without offering thanks to my husband, Rick Wise, and my son, Jenan Wise. They are the ones who suffer through any mistakes of the day and clap when it's all going well. I also offer special thanks to my longtime friend and sometime co-author, Susanna Hoffman, who has been completely generous in allowing me to redo for pressure cooking some of the recipes she and I initially did together for other cookbooks. This volume would not have been complete without them. I thank and will be eternally grateful to Berkeley Bowl Marketplace, the likes of which is not to be found anywhere. Whatever whim or gleam I ever have of a recipe idea from anywhere around the world, I head right there and am pretty sure to find the freshest, oddest, most seasonal ingredients to satisfy the notion or inspire another. And all the while, I can learn from the other shoppers, people from every culture I can think of, as I observe and talk to them over okra or cherries, hefting and tapping melons and pineapples, discussing the look of meat or fish offerings, deciding and wondering over the choys or bin of fresh corn for a price you can't resist, fingering the latest lush-from-nearby-farms tomatoes. That's truly inspiring.

Finally, as always, I am indebted to Susan Derecskey, freelance editor, whom I call "my mind backup" for all the things she knows and for keeping me focused and on track with every recipe.

*"Perfecting a dish
is a lifetime work."*
—Anonymous *mère de cuisine*

Introduction

When I was a young and eager amateur, chomping at the bit to explore the whole world of culinary possibilities, it seemed an outrageous idea that there would ever be time to return to any one dish, like re-reading a novel that even though much beloved must be set on the shelf, half-digested, in order to taste more and other literature. My outlook has changed dramatically over the years. Though I still find no time to re-read books, I do redo what has become a huge repertoire of recipes, sometimes to perfect them in their original but more often to play with their adaptability to other cooking techniques. And so, I have investigated what difference chopping in a food processor or pureeing in one has on the outcome of a dish; how a microwave rendition of salmon turns out differently from a grilled one; how beets boiled on the stove top vary from those oven roasted. For this book, it is the once customary, somewhat forgotten, new again pressure cooker that has taken my attention and piqued my curiosity. How can it enhance cooking in our modern kitchens? What can it do well and what not so well? How does it fit in with other appliances that make up our modern *batterie de cuisine?*

I intended the quest to be thorough—a fact-finding, precision project. For instance, it is clear the pressure cooker is no good at all for a fresh tossed salad, but it is highly useful for getting ready any grains or dried legumes that easily might be turned into a salad. Though it doesn't turn out crispy fried chicken or seared beef steak, it's a genius at rapidly rendering cut-up poultry and beef into melting tenderness. Pressure cooking beautifully handles large cuts, such as a salmon roast, lamb shanks, chicken or rabbit quarters, a pork shoulder roast.

And, you can brown meats, large cuts or small, right in the pressure cooker before locking on the lid to braise or stew them in the same pot. There's more: Every cook I know of who has delved into pressure cooking touts it for risotto. After several performance tests, I must say I agree. In fact, I have become convinced that, besides wok steaming or stir-frying, pressure cooking is the way to go for many a one-pot, quick-stop, homemade meal. It is also, hands down, the most expeditious way for basic preparations of most grains, legumes, and root vegetables.

Along the way, lots of new ideas pop up: Curries and chutneys become so easy, you might start thinking Indian style or Thai style for your entrée on a regular basis. Have a clambake in your own dining room without having to jury-rig a steamer. Put together a simmered pasta sauce in the time it takes to boil the pasta on the adjacent burner and everyone is happily chowing down in less than half an hour. For dessert, sweet corn pudding soaked in corncob syrup, chocolate almond pudding cake, and the perennial to-die-for cheesecakes are all within the pressure cooker's capabilities. Also, lots of old-fashioned ideas surface: braised oxtails, lamb tongue, veal breast that used to be part of Sunday family fare become feasible with the aid of the pressure cooker, which manages to turn out long-simmered flavors in so little time.

Not only that, with the time saving, the pressure cooker makes room for creative fun on the sidelines. While it hums away, you can turn your attention to elevating a plain bowl of grain, like steamed rice or bulgur, into a dish to remember by putting together a topping of pea sprouts or crispy shallot rings, setting out a small bowl of a special spice blend to sprinkle on, or assembling an assortment of garnishes that turn a mound of perfect tamales or Asian dumplings into something even more lip-smacking. I consider such embellishments and finishing touches part of what makes a meal enjoyable and part of what makes the making of the meal enjoyable for the cook. The pressure cooker allows time to indulge such whimsies.

In this volume you will find many of my old favorites culled from thirty years of professional cooking and many new favorites I discovered and developed in exploring the art and craft of pressure cooking. You might say my mission has been to encourage the novice cook; cheerlead the harried mom or dad, world-weary at the end of the day; and give an impetus to those who would yawn at cooking dinner tonight. In other words, I hope this book turns the joy of cookbook *reading* into the pleasure of home *cooking* by making it as seductive and easy as possible to move from the chair to the stove.

How to Use This Book

Each chapter contains beginner recipes, easy and uncomplicated for those who need to dip a toe in the water before plunging in for the big swim. Each chapter also includes pressure cooking tips, general cooking tips and techniques, and stories and conversation that express my lifelong passion for food and cooking. I've endeavored to make all the recipes, beginner or more complex, as close to one step as possible, though I do include the initial step of browning meats where it makes a difference for the taste and appearance of the dish.

The chapters begin with soups, a winner of a topic for pressure cooking. From there, I move to "main considerations," a collection of meat, poultry, and seafoods that braise or stew into a delectable meal on their own. The vegetable chapter includes vegetables I consider excellent candidates for pressure cooking. There are also several mixed and stuffed vegetable dishes because I love them, they're good family fare, and the pressure cooker does a primo job of cooking them. Grains and legumes make up a large part of the book. In fact, when I began, I had placed them together, but as I developed the recipes and contents, it became clear there were so many of each, they should be divided into two chapters. For each grain and legume, there is a basic recipe to serve as an easy launch for those who are unfamiliar with pressure cooking and also to give a guideline for those who have creative ideas of their own but would like the facts, please, just the facts, as groundwork.

About the Timing Instructions in the Recipes

All recipes include the time for bringing to pressure because that's part of the cooking. It can't be standardized. For instance, if the pot and its ingredients are already hot, it will take less time to come to pressure, whereas if you start with an unheated pot and ingredients, it will take longer, so each recipe is different.

All recipes allow time for the pressure to subside without any "quick cool down" that would require carrying a hot, steamy pot to the sink to run cool water over it. That's too cumbersome and somewhat dangerous. Instead, I have developed the recipes to allow a "natural" cool-down time as part of the cooking. That's what the "remove from the heat and let sit for *x* minutes" means. At the end of that time, you can safely use the slow release mechanism and, if there is still pressure, you can hasten the process by gently letting the steam escape in stages. Be sure to have the vent pointed away from your face as you do this.

Unlike for other appliances or cooking methods, I do not give an *until* instruction for the actual cooking time because there's no way to look in the pot without going through the process of cooling it down, and that would completely skew the given cooking time. In other, words, for this step, you need to set your timer.

Please note that if you would like to change a recipe's yield, the cooking time given can remain the same. However, there will be some time difference for bringing to pressure, and also some variance in how long it takes for the pressure to subside.

Minding the Pot

Working through and making precise-as-possible so many recipes led me to a certain flexibility, the kind that takes you a little away from hard-and-fast rules and a little into the realm of this-needs-this-now. Even though pressure cooking might seem automatic, "just bring to pressure and set the timer" it isn't. The pressure cooker is a helpmate, not a personal, in-house cook. There are two important things to watch after the ingredients come to pressure: the pressure gauge and the heat level under the pot. Each brand of cooker has a different style gauge; follow the manufacturer's instructions about when it is up and when it is over-up, or you may be surprised with the pressure cooker's version of boiling over, namely spewing steam through the steam escape vent in order to lower the pressure. That means you may need to adjust the heat, for instance down from medium-high to medium, to maintain the optimum pressure, just as you would with other stove-top cooking.

The Fear Factor

In discussing the topic of pressure cooking with people, two opposing notions have been expressed, often at the same time. They are: "Yeah, I love the idea of pressure cooking, having quick meals for the family," and "Gosh, aren't those things dangerous!"

Actually, there's a third reaction, usually sentimentally expressed: "I remember we had one of those when I was a kid."

Modern pressure cookers accentuate the yeah, eliminate the nay, and update the nostalgia. Here's how and why:

First, and most important, there's no way you can blow the top off a modern pressure cooker and wind up with spinach on the ceiling and fear in your heart. State-of-the-art modern pressure cookers don't allow that. There are two reasons: The design is largely based on a way for the pressure cooker to release excess steam in two ways, through the steam vent and also via the steam release dial or lever. Second, the pot simply won't budge to open until the pressure is at zero. What does that mean practically speaking? It means, though the cooker may whine, moan, or groan, you're safe; it's telling you, check me, I may need adjusting. In case you aren't present to heed that call, it will hiss and spew through the steam vent until it fixes the pressure problem itself. You, however, will have to fix any overflow mess yourself when it's done. I can't salve that with comforting words; it's just a clean-up job to do. However, I will take the opportunity to repeat the caution: *Always position the steam vent toward the back wall, away from your face, during cooking.*

The what-if-anyway? factor If the pressure builds too high for the moment and the cooker starts to send out sizzling steam, turn off the heat and wait until it calms down. Then turn on the heat again and, when the pressure has come back to level, adjust the heat so it cooks more gently. Continue counting the cook time all along. The interruption will not ultimately affect the timing of the dish.

The herniated gasket The first time I noticed that the gasket was poking out of one of the side vents during cooking, I gasped and thought, oh, no, it needs replacing already and the whole recipe needs redoing. Not so. That's part of the state-of-the-art modern pressure cookers. I can't tell you why scientifically speaking, but it's good.

Equipment

The recipes in this book have been tested primarily with three different brands of 6- to 8-quart pressure cookers, although I have put to the test a 4-quart cooker, and a cute, 3-quart sauté-pan-shaped cooker. Most of the cookers are the streamlined modern version sort with pressure gauges that pop up and down to indicate the pressure level. One is of the more old-fashioned, jiggle-top type, but with the modern blow-proof design. All are highest-quality, heavy-gauge stainless steel. Once I learned the quirks and small differences among them, I would be hard-pressed to choose. One spits a little when it's at high pressure, one hums when it comes to pressure, another hisses as it cooks. Another sounds like a one-man rock and roll band. I came to regard these variations as personality differences; all are safe and all cook well.

Ease of use I must admit, figuring out how properly to seat the lid on the pot was one of the most exasperating small skills to learn for all the pressure cookers I used. That's partly because I had no experience and partly because it's a precise fit that must be so in order to lock together the lid and pot for safety and good cooking purposes. However, as with all such simple mechanics, the mantra is: Don't force it. When it's a fit, it's smooth and easy. I found no difference of ease or difficulty among the pots I tried—it was patience and three or four go-rounds for each kind.

Cost Ounce for ounce and quart for quart, the price difference is insignificant among the cookers I use, namely, $100 to $150. That may at first be a shocking sticker price for a pot. But it's not; in fact, it's a downright bargain when you consider what you get: quality cookware that is useful not only for pressure cooking but for any other stove-top use you might want, from boiling up the water for pasta to reducing down a pot of jam.

Most convenient size(s) In the world of "if wishes were kings," and I were purchasing pressure cookers for the first time, I would choose two, namely:

- An 8-quart pot. For normal family use, including soups or stews or risottos for four to six and the occasional pot roast or brisket for eight or so, including guests. Also for making individual custards that need stacking. This size is appropriate for making all of the recipes in the book.

- A 3-quart, sauté-pan shape. I'm enamored of it because its shape and size suit cooking small amounts of, for instance, a vegetable or shrimp or clams for two or three, and its handsome look makes it stove top to table worthy for casual family dining. It has the added advantage that it's easy to transfer the cooked food from pot to plate without having to raise your elbows high and use long tongs or risk mashing or mangling such ingredients as asparagus spears or steamed bananas.

In addition, a 12-quart or larger pressure cooker comes in handy for special tasks, like preparing tomatoes to can or tomato sauces to store in the freezer or cooking up a clambake or gumbo for a crowd.

Backup Tools

For pressure cooking, as with any cooking, backup tools are key.

Kitchen timer I cannot emphasize enough that a kitchen timer is part of the process of pressure cooking. Unlike a microwave, stove-top pressure cookers don't have built-in timers. You need to have a separate one to clock the cooking time so it all turns out right.

Food processor I simply don't chop piles of vegetables any other way except for the few dishes that, for elegance, require the look of uniform pieces chopped by hand.

Knives A chef's knife with an 8-inch or 10-inch blade, depending on what feels comfortable in your hand, for doing most of the cut and chop work.

A straight blade 4-inch paring knife and a curved blade 6-inch paring knife, for peeling and slicing things like garlic and shallots.

An 8- to 10-inch serrated knife for cutting bread, neatly slicing tomatoes, and whatever other tasks you find for it once you know what it can do.

A curved boning knife for those cooks who sometimes bone a chicken breast,

Safety Considerations

In pressure cooking, as in microwave cooking or any other closed pot cooking on the stove top or in the oven, a lot of steam is generated. Always use terry cloth hot pads or dry terry cloth kitchen towels for lifting off the lid and always open it away from your face, taking care to keep your wrists and elbows out of the way too.

It is also important always to position the steam release vent away from your face both during cooking and when releasing any remaining steam at the end of the sit time.

Creating a Sling to Lift Out the Dish

Many pressure cookers come with a trivet with a handle, presumably so you can lift out the trivet and its contents when the cooking is done. This works fine for dishes like steamed scallops where the load is light and the trivet won't tilt and wobble when it's lifted out. If the trivet does not have a handle and the load is heavy (as with most dishes), there needs to be a Plan B.

Take a length of aluminum foil long enough to fit under and around the dish you are cooking plus a lot of extra length to reach up over the dish and twist at the top. Fold the foil lengthwise, leaving it wide enough to brace the trivet and make a strong sling. Set the foil sling under the trivet, bringing up its ends over the trivet. Place the dish you are cooking on the trivet. Twist together the ends of the foil to make a kind of basket handle over the dish. Use this handle to lower in and then lift out the trivet when the steam has subsided.

A note of caution: Nifty as the contraption is, the aluminum foil sling still requires care in lifting the dish out of the pot to avoid being burned by escaping steam or hot water splashes.

And here's a Plan C: For foods such as the large salmon roast that need to be lifted out intact and left undisturbed while they set up (see page 155), cheesecloth is the perfect solution. Enclose the food in a double layer of cheesecloth long enough to wrap around the food with several inches to spare at either end to serve as handles. Similarly, for a single large soufflé dish or glass bowl, enfold it with cheesecloth that has enough length to gather into a topknot tie and use it to lift out the dish when the steam has subsided.

The cheesecloth improv could also work for individual custard cups that are definitely tricky to lift out safely while they're still hot, but it's a fuss to wrap each one. I prefer to wait until the pot has cooled a bit and then use terry cloth kitchen towels, *not* hot pads, to grasp the cups and remove them one by one. None of the dishes in this book, specifically the custards, suffers from a bit of extra cool-off time.

cut up a duck or rabbit, separate the bone from the meat on a pork butt roast or beef chuck blade.

Spoons A slotted spoon, a Chinese-style strainer spoon, two sizes of ladles, and several different size wooden spoons are basic implements for functioning easily in the kitchen.

Tongs One of the most useful tools that shouldn't be forgotten. With tongs, you can extend your hand without burning your fingers with a mere pinch of its two prongs to pick up or turn over hot things. I suggest having a short pair of 12 inches and another of 18 inches for different jobs.

Colanders Have at least four of the plastic basket kind in different sizes. They're inexpensive, come in colors, last forever, and don't clank when you use them.

Microwave oven From toasting nuts and coconut flakes to melting chocolate and butter to wilting greens for a stuffing, and many more prep tasks, there's no way in the cooking of today that the microwave doesn't fit in. It's a part of the modern *batterie de cuisine*.

Hot pads The things with cute pictures on one side and slippery surfaces on the back or cute pictures on both sides are not what you should use for cooking. If you like the art, hang them on the wall, but don't use them for picking up a hot pot. For serious business, purchase large terry cloth hot pads. Even the gorgeous, all-cotton designer kitchen towels are not meant for handling hot pots, though they might do a nice job drying glasses and plates. The only towel for function and safely handling hot things in the kitchen is a thick, white terry cloth towel, and, *very important*, the towel must be dry. If you try to grasp a hot pot with a wet towel, you risk a steam burn when the heat of the pot and the moisture of the towel meet in the middle of your hand. The plain white terry cloth towels are not expensive if you shop the bed and bath or hardware stores—have a good stack of them on hand.

Aluminum foil For covering custard cups and creating a sling handle to lower in and lift out various steamed dishes.

Optional tools A 1-quart soufflé dish, 7-inch springform pan, and 7-inch Chinese steamer basket to fit inside the pressure cooker are optional but useful items to have for puddings, cheesecakes, and steamed dishes of all sorts.

Finishing Touches:
Simple Ways to Glamorize a Dish

The two basic elements to consider in the presentation of a dish are the way it's put on the plate and its finishing touches. These are the details that turn your cooking effort from plunked-down food to an enticement for eye and nose, satisfaction for the palate, and satisfaction for yourself.

Layout

Layout is the first consideration in expressing that the dish you are serving is worthy of the endeavor to make it (that means both family and company fare). A pot of hot soup or steaming rice from the stove top to table might be all that's needed for ensuring that home is here. Then again, if you would like to serve a pretty plate, the soup can be ladled into individual bowls; a stew can be dished out onto a platter with attention to its individual elements; a plate of vegetables or bowl of good-for-you grain can be festooned with colorful edibles to lift it above the ordinary.

Garnishes

The garnish is the second consideration, and the saving grace of many a dish that didn't turn out exactly as you saw it in your mind's eye. Even if the taste outcome of the cooking is good, to make the dish picture-perfect, keep in mind:

Color If a dish is looking boringly monochromatic and needs a color boost, contrasting hues are an easy fix. Think impressionistically: Cézanne vivid green, Van Gogh brilliant yellow, Monet subdued orange, Goya black.

For color from the red/orange/yellow spectrum:

Diced tomato, red bell pepper, or carrot
Pureed yam (see page 190) as a small side garnish
Ground spices, turmeric, or saffron stirred into the dish or
    paprika sprinkled over the top
Citrus zest, lemon or orange

For vivid greens, the choices are virtually endless. The favorites I rely on are:

Parsley
Dill
Chives
Scallion greens, finely chopped or slivered
Fennel fronds
Basil
Cilantro sprigs
Watercress leaves

For a potpourri of color, edible flower petals (those that have been grown pesticide-free):

Herb flowers of almost any sort, especially rosemary, sage, and thyme
Onion, chive, or garlic flowers, chopped
Mustard flowers of mizuna, broccoli, turnips, or radish or arugula that is bolting to seed
Nasturtium petals
Rose petals
Marigold petals
Chrysanthemum petals
Violets for blue

For a darker accent, blacks are available as:

Cracked black pepper
Black sesame seeds
Salted and fermented black beans
Caviar

Texture Crispy, crunchy toppings add texture and taste appeal. Depending on the dish, I use:

Sesame seeds, toasted (see page 41)
Sunflower seeds and roasted pumpkin seeds
Almonds, slivers or slices, toasted (see page 41)
Peanuts, chopped and toasted (see page 41)
Pine nuts, toasted (see page 41) or untoasted
Coconut flakes, toasted (see page 218)
Fried garlic slivers (see page 153)

Crispy Shallot Rings (page 54)
Crispy Mai Fun Noodles (page 57)
A lightly salted raw vegetable slaw, such as fennel, cabbage, daikon, radish, or turnip
Scallion brushes

Taste boosts Sometimes, a dish needs a bit of relish on the side to boost the taste. Try:

Kumquat and Red Chile Pepper Relish (page 303)
Red Bell Pepper Marmalade (page 302)
Cranberry Sauce with Ginger and Tangerine (page 299)
Plums Pickled in Port Wine and Balsamic Vinegar (page 311)
Spiced Peaches, an Old-Fashioned Favorite (page 309)
Mango and Dried Plum Chutney (page 304)

Yesterday's bread Leftover bread is one of the finest finishing touches. Peasants on the penny to chefs in toques know not to let go of a crumb of precious bread unless it's kindly given to the birds. In the kitchen it can be used every which way, and in this volume you will find:

Fried bread cubes (see page 16)
Herbed Croutons (page 25)
Cheese Toasts (page 31)
Duck Liver Crostini (page 143)
Crumbs, bread or cracker, toasted (see page 187)

In addition, yesterday's bread can be the base of savory and sweet dishes. See:

Bread Pudding with Apples and Fennel Seeds (page 334)
Double-Thrift Savory Bread Pudding with Lettuce, Onion, and Cheese (page 325)

Splendid Soups

Soup has been part of every cuisine since man acquired fire and then figured out how to create a vessel to hold liquid and ingredients that could cook together over the fire. Sometimes the solids are more significant than the liquid, and such preparations are usually called stews. Sometimes the liquid, usually a flavorful, premade broth but sometimes water, preponderates, and these preparations are usually called soups. The distinction, however, eventually blurs because a stew can be soupy and a soup can be stewy. The dishes in this chapter run the gamut from broth and delicate consommé to hearty-enough-to-be-a-meal almost-stews. Your pressure cooker can handle any one of them with good-as-gold results. Not only that, the energy-saving aspect of pressure cooking is important in modern times. Consider how much stove-top heat is required to bring a pot of soup to a boil or how long it takes to simmer a pot of soup into divine goodness. When a soup is cooked in a third to half less time than usual, less thermal energy is required. The pressure cooker serves well to make soups, quick cooked or long simmered, that bring the pleasure of a steaming bowl of food to your home table tonight.

Splendid Soups

◇ **Beef Broth** *I suspect the impracticality of making rich beef stock—the expense, the volume, the time—contributed immensely to the decline of classic French cooking and the rise of the fresh-is-best, reduced-juices style of saucing. By and large, that's a healthful and practical trend. But, ah, those demi-glace sauces, rich onion soups, and hearty stews. . . . For a dish that is not just a mere shadow of itself, the pressure cooker can help with the making of the beef broth. It's quick enough to make the broth almost on the spur of the moment and you don't have to make so much at a time. Still, the expense is not insignificant: Meaty bones are the only way to achieve a fine beef broth, and they're pricey by the pound.*

Makes 12 cups

2 pounds beef shank
2 pounds soup bones
½ medium-size yellow or white onion, coarsely chopped
1 small carrot, coarsely chopped
1 rib celery with top, coarsely chopped
1 large clove garlic, halved
6 sprigs fresh flat-leaf parsley
2 sprigs fresh thyme, or ½ teaspoon dried
1 bay leaf
½ cup dry white wine
12 cups water

Beef Broth Tips

- The step of roasting the bones first is important for obtaining a well-colored, flavorful broth.
- Salt is never added to beef broth until making the dish for which it is intended.
- If storing the broth, leave the fat on the top until just before using; it rises to the top, congeals, and helps seal out air, thus extending the storage life of the broth.

1. Preheat the oven to 350°F. Spread the shank and soup bones on a baking sheet and roast in the oven for 30 minutes.

2. Transfer to the pressure cooker and add the remaining ingredients. Lock on the lid and bring to pressure over high heat, 17 to 18 minutes. Reduce the heat to medium–low and cook for 60 minutes. Remove the cooker from the heat and let sit for 20 minutes to finish cooking.

3. With the steam vent pointed away from your face, gently release any remaining pressure. Let cool enough to handle. Drain the broth through a fine-mesh strainer into a bowl. Discard the solids and let the broth cool completely. Spoon the fat off the top and use right away. Or store in the refrigerator, covered, for up to 10 days or in the freezer for up to 6 months. Remove the fat before using.

◇ Consommé à la Madrilène

Larousse Gastronomique *lists six pages of soups and broths. Of them all, Consommé à la Madrilène, a clear broth with tomatoes, luxurious and uncomplicated at the same time, is one of my favorites. Instead of the specified chicken broth, I use beef broth when I have it homemade and embellish the bowls with tiny fried bread cubes and a sprinkling of fresh thyme.*

Makes 4 servings

Eight ½-inch-thick slices French bread,
    preferably day-old baguette
Olive oil, for frying
5 cups Beef Broth (page 15) or Chicken Broth (page 18)
2 medium-size tomatoes, peeled (see page 24),
    seeded, and pureed (see Note), or 2 canned tomatoes,
    seeded and pureed
1 teaspoon salt
1 teaspoon chopped fresh thyme, for garnish

1. Cut the bread slices as evenly as possible into ¼-inch cubes. Pour olive oil into a large, heavy skillet to a depth of ¼ inch. Heat over medium-high heat until beginning to smoke. Add the bread cubes and fry, turning frequently, until golden all around, 3 to 5 minutes. Transfer to paper towels to drain.

2. Combine the broth, tomato puree, and salt in a microwave-safe bowl or medium-size saucepan. Heat on high in the microwave or over medium-high heat on the stove top until steaming but not boiling.

3. Ladle the consommé into individual bowls. Garnish with the croutons and thyme and serve right away.

Note: Traditionally, the tomato would be pureed through a food mill or fine sieve. In today's world, a food processor works just fine, though it doesn't give as fine a puree.

Pasta in Brodo

Pasta in brodo *means pasta in broth in Italian. It can take many forms, from substantial, with other elements included, to quite simple, as here, in a warming consommé to begin a cozy autumn meal. The broth could as well be chicken or vegetable.*

Makes 4 servings

5 cups Beef Broth (page 15)
1 teaspoon salt
2 ounces angel hair or vermicelli pasta, broken up
2 teaspoons chopped fresh flat-leaf parsley, for garnish
Several fine shreds lemon zest, for garnish
½ cup freshly grated parmesan cheese, for serving

1. Bring the broth and salt to a boil in a medium-size saucepan. Add the pasta and cook until *al dente* according to the package instructions.

2. Ladle the broth and pasta into individual bowls. Garnish each with parsley and zest. Serve right away with the cheese on the side.

◇ Japanese-Inspired Beef Consommé with Tofu and Scallion Slivers

With a good and healthful homemade beef broth on hand, a spur-of-the moment, restoring consommé or elegant start to a special meal is but a few slices away.

Makes 4 servings

5 cups Beef Broth (page 15)
2 tablespoons low-sodium soy sauce
½ teaspoon salt
4 ounces soft tofu, cut into 4 equal-size cubes
1 scallion (white and light green parts only),
   cut into 3-inch-long slivers, for garnish

1. Combine the broth, soy sauce, and salt in a microwave-safe bowl or medium-size saucepan. Heat on high in the microwave or over medium-high heat on the stove top until steaming hot but not boiling.

2. Place 1 tofu cube in the bottom of each of 4 bowls. Divide the broth among the bowls and garnish each with scallion slivers. Serve right away.

◇ Chicken Broth

There are some distinct advantages to making chicken broth in the pressure cooker. First, there's no volume lost to evaporation during cooking. Second, the broth comes out clear, not cloudy, because there's not a chance of its boiling too hard in a moment of inattention. Third, rather than waiting an hour and a half, you have a delicious broth in less than an hour.

Makes about 10 cups

3 pounds chicken parts, such as backs, necks, and wing tips
1 medium-size carrot, coarsely chopped
1 small yellow or white onion, coarsely chopped
1 celery rib with top, coarsely chopped
6 sprigs fresh flat-leaf parsley
2 sprigs fresh thyme, or ¼ teaspoon dried
10 cups water

1. Place all the ingredients in the pressure cooker. Lock on the lid and bring to pressure over high heat, about 18 minutes. Reduce the heat to medium-low and cook for 20 minutes. Remove from the heat and let sit for 15 minutes to finish cooking.

2. With the steam vent pointed away from your face, gently release any remaining pressure. Let cool enough to handle.

3. Drain the broth through a fine-mesh sieve into a bowl. Discard the solids. Let the broth cool completely. Skim the fat off the top and use right away. Or refrigerate, covered, for up to 10 days or freeze for up to 6 months. Remove the fat before using.

◌ Consommé Belleview with Clams à la Michael Field

Chef Michael Field, who was also an acclaimed pianist even as he turned his attention to writing cookbooks, modestly leaves hanging the question of whether or not he was the inspired cook for this recipe. For sure, it's a slam dunk of a delicious dish if you have homemade, pressure-cooked chicken broth and some fresh clams. The ginger seasoning and pea sprout garnish, in place of his lemon zest and parsley, is my interpretation of another way to vary the surprises and delights of the dish.

Makes 4 servings

1 pound Manila or cherrystone clams, rinsed
5 cups Chicken Broth (page 18)
One 1-inch piece fresh ginger, cut into 4 pieces
Salt to taste
1 cup pea sprouts, for garnish

1. Combine the clams, broth, and ginger in the pressure cooker. Lock on the lid and bring to pressure over high heat, about 6 minutes. Remove from the heat and let sit for 6 minutes to finish cooking.

2. With the steam vent pointed away from your face, gently release any remaining pressure. Lift out the clams and ginger. Discard the ginger and remove the meat from the clam shells.

3. Add the salt to the broth and reheat it if necessary. Ladle into individual bowls. Divide the clam meat among the bowls, garnish with the pea sprouts, and serve right away.

"Every so often an inspired cook will throw together a couple of unlikely ingredients and the result will be a culinary triumph."

—Michael Field in *Michael Field's Cooking School*

Vegetable Broth

Making an excellent vegetable broth is not difficult, as long as you keep regard for the ingredients and proportion of vegetables to liquid. There must be enough vegetables, not necessarily picture-perfect ones but still fresh, so they barely float in the water. Not enough veggies and the broth will be too thin. Also, it's important not to cook the vegetables so long that they start to disintegrate in the liquid, or your broth will become murky and stale tasting. Following is a formula for making a clear vegetable broth that's herbaceous and rich enough to serve as a bouillon or use as a base for vegetarian soups. I always add the salt during the cooking for vegetable broth, unlike other broths; it seems to make a better brew. Makes 10 cups

4 medium-size tomatoes, coarsely chopped
1 medium-size yellow or white onion, quartered
2 large cloves garlic, halved

2 ribs celery with tops, coarsely chopped

2 medium-size carrots, cut into ½-inch-thick slices

4 large chard leaves, very coarsely chopped, well washed, and drained

2 medium-size zucchinis or other summer squash, cut into 1-inch chunks

12 pea pods

1 cup fresh flat-leaf parsley

½ cup fresh cilantro

2 sprigs fresh thyme, or ¼ teaspoon dried

1 bay leaf

2 teaspoons salt

10 cups water

1. Combine all the ingredients in the pressure cooker. Lock on the lid and bring to pressure over high heat, about 18 minutes. Reduce the heat to medium and cook for 20 minutes. Remove from the heat and let sit for 15 minutes to finish cooking.

2. With the steam vent pointed away from your face, gently release any remaining pressure. Let cool enough to handle.

3. Drain the broth through a fine-mesh sieve into a bowl. Discard the solids. Use right away or cool completely and store in the refrigerator, covered, for up to 1 week. May be frozen for up to 6 months.

Mushroom Consommé with Sherry and Shiitake Mushroom Slices

In the world of consommés, this one is special because it's such a surprise. The richest, meatiest broth is brewed from mushrooms and water. Then it's livened up with an expansive amount of shiitake mushroom slices, sparked with a sprinkle of sherry, and served. Nothing more. Through the years, I've experimented with embellishing the soup every which way—herbs, different mushrooms, different wine. Nothing surpasses its unadorned purity. It's a sophisticated extravagance of a soup, fit for any grand gathering from family Thanksgiving to state dinner.

Makes 6 servings

10 ounces fresh shiitake mushrooms
2 pounds button mushrooms, stems trimmed and coarsely chopped
10 cups water
1½ teaspoons salt
½ cup dry sherry

1. Rinse the shiitake mushrooms and remove the stems. Set aside half the caps and coarsely chop the rest with the stems.

2. Place the chopped shiitake stems and caps, button mushrooms, and water in the pressure cooker. Lock on the lid and bring to pressure over high heat, about 15 minutes. Reduce the heat to medium-low and cook for 12 minutes. Remove from the heat and let sit for 15 minutes to finish cooking.

3. With the steam vent pointed away from your face, gently release any remaining pressure. Let cool enough to handle.

4. Drain the broth through a fine-mesh sieve into a large bowl. Press down on the mushroom pieces in the sieve to extract any remaining juices. Discard the mushroom pieces.

5. Return the broth to the pressure cooker. Bring to a boil and cook over high heat until reduced to about 8 cups, about 15 minutes. Slice the set-aside shiitake mushroom caps and add to the soup along with the salt and sherry. Continue cooking at a simmer for 10 minutes. Ladle into individual bowls and serve piping hot.

◊ Almost Greek Manestra

How water can turn so flavorful with so few, uncomplicated ingredients is somewhat baffling. But it does in Greek tomato manestra *soup. The secret is that the tomatoes be red ripe and height-of-summer flavorful. Whether or not to peel them is up to the cook. I always do, but Greeks might think that a waste of perfectly good taste.*

Makes 4 servings

2 tablespoons olive oil
4 cloves garlic, finely chopped
1 medium-size yellow or white onion, finely chopped
4 medium-size tomatoes or 8 Roma or plum tomatoes,
    peeled (see page 24) or not, and coarsely chopped
2 teaspoons chopped fresh oregano, or 1 teaspoon dried
4 cups water
½ cup freshly grated parmesan cheese, for serving

Manestra That's More

If you would like real Greek *manestra*, add 2 ounces orzo or pastina pasta after the soup has cooled down and you've released any remaining pressure. Simmer over medium heat until the pasta is just done, about 5 minutes. Or instead of orzo, use vermicelli broken into 1-inch pieces or ¾ cup cooked rice. Garnish the soup with shredded fresh mint or basil leaves. Accompany with a Greek grating cheese, such as *kefalotyri* or *mizithra*, available in gourmet cheese shops and many supermarkets.

1. Heat the oil in the pressure cooker over medium-high heat until beginning to smoke. Add the garlic and onion and cook, stirring, over medium heat until softened, about 3 minutes. Add the tomatoes, oregano, and water and stir to mix. Lock on the lid and bring to pressure over high heat, about 6 minutes. Reduce the heat to medium and cook for 15 minutes. Remove from the heat and let sit for 8 minutes to finish cooking.

2. With the steam vent pointed away from your face, gently release any remaining pressure. Ladle into individual bowls and serve hot, with the cheese on the side.

◎ Cream of Tomato Soup

Cream of tomato soup is a snap to whip up in a pressure cooker. It's also versatile and freezes well, so when there's an abundance of tomatoes you can make several batches to store in the freezer and serve it a different way each time.

Makes 4 to 6 servings

1 tablespoon vegetable oil
1 tablespoon butter
1 large yellow or white onion, finely chopped
3 pounds tomatoes, peeled (see left), seeded, and coarsely chopped, with juices
2 teaspoons chopped fresh thyme, or 1 teaspoon dried
1 teaspoon salt
¼ teaspoon freshly ground black pepper
½ cup Vegetable Broth (page 20) or water
¾ cup heavy cream
Herbed Croutons (optional, recipe follows), for garnish

To Peel or Not to Peel?

There are actually several ways to get a smooth puree. If using only a food processor, you must peel the tomatoes: Drop them into boiling water, count to 20, and drain them. When cool enough to handle, peel, then halve them and remove the seeds with your fingers. If you prefer to have the flavor and vitamins of the peel in the soup, you can cook the tomatoes unpeeled, then puree the soup through a food mill, which will hold back the skins and seeds. Or you can leave the tomatoes unpeeled and puree the soup in a food processor, then press it through a fine-mesh sieve to strain out the skins and seeds.

1. Heat the oil and butter in the pressure cooker over medium-high heat until the butter melts. Add the onion and cook, stirring occasionally, until wilted, about 5 minutes. Add the tomatoes and their juices, thyme, salt, pepper, and broth and stir to mix. Lock on the lid and bring to pressure over high heat, about 4 minutes. Reduce the heat to medium-high and cook for 15 minutes. Remove from the heat and let sit for 10 minutes to finish cooking.

2. With the steam vent pointed away from your face, gently release any remaining pressure. Let cool enough to handle,

3. Transfer the soup to a food processor and puree. If using right away, stir in the cream and reheat gently without boiling, then serve. Or store in the refrigerator until ready to use; then stir in the cream, heat, and serve. Garnish with the croutons, if desired.

Tomato Soups Galore

On the principle that there are never too many tomato soup recipes, you can put your imagination to work and vary the basic tomato puree in numerous ways.

- Use crème fraîche or sour cream instead of cream.
- Omit the cream altogether and garnish the soup with a chopped fresh herb, such as parsley, cilantro, basil, or mint.
- Use marjoram, oregano, or tarragon for the herb instead of thyme.
- Add spices when cooking the soup, like cumin, cayenne, hot paprika, Aleppo pepper, ground ginger, or turmeric (which will also add a zing to the color).

Herbed Croutons *As well as garnishing soup, these croutons can add crunch to a Caesar-type romaine salad. They also make a delightful snack on their own.* Makes 2 cups

Olive oil, for frying
2 cups ½-inch cubes country-style bread or good-quality French bread
1 tablespoon chopped fresh thyme, oregano, marjoram, or rosemary,
    or 1½ teaspoons dried
2 tablespoons freshly grated parmesan cheese (optional)

1. Pour olive oil into a large, heavy sauté pan to a depth of ½ inch. Heat over medium–high heat until a cube of bread sizzles when dropped in. Add the bread cubes and fry, stirring and turning, until golden all around, about 5 minutes. With a wire strainer or slotted spoon, transfer the cubes to paper towels.

2. Sprinkle the herbs and parmesan, if using, over the cubes and toss to coat. Serve right away or within several hours.

◈ Garlic Soup with Ancho Chile and Lime

From the time the Moors introduced to Spain a soup of garlic and almonds pounded together and thickened with eggs and cooks from the New World updated it with tomatoes and chiles, omitting the almonds, garlic soup has been embraced in Mediterranean and Latin cuisines almost as a blessing. I feel I bring good health when I prepare such a soup and partake of a blessing when I eat one. This Mexican version, which I first enjoyed on a balcony overlooking the zocolo in Oaxaca, Mexico, is ardently delicious, deep-red beautiful, and blessedly easy to make, especially in the pressure cooker.

Makes 3 to 4 servings

2 tablespoons olive oil

10 large cloves garlic, chopped not too fine

1 large dried ancho chile pepper, seeded and finely chopped

2 medium-size tomatoes, peeled (see page 24), seeded, and
    coarsely chopped, with juices

5 cups Vegetable Broth (page 20) or Chicken Broth (page 18)

½ teaspoon salt

1 recipe Mexican Meatballs (optional, recipe follows)

Eight 1-inch-thick slices baguette, brushed with olive
    oil and toasted, for garnish

1 lime, quartered, for garnish

1. Heat the oil in the pressure cooker over medium-high heat until it begins to smoke. Add the garlic and cook, stirring occasionally, until lightly golden, about 1 minute.

2. Stir in the chile pepper and tomatoes and their juices, then add the broth and salt and stir again. Lock on the lid and bring to pressure over high heat, about 4 minutes. Reduce the heat to medium-low and cook for 5 minutes. Remove from the heat and let sit for 8 minutes to finish cooking.

3. With the steam vent pointed away from your face, gently release any remaining pressure. If adding the meatballs, brown them as in Step 2 in the recipe that follows and add them to the soup. Let rest another 3 minutes with the lid ajar, until the liquid is no longer bubbling. Ladle into bowls and garnish each with toasted bread and a lime wedge. Serve right away.

Mexican Meatballs *Meatballs are called* albóndigas *in Spanish; I've always thought of them as meatballs with a dramatic name. Poaching them in a garlic soup is a typical, and irresistible, way both to cook the meatballs and turn the soup into a meal. But that's not their limit. They do as well plumping a pasta sauce or rolling around a plate of hors d'oeuvres to be passed at a cocktail party (toothpicks help here).* Makes 12 to 14 walnut-size meatballs

½ pound lean ground beef
2 tablespoons finely chopped yellow or white onion
1 tablespoon coarse bread crumbs (see page 187)
½ tablespoon chopped fresh mint, or ½ teaspoon dried
½ teaspoon chopped fresh oregano, or ¼ teaspoon dried
¼ teaspoon chili powder
½ teaspoon salt
1 large egg

1. Combine all the ingredients in a medium-size bowl. Using your hands, blend thoroughly, working the ingredients into a cohesive mixture. Roll into small balls about the size of walnuts. Set aside at room temperature for up to 30 minutes or refrigerate for up to 3 days.

2. When ready to use, brown the meatballs in a lightly greased skillet over medium-high heat for 5 minutes, then proceed with the main recipe.

◈ Beet and Orange Soup with Mint, Orange Zest, and Sour Cream
Whether smooth or somewhat chunky (it's really a matter of taste), this soup is an appetite opener, a hunger salve, a fulfilling warmth for a small meal.

Makes 6 servings

3 medium-size beets (about 1 pound)
1 medium-size yellow or white onion, quartered and sliced ¼ inch thick
2 carrots, peeled and cut into ¼-inch dice
⅓ cup freshly squeezed orange juice
⅓ cup balsamic vinegar
1 bay leaf
6 cups water
Shredded fresh mint, for garnish
Slivered orange zest, for garnish
Sour cream, for garnish

1. Combine the beets, onion, carrots, orange juice, vinegar, bay leaf, and water in the pressure cooker and stir to mix. Lock on the lid and bring to pressure over high heat, about 10 minutes. Reduce the heat to medium and cook for 6 minutes. Remove from the heat and let sit for 10 minutes to finish cooking.

2. With the steam vent pointed away from your face, gently release any remaining pressure. Lift out the beets with a slotted spoon and set aside until cool enough to handle, then peel them. Remove and discard the bay leaf and set the pot aside.

3. *For a smooth soup,* mix the beets with the ingredients in the pot and puree them all together. You can use a food processor, pureeing in batches, or a food mill for a smoother puree.

For a chunky soup, cut the beets into ¼-inch dice. Add them to the pot with the rest of the ingredients and stir to mix.

4. When ready to serve, heat the soup until boiling. Ladle into individual soup bowls and garnish each with a pinch of shredded mint, 3 or 4 slivers of orange zest, and a small dollop of sour cream. Serve piping hot.

◇ Spring Spinach and Scallion Soup

So restoring is this soup that I often think of it as a medicinal brew, a simple cup of which is good for what ails you. I also think of it as an elegant beginning for a spring meal when the weather is still on the chilly side or as a light luncheon in early summer when the days have warmed. Either way, warm bread and good butter should accompany.

Makes 4 servings

2 tablespoons butter
8 scallions, trimmed and thinly sliced
1 clove garlic, finely chopped
1½ pounds spinach, tough stems removed, leaves coarsely chopped, well
    washed, and drained
6 cups Chicken Broth (page 18)
½ teaspoon salt
Warm country-style bread and very fresh sweet butter, for serving

1. Melt the butter in the pressure cooker over medium-high heat. Add the scallions and garlic and cook, stirring occasionally, until wilted but not browned, about 1 minute. Add the spinach and stir to mix a bit. Stir in the broth and salt, lock on the lid, and bring to pressure over high heat, 6 to 7 minutes. Remove from the heat right away and let sit for 8 minutes to finish cooking.

2. With the steam vent pointed away from your face, gently release any remaining pressure. Serve hot, with warm bread and butter.

◈ Blond Onion Soup

Set aside any images of still-dark-with-a-little-early-light mornings in a bistro in Les Halles, spooning deeply into a bowl of rich brown, dense onion soup after a hard day's night at the produce market. Today's onion soup is blond, but it's still thick and oniony and lacks no flavor if you make it with homemade beef broth. The romance continues, at home, with the help of the pressure cooker. It's still a two-stage process, as on the stove top, because the onions need long cooking until they're practically melted before simmering them in the broth.

Makes 4 servings

1 tablespoon olive oil
2 tablespoons butter
3 medium-size yellow onions, quartered and sliced ¼ inch thick
1 teaspoon sugar
2 teaspoons salt
5 cups Beef Broth (page 15)
½ cup dry white wine
1 recipe Cheese Toasts (recipe follows)

1. Heat the oil and butter in the pressure cooker over medium heat until the butter melts. Stir in the onions and cook, stirring, until the onions begin to wilt, about 5 minutes. Stir in the sugar and salt. Add 1 cup of the beef broth, lock on the lid, and bring to pressure over high heat, about 2 minutes. Reduce the heat to low and cook for 15 minutes. Remove from the heat and let sit for 4 minutes to finish cooking.

2. With the steam vent pointed away from your face, gently release any remaining pressure. Add the remaining 4 cups broth and the wine. Lock on the lid and bring to pressure again over high heat, 4 to 5 minutes. Reduce the heat to medium and cook for 15 minutes. Remove from the heat and let sit for 5 minutes to finish cooking.

3. With the steam vent pointed away from your face, gently release any remaining pressure. Ladle the soup into bowls and top each with two or three of the cheese toasts. Serve right away.

Cheese Toasts *For onion soup, a flavorful melting cheese like Gruyère or emmental is a perfect choice. For other dishes, you can use another kind of melting cheese, such as kefalotyri, sharp cheddar, or Monterey Jack spiked with a sprinkle or two of grated parmesan, romano, or aged asiago. If you don't have day-old bread on hand, cut slices from a fresh loaf and pretoast them until dried out but not yet golden.*

Makes 12 toasts

Twelve ½-inch-thick slices day-old baguette
1 cup freshly grated melting cheese

Preheat the oven to 350°F. Top each slice of bread with 1 heaping tablespoon cheese. Place on a baking sheet and toast in the oven until the cheese melts, about 5 minutes. Use right away, while the cheese is still soft.

Carrot Bisque with Vodka and Chervil *It was my friend Lindsey Shere, longtime pastry chef at Chez Panisse restaurant, now retired, who taught me total respect for the carrot. It was at a dinner at her home, and the first course was a carrot quiche. It was quite a shocking revelation that carrots could be made into something so sophisticated and grand. In her usual modest way, Lindsey explained that it wasn't actually her idea, that it was from Maxim's cookbook. My culinary excitement mounted as I exhorted her to supply the recipe—better yet the whole cookbook. She kindly made me a copy, because the book was by then out of print, and it's remained a treasure in my library. In later years, the carrot quiche turned into carrot bisque, still perked up with vodka and with a fillip of chopped chervil.*

Makes 4 servings

¼ cup (½ stick) butter

1 medium-size yellow or white onion, finely chopped

4 large carrots, peeled and coarsely chopped

¼ cup rice, preferably Arborio

1 teaspoon salt

¼ teaspoon freshly ground pepper, preferably white

1 cup Chicken Broth (page 18)

3 cups water

1 tablespoon vodka

1 tablespoon chopped fresh chervil, for garnish

1. Melt the butter in the pressure cooker over medium heat. Stir in the onion and cook, stirring occasionally, until it begins to wilt, about 2 minutes. Add the carrots, rice, salt, pepper, broth, and water. Lock on the lid and bring to pressure over high heat, about 8 minutes. Reduce the heat to medium and cook for 5 minutes. Remove from the heat and let sit for 10 minutes to finish cooking.

2. With the steam vent pointed away from your face, gently release any remaining pressure. Let sit until cool enough to handle, then transfer the contents of the pressure cooker to a food processor and puree. Just before serving, reheat and stir in the vodka. Garnish with the chervil and serve.

Butternut Squash Soup

Butternut squash diverts the most die-hard away from a conviction that winter squash is better for looking at than for eating. Its intense, madder orange color; dense, not mealy, texture; and buttery taste cause those who would turn up their noses to lean over and see, smell, savor a soup of it. For that matter, a side dish of butternut squash elicits the same positive response (see page 34).

Makes 3 to 4 servings

1½ pounds butternut squash, quartered and seeded
2 tablespoons olive oil
3 cloves garlic, coarsely chopped
1 medium-size yellow or white onion, finely chopped
1 tablespoon chopped fresh sage, or 1½ teaspoons dried
¾ teaspoon salt
3 cups water
3 to 4 pats butter, for garnish
Large pinch of ground nutmeg, for garnish

1. Place the squash, cut side down, on a trivet in the pressure cooker. Pour in 1 cup water, lock on the lid, and bring to pressure over high heat, 2 to 3 minutes. Reduce the heat to medium and cook for 7 minutes. Remove from the heat and let sit for 3 minutes to finish cooking.

2. With the steam vent pointed away from your face, gently release any remaining pressure. Transfer the squash to a kitchen plate.

3. In a clean pressure cooker, heat the oil over medium heat until beginning to smoke. Add the garlic, onion, and sage and cook, stirring occasionally, until thoroughly wilted, about 6 minutes.

4. Scrape the squash pulp away from the skin. Coarsely chop the pulp and add it to the garlic and onion mixture, along with the salt and water. Lock on the lid and bring to pressure over high heat, 4 to 5 minutes. Reduce the heat to medium and cook for 10 minutes. Remove from the heat and let sit for 10 minutes to finish cooking.

5. With the steam vent pointed away from your face, gently release any remaining pressure. When cool enough to handle, transfer the contents of the pressure cooker to a food processor and puree.

6. When ready to serve, reheat without boiling and garnish with the butter and nutmeg.

◇ ◇ ◇

Butternut Squash Besides Soup

Butternut squash redefines the reputation of winter squash from "okay but I could do without it" to "oh, boy, butternut squash tonight!" That may be a bit of an overstatement, but there's no doubt it sums up the essence of squash goodness. Beginning with the cooked and peeled quarters (Steps 1, 2, and 4 on page 33), here are some other ways to serve butternut squash.

Set the quarters on a serving platter and garnish with:

- Butter and lots of freshly ground black pepper
- Butter and a little bit of minced garlic
- Crisped pancetta bits and fresh parsley

Or serve for Thanksgiving instead of candied yams: Put the quarters in a small, oven-to-table baking dish, sprinkle with 2 tablespoons of finely chopped walnuts, drizzle 2 tablespoons of maple syrup over the top, dot with butter, and bake in a 350°F oven until everything is bubbling, about 20 minutes.

◈ Cream of Cauliflower Soup du Barry

The fancy title comes from the first days of my food career (really before it was a career, more of a fantasy), when Michael Field, the too-soon-departed pianist and food writer par excellence, became my mentor through his writing. The notion of cauliflower and Madame du Barry fit perfectly into my wild imagination— a cauliflower, high-rise, Sixties bubble hairdo. The soup is more down-to-earth, and a very good thing to do with cauliflower.

Makes 4 to 6 servings

1 large head cauliflower (about 2 pounds),
    including stems, cut into ½-inch pieces
¼ cup freshly squeezed lemon juice
3 tablespoons butter
½ medium-size yellow or white onion, coarsely chopped
2 tablespoons all-purpose flour

5 cups Chicken Broth (page 18) or half broth and half water

1 teaspoon salt

½ cup heavy cream

Pinch of cayenne, for garnish

1 tablespoon chopped fresh chives, for garnish

1. Combine the cauliflower, lemon juice, and water to cover in a large bowl. Set aside for 15 to 30 minutes.

2. Melt the butter in the pressure cooker over medium heat. Add the onion and cook, stirring occasionally, until wilted, about 2 minutes. Stir in the flour and continue cooking for 1 minute.

3. Drain the cauliflower and add it to the pot. Add the broth and salt and stir to mix. Lock on the lid and bring to pressure over high heat, about 8 minutes. Reduce the heat to medium and cook for 5 minutes. Remove from the heat and let sit for 15 minutes to finish cooking.

4. With the steam vent pointed away from your face, gently release any remaining pressure. Let cool enough to handle.

5. Puree the soup in a food processor or through a food mill. Stir in the cream and serve, garnished with the cayenne and chives.

Potato, Leek, and Celery Soup

Celery became a star ingredient in my potato soup the first time I had my own kitchen and wanted to reproduce the treasured comforts of home. My mother's potato soup didn't have leeks, nor ever celery. Celery was a different soup altogether, one I also adored. Somehow, though, the potatoes and celery wound up in the same soup pot, and I added leeks because, well, because I was exploring. Through the years, I have continued to extend the variations in my repertoire (see the recipes that follow). I remain devoted to potato soup, almost any kind, as the best of any soup.   Makes 4 to 6 servings

Salting the Soup

Soups need salt to bring out flavor—potato soups, in particular. They require a noticeable amount of salt during cooking, not after, to reach their peak of taste. So, don't be daunted by the amount called for in the recipes for potato soups. If you are maintaining a low-sodium diet, reduce the amount to suit your needs and replace the salt flavor with a squeeze of lemon juice and lots of freshly ground black pepper.

3 large russet potatoes (2½ pounds), peeled and cut into 1½-inch chunks

1 large leek, trimmed, coarsely chopped, well washed, and drained

6 ribs celery, trimmed and cut into ¼-inch-thick slices

2 teaspoons chopped fresh thyme, or 1 teaspoon dried

2 teaspoons salt

4 cups water

4 to 6 pats butter, for garnish

1½ tablespoons chopped fresh chives, for garnish

1. Place the potatoes, leek, celery, thyme, salt, and water in the pressure cooker and stir to mix. Lock on the lid and bring to pressure over high heat, about 5 minutes. Reduce the heat to medium-low and cook for 5 minutes. Remove from the heat and let sit for 4 minutes to finish cooking.

2. With the steam vent pointed away from your face, gently release any remaining pressure. Whisk to mash the potatoes into a chunky puree, with the leeks and celery remaining somewhat whole. Ladle into 4 to 6 individual bowls. Garnish each with a pat of butter and a teaspoon or so of chives. Serve right away.

Potato, Garlic, and Celery Root Soup *Water works! No broth required.*

Potato soups are easy on the ingredient list and allow dozens of variations. Any potato soup is also a good keeper and will last in the refrigerator for up to five days. You may need to thin it with a little water, milk, or cream to bring it back to soup consistency before serving.

Makes 4 to 6 servings

1 large celery root (1½ pounds), peeled (see top right) and cut into 1½-inch chunks

3 medium-size russet potatoes (1¼ pounds), peeled and cut into 1½-inch chunks

6 large cloves garlic, halved

2 teaspoons salt

Peeling Celery Root

The knobby, creviced celery root looks unapproachable at first glance. And it is, a little. You must take away its peel in order to reach the good part. The best way to do that is first to cut off the top and bottom to make flat surfaces. Then peel the celery root with a vegetable peeler. Use a small, sharp paring knife to dig into the crevices and cut away what peel remains. It's a little like removing the eyes of a potato or pineapple after peeling the outside.

4 cups water
4 to 6 pats butter, for garnish
Freshly ground black pepper to taste, for garnish

1. Place the celery root, potatoes, garlic, salt, and water in the pressure cooker. Lock on the lid and bring to pressure over high heat, about 5 minutes. Reduce the heat to medium-low and cook for 5 minutes. Remove from the heat and let sit for 4 minutes to finish cooking.

2. With the steam vent pointed away from your face, gently release any remaining pressure. Whisk to mash the vegetables and make a chunky puree. Ladle into 4 to 6 individual bowls and top each with a pat of butter and several grinds of black pepper. Serve right away.

◇ Chilled Potato Soup Mexican Style, with Cantaloupe and Toasted Almonds

Since my first time in Spain, I have been intrigued by chilled soups. It was the gazpacho in Granada that showed, in the right setting at the right time, cold soup is an oxymoron of a notion but a lilt in the day's repasts. In a delicious Mexican version of chilled soup, potato and cantaloupe are combined in a vichyssoise way that suits both warm weather dining and a svelte crowd.

Makes 6 servings

3 medium-size russet potatoes (1¼ pounds), peeled and
    cut into 1½-inch chunks

1 jalapeño or serrano chile pepper, halved and
    seeded

1 teaspoon salt

4 cups milk

1 medium-size cantaloupe, halved, seeded and
    cut into 2-inch chunks

1 tablespoon freshly squeezed lime juice

¼ cup sliced almonds, lightly toasted (see page 41), for garnish

6 sprigs fresh cilantro, for garnish

1 lime, cut into 6 thin rounds, for garnish

1. Place the potatoes, chile pepper, salt, and milk in the pressure cooker. Lock on the lid and bring to pressure over high heat, about 5 minutes. Cook on medium heat for 5 minutes. Remove from the heat and let sit for at least 4 minutes (more is okay in this case because the soup is to be served chilled), to finish cooking.

Avocado Vichyssoise

Prompted by the chilled potato and melon soup I developed when writing *The Vegetarian Table: Mexico*, avocado, one of the supreme south-of-the-border fruits, suddenly melded in my mind with another version of chilled potato soup, the classic vichyssoise. The recipe was published there, and so tasty is the dish, I adapted it to pressure cooking for this volume.

To make 6 servings, make Potato, Leek, and Celery Soup (page 35) through Step 1, substituting a second large leek for the celery and adding 1 jalapeño chile pepper, halved. When cool enough to handle, puree, along with 3 medium-size, ripe Haas avocados, peeled and pitted. Refrigerate until thoroughly chilled, several hours but not overnight or the avocado will discolor. When ready to serve, stir in ¼ cup freshly squeezed lime juice and ½ cup sour cream. Garnish with ¼ cup chopped fresh chives and serve cold.

2. With the steam vent pointed away from your face, gently release any remaining pressure. Let cool enough to handle.

3. Remove the chile pepper halves and puree the soup and cantaloupe together in a food processor. Transfer to a storage container and chill for at least 3 hours, or up to overnight.

4. When ready to serve, stir the lime juice into the soup. Ladle into individual bowls. Garnish each bowl with toasted almonds and a cilantro sprig. Set 1 slice of lime alongside the garnishes and serve.

◇ Leek, Kale, and Lentil Soup with Salted Lemon Rounds

I prefer the small, green, nutty-tasting French lentils in soup because they retain their shape even as

they soften. If they aren't available, regular brown lentils will do. Or you can use cranberry beans

or navy beans in place of the lentils and let the soup cook for 25 minutes instead of 4 in Step 1

before sitting.

Makes 4 servings

Cooking Lentils

It may seem counterintuitive to cook the lentils for such a short time and let them sit for a much longer time; it's because lentils tend to foam up during cooking and so the pressure subsides more slowly than with other legumes. The cool down is part of the cooking, though, so don't use a quick cool method or the lentils will be underdone.

2 tablespoons olive oil
3 medium-size leeks, trimmed, sliced ¼ inch thick,
    well washed, and drained
3 cups thinly shredded kale, well washed and drained
¾ cup lentils
1 teaspoon salt
6 cups Chicken Broth (page 18) or Vegetable Broth (page 20)
1 tablespoon freshly squeezed lemon juice
8 Salted Lemon Rounds (page 40), for garnish

1. Heat the oil in the pressure cooker over medium-high heat until beginning to smoke. Add the leeks and cook, stirring occasionally, until slightly wilted, about 1 minute. Stir in the kale, then add the lentils, salt, and broth and stir to mix. Lock on the lid and bring to pressure over high heat, about 6 minutes. Reduce the heat to medium-low and cook for 4 minutes. Remove from the heat and let sit for 15 minutes to finish cooking.

2. With the steam vent pointed away from your face, gently release any remaining pressure. Stir in the lemon juice and serve right away, garnished with the lemon rounds.

Salted Lemon Rounds *Similar to preserved lemon, these are not as soft because they don't cure as long.*

Makes 8 rounds

1 lemon, thinly sliced into rounds
Salt to taste

Spread the lemon slices on a plate and sprinkle with salt. Set aside for 20 to 30 minutes, or until softened. Rinse before using, if desired.

◈ Split Pea Soup *Split pea soup is not one to oomph or labor over. Nor is it one to cook very long. At least for my taste. I like my split pea soup like a dal (see page 266), meaning vegetarian style—essence of green split peas with the peas retaining some shape. In the pressure cooker, you don't have to worry about burning on the bottom, and the flavors condense without the liquid boiling away.*

Makes 4 to 6 servings

2 tablespoons butter
1 medium-size yellow or white onion, finely chopped
1 medium-size carrot, peeled and finely chopped
2 cups green split peas
2 teaspoons chopped fresh thyme, or ¾ teaspoon dried
1 teaspoon salt
6 cups water
4 to 6 pats butter, for garnish
2 tablespoons thinly shredded fresh mint, for garnish

1. Melt the 2 tablespoons butter in the pressure cooker over medium-high heat. Add the onion and cook, stirring occasionally, until beginning to wilt, about 2 minutes. Add the carrot and peas and stir to mix. Add the thyme, salt, and water. Lock on the lid and bring to pressure over high heat, about 6 minutes. Reduce the heat to medium-low and cook for 5 minutes. Remove from the heat and let sit for 15 minutes to finish cooking.

2. With the steam vent pointed away from your face, gently release any remaining pressure. Ladle into individual bowls and garnish with the butter and mint. Serve right away.

Navy Bean and Ham Hock Soup

Dried small white beans, or pea beans, are a type of haricot bean, many varieties of which have been cultivated in the New World for 5,000 years. They came to be called navy beans for their role as a mess staple on navy ships. As navy bean soup evolved, the addition of a smoked ham hock to the pot was a natural development. Not only is it a source of protein that could be stored on seafaring journeys, it is also a source of the per-

fect flavor to complement and enhance the somewhat bland beans. For the same reasons, the soup naturally made its way into American home cooking, where it remains a favorite for uplifting gloomy winter days. Using both a hock and a shank means the soup gets the depth of flavor bone offers plus plenty of meat, which the shank offers. One or the other is okay, though, if you can't find both.

Makes 4 servings

1½ cups dried small white (navy) beans
5 cups water
1 bay leaf
5 large sprigs fresh thyme, or ¼ teaspoon dried
¼ cup chopped celery leaves
One ¾-pound piece smoked ham hock
One ¾-pound smoked ham shank
1 small yellow or white onion, halved
2 whole cloves, stuck into the onion halves
1 teaspoon salt, or more to taste
Freshly ground black pepper to taste
Chopped fresh flat-leaf parsley (optional), for garnish

Keeping an Eye on the Pot

It's important to remember to keep an eye on the pressure indicator when cooking peas and beans. Usually the burner heat needs adjusting once or twice to make sure the pressure remains high enough to cook the ingredients in the time given, yet not so high that the contents boil over.

1. Place the beans, water, bay leaf, thyme, celery leaves, ham hock, ham shank, and clove-stuck onion halves in the pressure cooker. Lock on the lid and bring to pressure over high heat, about 8 minutes. Reduce the heat to medium-low to low and cook for 20 minutes. Remove from the heat and let sit for 15 minutes to finish cooking.

2. With the steam vent pointed away from your face, gently release any remaining pressure and carefully remove the lid. Lift out and discard the bay leaf, thyme sprigs, and onion. Lift out the ham, cut the meat off the bone, and return the meat to the pot. Stir in the salt. Serve piping hot, reheating if necessary, sprinkled with freshly ground black pepper and parsley, if using.

◇ Garlicky White Bean Soup with Red Bell Pepper Puree

If you can find the meaty, sweet Italian cannellini beans, also known as white kidney beans, use them instead of Great Northerns.

Makes 4 to 6 servings

Red Bell Pepper Pesto

Red Bell Pepper Puree (page 44) can be easily transformed into a pesto suitable to sauce pasta or simply cooked chicken breast, to dip bread or blanched cauliflower florets into, or to use as a sandwich spread.

Makes about 1 cup

2 cloves garlic, minced
1 tablespoon pine nuts
2 tablespoons freshly grated parmesan cheese
2 tablespoons extra virgin olive oil

Add the garlic, pine nuts, cheese, and oil to the peppers while pureeing.

2 tablespoons butter
1 large head garlic, cloves separated, peeled, and very coarsely chopped
1 small yellow or white onion, finely chopped
2 teaspoons chopped fresh sage
1½ cups dried Great Northern or cannellini beans
4 cups Chicken Broth (page 18) or half broth and half water
1½ teaspoons salt
⅔ cup Red Bell Pepper Puree (page 44), for garnish

1. Melt the butter in the pressure cooker over medium-high heat. Add the garlic and onion and cook over medium heat, stirring occasionally, until beginning to wilt, about 2 minutes. Stir in the sage, then add the beans and broth and stir to mix. Lock on the lid and bring to pressure over high heat, about 6 minutes. Reduce the heat to medium and cook for 5 minutes, then reduce the heat to low for 20 minutes. Remove from the heat and let sit for 15 minutes to finish cooking.

2. With the steam vent pointed away from your face, gently release any remaining pressure. If the beans are not quite tender, boil the soup for a few minutes more (see Note). Lift out ½ cup of the beans and puree them in a food processor or through a food mill. Add the puree back to the pot and stir in the salt. Reheat the soup, if necessary, and ladle into individual bowls. Swirl about 2 tablespoons of the red pepper puree across the top of each bowl and serve.

Note: Remember that the cooking time for dried beans varies according to how long they have been stored.

Red Bell Pepper Puree

Makes about ⅔ cup

3 medium-size red bell peppers
Salt to taste

1. Preheat the oven to 425°F. Set the peppers on the oven rack with a length of aluminum foil on the rack below to catch the juices. Roast until the peppers are collapsed and charred, 20 to 25 minutes. Remove them to a kitchen plate, cover them with a cloth towel, and let sit for 15 minutes or so.

2. With your fingers, peel the peppers, then cut off the stems and seed them, saving as much of the juices as you can. Puree the peppers and juices, including any collected on the plate, in a food processor. Stir in the salt. Use right away or store in the refrigerator for up to 1 week.

◈ Corn and Chile Chowder, with or without Butterflied Shrimp

Though I don't usually specify precise form for chopped vegetables, for looks, dice is nice for this dish. The shrimp addition makes the chowder more of a meal, and it's also pretty, but the chowder can stand on its own if you'd like a lighter first course or luncheon soup.

Makes 4 servings

2 large fresh green chile peppers, such as pasilla or Anaheim
1 large jalapeño chile pepper
2 tablespoons butter
½ cup diced yellow or white onion
1 cup fresh corn kernels plus juices scraped from the cob
1 small creamer potato, preferably Yukon gold,
    cut into ¼-inch dice
5 cups Chicken Broth (page 18)
½ teaspoon salt

The potatoes for chowder
certainly could be red or
white creamers, the more
familiar varieties of waxy
potatoes for potato salads
and plain boiling. But
the Yukon golds are deli-
cious in an unmatchable
way, especially since they
retain their fresh-from-the-
field flavor even miles into
the city. Fortunately, they
have become more and
more available, even in
supermarkets.

8 large fresh shrimp (optional), shelled, deveined if necessary, and butterflied

8 sprigs fresh cilantro, for garnish

1 lime, quartered, for garnish

1. Roast the chile peppers in a preheated 425°F oven or over a charcoal grill until wilted and wrinkly but not charred, about 15 minutes. Remove and let cool a minute or two, then seed but don't peel them. Cut into thin strips and set aside.

2. Melt the butter in the pressure cooker over medium heat. Stir in the onion and cook, stirring occasionally, until beginning to wilt, about 1 minute.

3. Add the chile pepper strips, corn and its juices, potato, broth, and salt. Lock on the lid and bring to pressure over high heat, about 5 minutes. Reduce the heat to low and cook for 2 minutes. Remove from the heat and let sit for 15 minutes to finish cooking.

4. With the steam vent pointed away from your face, gently release any remaining pressure. If using the shrimp, add them to the pot, cover without locking on the lid, and let sit for 3 minutes. Serve right away, garnished with the cilantro and lime wedges.

Soup, Stew, or Chowder?

So alluring has the notion of chowder become, it's popping up in trendy restaurants across the nation and home cooking books, like this one. The expansion beyond its original East Coast venue naturally brings with it new interpretations. There's chowder with other seafood besides clams—lobster was probably the first stretch in this direction, back in the 1700s, and still on the East Coast. Now shrimp, salmon, and sea bass are concocted into robust soups called chowders. There's chowder with other vegetables besides potatoes and/or tomatoes, even chiles; with no bacon at all; with no seafood at all but only vegetables. Appropriately, the chowder-devising game seems to have halted there. I've never seen, nor can I imagine, a chowder of beef, lamb, pork, or poultry. Those would be stew. I admit, I've joined the fun: There are four chowder recipes in this chapter.

The Trick Is in the Timing, and a Revelation

Actually, the trick is *always* in the timing. That's why cookbooks offer up so many measurements for each stage of the cooking process from raw ingredients to lovely plate on the table. The timing measurements especially were paramount in developing outstanding recipes for the pressure cooker. The revelation was realizing that delicate fish chowders can be pressure cooked without the seafood being overdone. There are three methods:

- Eliminate any additional cooking time between bringing the pot to pressure and removing it to sit (as in Sea Bass, Sweet Potato, and Black Bean Chowder, page 50).
- Add the fish only after the dish is off the burner and let it steep to cook, like tea (as in Corn and Chile Chowder with Butterflied Shrimp, page 44)
- Use a combination of the two (as in Salmon and Fennel Chowder with Green Peppercorn Mayonnaise, page 47).

Clam Chowder, the Red and the White Together

Fresh clam chowder is a remarkable dish. President Kennedy requested it often, not only for his own comfort but also for important guests. Whether Boston white, as René Verdon, chef to the Kennedys, served it at the White House, or Manhattan red, as you find it at the Grand Central Station Oyster Bar and Restaurant in midtown New York City, it's an all-American dish. Here the red and the white join to make a creamy, tomatoey clam chowder. The pressure cooker makes it so easy to have that you only need fuss about getting the clams fresh.

Makes 4 servings

2 pounds clams, rinsed
½ cup water
1 tablespoon butter
2 ounces blanched salt pork (see Note page 70) or pancetta, cut into ½-inch pieces
1 small yellow or white onion, cut into ¼-inch dice
½ medium-size green bell pepper, seeded and cut into ¼-inch dice
1 medium-size tomato, seeded and cut into ¼-inch dice, with juices reserved

2 medium-size creamer potatoes, preferably Yukon gold, cut into ¼-inch dice

2 cups milk

1 bay leaf

½ teaspoon salt

¾ cup heavy cream

1 tablespoon chopped fresh chives or flat-leaf parsley, for garnish

1. Place the clams and water in the pressure cooker, lock on the lid, and bring to pressure over high heat, 2 to 3 minutes. Remove from the heat right away and let sit for 2 minutes to finish cooking.

2. With the steam vent pointed away from your face, gently release any remaining pressure. Drain, reserving the juices. When cool enough to handle, shuck the clams and set aside.

3. Melt the butter in the pressure cooker over medium–high heat. Add the salt pork and cook, stirring occasionally, until limp, about 1 minute. Add the onion, bell pepper, tomato and its juices, potatoes, milk, bay leaf, and salt. Lock on the lid and bring to pressure over high heat, about 4 minutes. Reduce the heat to medium and cook for 2 minutes. Remove from the heat and let sit for 5 minutes to finish cooking.

4. With the steam vent pointed away from your face, gently release any remaining pressure. Remove the bay leaf and stir in the cream, shucked clams, and reserved juices. Heat over medium–high heat just until beginning to boil. Serve right away, garnished with the chives.

◈ Salmon and Fennel Chowder with Green Peppercorn Mayonnaise
Like tomatoes and basil, salmon and fennel are natural companions on the plate. One almost suggests the other. Potatoes fit right in to form a happy threesome, and napped with tangy Green Peppercorn Mayonnaise, the four make a substantial chowder.

Makes 4 servings

One 1½-pound salmon fillet, skinned
1 tablespoon freshly squeezed lemon juice
1 tablespoon olive oil
1 medium-size leek, trimmed, thinly sliced, well washed, and drained
1½ teaspoons salt
1 medium-size fennel bulb, quartered lengthwise and
    sliced ½ inch thick
¾ pound Yukon gold potatoes, cut into ¼-inch dice
4 cups water
1 bay leaf
1¼ cups Green Peppercorn Mayonnaise (recipe follows)
Green peppercorns (see right), for garnish

1. Cut the salmon into 4 pieces and sprinkle on both sides with the lemon juice.

2. Heat the oil in the pressure cooker over medium-high heat until beginning to smoke. Reduce the heat to medium, stir in the leek and salt, and cook, stirring occasionally, until wilted, about 2 minutes.

3. Add the fennel and potatoes, pour in the water, and drop in the bay leaf. Lock on the lid and bring to pressure over high heat, about 7 minutes. Remove from the heat right away and let sit for 7 minutes to finish cooking.

4. With the steam vent pointed away from your face, gently release any remaining pressure. Remove the lid and lower the salmon pieces into the pot. Set the lid ajar and let sit for 5 minutes.

5. Ladle the chowder into individual bowls, taking care not to break up the salmon pieces. Place a large dollop of the mayonnaise on top and garnish with the peppercorns. Serve right away, with the remaining mayonnaise on the side.

Green Peppercorns, the Sass and Suppleness of Youth

Green peppercorns are the unripe berries of the Old World pepper bush, *Piper nigrum*, which also gives us one of our most indispensable table and kitchen spices, black pepper. Not botanically related to the New World chile peppers of the capsicum family, *Piper nigrum* berries fulfill a very similar culinary niche, that of adding punch to food both from within, during cooking, and without, as garnish.

You can find green peppercorns brined, usually imported from France. You can also find them freeze-dried in little jars on the spice rack in better grocery stores. I prefer the freeze-dried because they are pure pepper exuberance without any pickle overtones.

To use brined green peppercorns, drain, rinse, and chop them. To use freeze-dried green peppercorns, soak them for 5 minutes in warm water, then drain and chop them.

Green Peppercorn Mayonnaise *Where fish goes, mayonnaise comes; at least that's so in my house. Once you have the technique of swirling the eggs and oil together in the food processor, a matter of seconds, this classic sauce of French and continental cuisine is at your fingertips, along with a boundless number of variations. For a basic mayonnaise, follow the recipe through Step 2. Then make variations according to the dish you are saucing and the whim of the moment. Because of the health risk associated with consuming uncooked eggs, be sure the eggs are very fresh and keep the mayonnaise refrigerated until ready to serve.* Makes 1¼ cups

2 large egg yolks
1 teaspoon Dijon mustard
1 teaspoon freshly squeezed lemon juice
1 cup extra virgin olive or peanut oil, or a mixture
1 tablespoon very hot water, or more if necessary
3 tablespoons green peppercorns, chopped (see above)
Salt to taste

1. Place the egg yolks, mustard, and lemon juice in the food processor. Process until well blended and creamy looking.

2. With the processor still running, slowly pour in the oil to make a thick mixture. Add the 1 tablespoon hot water and continue processing until blended. Transfer to a bowl and whisk to incorporate the oil from the bottom of the processor bowl. Stir in more hot water, if necessary, to make a mayonnaise of the consistency you'd like.

3. Add the green peppercorns and salt. Cover and refrigerate for 15 minutes or so for the peppercorns to infuse the mayonnaise. Use right away or store in the refrigerator for up to 1 week.

◫ Sea Bass, Sweet Potato, and Black Bean Chowder

Sea bass is one of the most delicious white ocean fishes. Before that was so widely known, it used to be a bargain. Now it's downright expensive. But when it's chunked into a chowder, you don't need so much, and it can make a special meal with half of what you'd need if serving it on plates.

Makes 4 servings

1 pound sea bass fillets, cut into 1½-inch chunks
1 smallish sweet potato (5 to 7 ounces), peeled and cut into ½-inch dice
1 large fresh green chile pepper, such as pasilla or Anaheim,
    seeded and cut into long, thin strips
1 cup cooked black beans (see page 279)
4 cups water
1 teaspoon salt
2 tablespoons coarsely chopped celery leaves from the tender
    inner ribs, for garnish
1 lime, quartered, for garnish

1. Place the sea bass, sweet potato, chile pepper, black beans, water, and salt in the pressure cooker. Lock on the lid and bring to pressure over high heat, about 7 minutes. Remove from the heat right away and let sit for 8 minutes to finish cooking.

2. With the steam vent pointed away from your face, gently release any remaining pressure. Ladle the soup into individual bowls. Garnish each bowl with celery leaves and a lime wedge hooked to the side of the bowl. Serve right away.

◊ Old-Fashioned Cream of Chicken Soup   *When I was young, soup was*

a standby, and even though my mother cooked, canned soup was a super standby. Mostly, or

maybe only, the brand was Campbell's. The main selections were cream of mushroom, always a

reject as far as I was concerned, cream of tomato, and cream of chicken, which vied with tomato for

choice of the hour. Both have entered my repertoire of family cooking. The cream of tomato is on

page 24. Here's the cream of chicken, which I will say has nothing to do with canned cream of

chicken as I discovered when I sampled grocery store shelf offerings to jog my memory. This one is

what I think a cream of chicken soup should be, and the pressure cooker does it just right. The veg-

etables can be chopped quickly in a food processor instead of neatly diced by hand, but do take care

not to turn them into a mince.   Makes 6 servings

2 tablespoons butter

2 ribs celery, finely chopped

1 medium-size carrot, peeled and finely chopped

1 medium-size yellow or white onion, finely chopped

1 whole boneless, skinless chicken breast (1 to 1¼ pounds),
   cut into ½-inch pieces

2 boneless, skinless chicken thighs (about ½ pound), cut into ½-inch pieces

3 cups Chicken Broth (page 18)

2 sprigs fresh thyme, or ½ teaspoon dried

1 teaspoon salt

¼ teaspoon freshly ground black pepper

1 cup shelled fresh peas (see Note on page 52)

1 cup heavy cream

1. Melt the butter in the pressure cooker over medium heat. Add the celery, carrot, and onion and cook, stirring occasionally, until beginning to soften, about 2 minutes.

2. Add the chicken breast and thigh pieces, broth, thyme, salt, and pepper. Stir to mix. Lock on the lid and bring to pressure, 4 to 5 minutes. Reduce the heat to medium and cook for 2 minutes. Remove from the heat and let sit for 5 minutes to finish cooking.

3. With the steam vent pointed away from your face, gently release any remaining pressure. Add the peas and stir. Stir in the cream. Serve right away.

Note: Although I am usually adamant about peas being fresh, for this all-weather comfort soup I sometimes relent and use frozen peas.

Curried Chicken Soup with Young Ginger, Coconut Milk, and Crispy Shallot Rings

The drama and delight of curries are the array of condiments served alongside. There are toasted coconut flakes (see page 218) for a sweet taste, and pickled vegetables or hot-tart pineapple salsa (see page 321) for tang. Here, I suggest some that are typical of Southeast Asian curry presentations and not difficult to prepare for a home meal.

The fish sauce, also known as nam pla, *adds a depth of flavor to Southeast Asian dishes much as soy sauce does to Chinese or Japanese dishes. Like soy sauce, it can vary widely in excellence; I suggest going for a quality brand from Thailand that is fermented from water, salt, and anchovy only, with no lesser fish thrown in for bulk.*

Makes 3 to 4 servings

2 tablespoons peanut oil
½ medium-size yellow or white onion, finely chopped

Marinated Young Ginger

Young ginger can be likened to spring garlic in that its texture is moister and its taste softer than the mature plant. Its skin has not yet toughened, and you can peel it with a vegetable peeler or just scrub it and not peel it at all. In fact, I love its flavor so much, I sometimes shred it through the large holes of a grater, toss it with a few drops of good fish sauce, and serve it on a little plate as yet another condiment for curried soup.

½ teaspoon ground turmeric

1 whole boneless, skinless chicken breast (1 to 1¼ pounds), cut into ½-inch pieces

2 boneless, skinless chicken thighs (about ½ pound), cut into ½-inch pieces

1 tablespoon peeled and not-too-finely chopped young ginger (see left)

½ teaspoon hot paprika, preferably Hungarian

½ teaspoon salt

1 tablespoon fish sauce (*nam pla*)

2 cups unsweetened coconut milk

1 cup water

⅓ cup Crispy Shallot Rings (page 54), for serving

½ cup salted roasted peanuts, very coarsely chopped, for serving

¼ cup chopped fresh cilantro, for serving

1 lime, quartered, for serving

1 small fresh red chile pepper (optional), chopped, for serving

Marinated Young Ginger (optional, see left), for serving

1. Heat the oil in the pressure cooker over medium–high heat until beginning to smoke. Stir in the onion and turmeric and cook, stirring occasionally, until wilted, about 3 minutes. Add the chicken breast and thigh pieces, ginger, paprika, salt, fish sauce, coconut milk, and water. Lock on the lid and bring to pressure over high heat, 2 to 3 minutes.

2. Reduce the heat to medium and cook for 3 minutes. Remove from the heat and let sit for 8 minutes to finish cooking.

3. With the steam vent pointed away from your face, gently release any remaining pressure. Ladle the soup into individual bowls and serve, with the shallot rings, peanuts, cilantro, lime wedges, red chile (if using) and young ginger (if using), on separate small plates.

Crispy Shallot Rings   *Surprisingly, shallots are a staple of Southeast Asian cooking, where they are used both as a seasoning within curries and as a condiment on top of curries. If you care to make a quadruple batch of shallot rings, you can have some left over to store.*

Makes ⅓ cup

4 large shallots, very thinly sliced and rings separated
Vegetable oil, for frying

1. Spread the shallots on a plate lined with paper towels and set aside to air dry for several hours, or up to overnight.

2. Pour the oil into a medium-size, heavy skillet or wok to a depth of ¼ inch and heat over medium-high heat until a shallot ring dropped in sizzles. Add the shallots and fry until golden and crisp, about 45 seconds. Transfer to paper towels to drain. Use right away or store in an airtight container for up to 2 weeks.

◑ Beef Plate Soup, Not Stew   *Plate soup may seem a somewhat strange name, but it exactly describes the way this dish is neither bowl soup nor regular stew, but rather a cross between the two. The closely trimmed, thinly cut beef riblet strips, sometimes called flanken or English short ribs, solve the problem of how to have a hearty, sturdy, stand-up-to-boiling cut of beef that will turn out both tasty and tender. The unobtrusive bones along the strip are actually added value for the soup because they contribute flavor that boneless beef stew meat doesn't.*

Plating the soup individually rather than serving it family style adds immeasurably to the visual appeal of the dish and, insofar as the eyes inform the palate, also to the taste of the dish.

Makes 4 to 6 servings

8 creamer potatoes, red, white, or Yukon gold, halved

1½ pounds beef riblet strips

1 tablespoon olive oil

2 large carrots, peeled and cut into ½-inch-thick diagonal slices

1 small yellow or white onion, quartered and sliced ¼ inch thick

One 14-ounce can plum tomatoes, with juices

1 teaspoon chopped fresh thyme, or ¼ teaspoon dried

4 cups Beef Broth (page 15)

½ teaspoon salt

¼ teaspoon freshly ground black pepper

½ tablespoon chopped fresh dill, for garnish

1 tablespoon chopped fresh flat-leaf parsley, for garnish

1. Cook the potatoes in a large pot of boiling salted water until tender, 6 to 8 minutes, depending on the size of the potatoes. Drain briefly, return to the pot, and set aside in a warm place.

2. Cut the riblet strips crosswise between the bones. Heat the oil in the pressure cooker over medium-high heat until beginning to smoke and add the riblet pieces. Cook until lightly browned all around, about 2 minutes.

3. Add the carrots, onion, tomatoes and their juices, thyme, broth, salt, and pepper and stir to mix. Lock on the lid and bring to pressure over high heat, about 6 minutes. Reduce the heat to medium and cook for 10 minutes. Remove from the heat and let sit for 12 minutes to finish cooking.

4. With the steam vent pointed away from your face, gently release any remaining pressure. Divide the potatoes among 4 large, high-lipped plates. Spoon the beef and vegetables over the potatoes. Ladle some of the juice over all and garnish with the dill and parsley. Serve right away.

◈ Chinese-Inspired Beef Soup with Star Anise and Crispy Mai Fun Noodles

Mai fun, also called rice sticks, have always seemed appropriately named to me because of the way they immediately puff up and turn into a crisp cloud of thin noodles when fried, an amusing surprise. Star anise is the dried fruit pod of an evergreen bush native to southwestern China. Its flavor and fragrance are like that of anise seeds, only far more pronounced. Both mai fun and star anise are available in better supermarkets. If you prefer, you can skip the step of deep-frying and substitute fresh or dried Chinese noodles or Japanese udon noodles. Like Italian pasta, they need to be precooked before adding to the soup.

Makes 3 to 4 servings

1 tablespoon peanut oil, plus extra for frying
1 pound tri-tip beef or beef riblet strips, cut into ½-inch pieces
1 star anise
3 small dried red chile peppers
4 strips orange peel (removed with a vegetable peeler)
1 tablespoon low-sodium soy sauce
½ teaspoon salt
3 cups Beef Broth (page 15)
3 cups water
Crispy Mai Fun Noodles (recipe follows)
8 sprigs fresh cilantro, for garnish

1. Heat the 1 tablespoon oil in the pressure cooker over high heat until beginning to smoke. Add the beef and brown over medium-high heat for 2 minutes. Add the star anise, chile peppers, orange peel, soy sauce, salt, broth, and water. Lock on the lid and bring to pressure over high heat, about 5 minutes. Reduce the heat to medium and cook for 25 minutes. Remove from the heat and let sit for 10 minutes or so while frying the noodles.

2. With the steam vent pointed away from your face, gently release any remaining pressure. Ladle the soup into individual bowls. Mound a handful of the crispy noodles on top of each bowl and garnish with cilantro sprigs. Serve right away, with the remaining noodles on the side.

Crispy Mai Fun Noodles *Part of the fun of* mai fun *is that they can be crisped (or softened) for other dishes quickly. Their role in a dish is to provide crunchy or soft texture rather than flavor. If crisping them, the oil for frying can be used again because it isn't tainted by overheating or an intrusive flavor.*

Makes as much as you want

Vegetable oil, for frying
Mai fun noodles (rice sticks), as much as you want, pulled apart into small
   bunches

1. Pour the vegetable oil into a heavy frying pan to a depth of $\frac{1}{2}$ inch and set over high heat until a noodle dropped in sizzles and immediately rises to the top.

2. Add a handful of the noodles, and when they rise to the top, almost right away, turn them over using a wire strainer and wooden spoon. Cook on the other side until puffed all around, about 30 seconds. Remove to paper towels to drain and continue with another round until all the noodles are fried. Use right away, while still crisp.

Meat:
Homey to Haute

Meat in the pressure cooker is not a tricky business. Of course, there are considerations. Large cuts like shanks and pot roasts and succulent cuts like pork shoulder, lamb neck, or veal breast are a cinch. So are stews and braises as long as the meat is not too lean. (For instance, veal stew doesn't work, although quick-cooked veal scaloppine rolls braised in broth do.) Chops and cutlets are out of the question, though a thick beef rib-eye steak makes a superlative, medium-rare black pepper pot steak, plus sauce. Tongue and brisket, old-fashioned family treats, take half the time cooked under pressure and turn out at least as good, if not better, than from the oven or stove top because pressure cooking compresses the flavors into the meat rather than letting them dissipate as the liquid evaporates during long cooking. Meat loaves, from the familiar American kind to the more esoteric ones, called terrines, of French cooking, also take well to the steam bath as long as you don't need to have the top too browned. Following is an adventurous collection of meats that shine with pressure cooking, plus lots of accompaniments that make the meal worth its salt.

Meat: Homey to Haute

◇ Pot Roast with Baby Carrots, Pearl Onions, and Cranberry Beans

For pot roast, in the oven or in the pressure cooker, the cut counts. It must be a thick flatiron (blade) steak, cut from the chuck, or a cross rib roast. Other pot roast cuts, such as bottom round or rump roast, won't do; they are too tough. In my opinion, so too is the seven-bone chuck roast, though many think it works fine. To add elegance in this recipe, the carrots are babies and the onions are pearls, and they're cooked separately from the roast so they don't turn to mush while the meat braises away. The cranberry beans, which don't need soaking when pressure cooked, add a certain unexpected verve to the meat and vegetable combination, but they're a little difficult to find unless you have a market that carries grains and legumes in bulk. Pink beans are a good substitute.

Makes 6 servings

One 2-inch-thick flatiron (blade) steak (about 2½ pounds),
　　or one 2½-pound cross rib roast
Salt and freshly ground black pepper to taste
1 tablespoon olive oil
1 medium-size carrot, peeled and cut into 2-inch chunks
1 rib celery, cut into 2-inch chunks
1 small yellow or white onion, halved
2 large cloves garlic, coarsely chopped
¼ cup tomato paste
3 sprigs fresh thyme, or ½ teaspoon dried
½ tablespoon black peppercorns
¾ cup dry white wine
½ cup dried cranberry or pink beans
2 cups Beef Broth (page 15)
18 baby carrots, preferably with tops; tops removed, leaving
　　1 inch of green stem
18 pearl onions, peeled
2 tablespoons chopped fresh flat-leaf parsley, for garnish
1 tablespoon chopped fresh chives, for garnish

1. Sprinkle both sides of the meat with a liberal amount of salt and pepper. Heat the oil in the pressure cooker over medium-high heat until beginning to smoke. Add the meat and brown on both sides, about 2 minutes altogether.

2. Add the carrot chunks, celery, onion, garlic, tomato paste, thyme, peppercorns, wine, beans, and broth. Stir to mix, lock on the lid, and bring to pressure over high heat, about 5 minutes. Reduce the heat to medium and cook for 40 minutes. Remove from the heat and let sit for 10 minutes to finish cooking.

3. With the steam vent pointed away from your face, gently release any remaining pressure. Transfer the meat to a kitchen plate and set aside in a warm place.

4. Remove and discard the carrot, celery, and onion pieces and the thyme sprigs. Pour the juices through a fine-mesh strainer set over a bowl. Set aside for the fat to rise, at least 15 minutes. Also set aside the beans in the strainer.

5. Skim off the fat and return the juices to the pot, along with the beans. Add the baby carrots and pearl onions, lock on the lid, and bring to pressure over high heat, about 5 minutes. Remove from the heat right away and let sit for 3 minutes to finish cooking. With the steam vent pointed away from your face, gently release any remaining pressure and remove the lid.

6. Cut the beef across the grain into 1-inch-thick slices and add to the pot. Heat, uncovered, until just beginning to boil, 2 to 3 minutes.

7. To serve, arrange the beef slices in the center of a serving platter. Arrange the baby carrots and pearl onions around the beef. Spread the beans around the vegetables and spoon the juices over all. Garnish with the parsley and chives and serve.

Note: The peppercorns that remain in the strainer with the beans will have cooked long enough to be chewable, like a soft berry. They can be returned to the pot with the beans.

Beef Brisket with Sauerkraut and Creamy Horseradish Sauce

This recipe has become something of a shaggy-dog story in my cookbook writing career. It began with a delightful dinner at my to-be-agent Martha Casselman's. She offered me the recipe, and it appeared in my first book, American Charcuterie: Recipes from Pig-by-the-Tail. *The dish appeared in several later cookbooks and often on my own table, a halcyon offering to friendly winter occasions. "But hold off," said Martha, "I received that recipe from a friend, and now I find the friend might have learned it from* Joy of Cooking! *What now?" Well, here it is again, pressure cooked and, I hope, all parties duly attributed. Some recipes call for rinsing the sauerkraut. I don't because I think taking the sour out of the kraut makes it too bland.*

Makes 6 to 8 servings

2 tablespoons butter

2 ounces blanched salt pork (see Note page 70), coarsely chopped

1 large yellow or white onion, halved and sliced ½ inch thick

One 2- to 3-pound untrimmed beef brisket, from the front cut,
    including the fatty end piece

2 teaspoons freshly ground black pepper

1½ pounds sauerkraut, drained

¾ cup dry white wine

3 cups water

½ cup Creamy Horseradish Sauce (page 65), for serving

1. Heat the butter in the pressure cooker over medium heat until melted. Add the salt pork and cook, stirring occasionally, until beginning to brown, about 2 minutes. Add the onion and continue to cook, stirring occasionally, until beginning to wilt, about 3 minutes.

2. With the brisket fat side up, pat the pepper all across the top, then set it on the onions. Spread the sauerkraut over all and pour in the wine and water. Lock on the lid and bring to pressure over

Turning a Brisket into Corned Beef

If St. Patrick's Day is one you toast or even if you just like corned beef, you can easily transform a beef brisket into corned beef by soaking it in a pickling brine for a week. The only tricky part is finding a container large enough to hold the brine and brisket—an enameled turkey roaster is perfect—and then giving up refrigerator space while the brine works its magic. To make corned beef from beef brisket, purchase the far more flavorful and moist front cut with the fatty edge. Then:

Prepare a double batch of brine as described on page 80. Prick the brisket all over with a long-tined fork so the brine can penetrate into the center of the meat. Set the meat in the brine and place in the refrigerator for 1 week, or up to 3 weeks. When ready to cook, drain and pressure cook for the same amount of time as for beef brisket cooked as pot roast.

high heat, about 8 minutes. Reduce the heat to medium and cook for 1½ hours. Remove from the heat and let sit for 30 minutes to finish cooking.

3. With the steam vent pointed away from your face, gently release any remaining pressure and let sit with the lid ajar for 15 minutes more. The pot roast may be refrigerated in the liquid overnight, covered, and reheated before serving.

4. To serve, move aside the sauerkraut. Transfer the brisket to a cutting board and thinly slice it using a sharp knife to avoid shredding the meat. Arrange the slices on a serving platter and spread the sauerkraut over them. Serve with the horseradish sauce on the side.

Shredded Beef, from Hash to Picadillo

Leftover beef brisket is an excellent candidate for shredding and hashing in several ways:

- American diner hash: Cooked meat, usually beef, rounded out with vegetables, commonly potatoes and onions, sometimes green pepper, and seasoned according to the style of the cook, can be pressed into a heavy skillet and pan-fried into a golden cake. When the cake is topped with a poached egg, as for corned beef hash, or baked with mashed potatoes into a shepherd's pie, hash takes on true nostalgia status.
- Hash stuffing: Shredded brisket can be combined with chopped onion and tart apple to use as an unusual stuffing for cabbage leaves (see page 209).
- Picadillo: Mixed with raisins and walnuts and seasoned with cinnamon and cloves, the hashed beef becomes picadillo, used in Mexican-style cooking to fill tamales, empanadas, or chiles.

Beef Versus Chicken Broth for Stews

Only a few recipes in this book call for beef broth. That's because chicken and vegetable broths have become more popular for their lighter taste, and beef broth has fallen from favor also because it is costly and time-consuming to make a good one at home. The costly part remains unchanged, but the pressure cooker takes care of the time part (see page 15). Still, if you're not inclined to produce homemade beef broth, substitute chicken broth instead. There are good commercial chicken broths available, whereas there are no good commercial beef broths. I always keep Swanson's low-sodium fat-free chicken broth in aseptic packages in my pantry for on-the-spot emergencies when I don't have homemade broth on hand in the fridge or freezer.

Creamy Horseradish Sauce

Makes ½ cup

½ cup peeled and grated fresh horseradish
2 tablespoons red wine vinegar
2 tablespoons heavy cream

Combine all of the ingredients in a small bowl. Use right away or keep in the refrigerator, covered, for up to 2 weeks.

◈ Mid-Country Beef Stew
Seasonings from the cupboard (malt vinegar, caraway, cloves), vegetables from the root cellar (onions and carrots), tomatoes from the can, and dried herbs make up a substantial beef stew in a hallmark dish of Midwestern cooking. Serve this with noodles on the side and sour cream to top, and you can settle into indoor comfort without further thought of the cold outside.

Makes 4 servings

1 tablespoon vegetable oil

3 cross-cut beef shanks with bone (3 to 3½ pounds)

1 tablespoon all-purpose flour

1 medium-size yellow or white onion, halved and sliced ¼ inch thick

3 medium-size carrots, cut into 2- to 2½-inch chunks

4 canned tomatoes, broken up, with juices

1 bay leaf

1 teaspoon dried marjoram

½ teaspoon caraway seeds

4 whole cloves

⅛ teaspoon ground allspice

1½ teaspoons salt

½ teaspoon freshly ground black pepper

1 tablespoon malt vinegar

4 cups Beef Broth (page 15)

6 ounces extra-wide egg noodles, cooked, drained, and kept warm, for serving

1 cup sour cream, for serving

1. Heat the oil in the pressure cooker over medium–high heat until beginning to smoke. Add the beef shanks and cook, turning once, until browned on both sides, about 5 minutes. Add the flour and turn to coat. Add the onion, carrots, tomatoes and their juices, bay leaf, marjoram, caraway, cloves, allspice, salt, and pepper and turn to mix. Add the vinegar and broth and bring to a boil over high heat.

2. Lock on the lid and bring to pressure over high heat, 2 to 3 minutes. Reduce the heat to medium and cook for 35 minutes. Remove from the heat and let sit for 15 minutes to finish cooking.

3. With the steam vent pointed away from your face, gently release any remaining pressure and let sit for 5 minutes more. Transfer the meat to a serving platter, taking care to keep the center marrow of each bone intact. Discard the bay leaf. Surround the meat with the vegetables and spoon the sauce over all. Serve right away with the egg noodles and a dish of sour cream on the side.

Luxurious Marrow

The marrow is a prized morsel of meat shanks—lamb, veal, or beef. Traditionally, it is served separately on top of warm toasted bread. If you care to take that extra step and present it as the treat it is, place some marrow on top of toasts and arrange them around the edges of the serving platter for a special garnish.

◇ Meat and Potatoes Korean Style

Korean dishes are sometimes thought to be "too hot to handle." Spice is a factor, it's true, but if you raise your palate thermometer half a notch, you can enjoy the heat without sweat as you savor the complex flavors of this robust cuisine.

Makes 3 to 4 servings

1 tablespoon peanut oil

1½ pounds boneless beef short ribs, cut into 1½-inch chunks

1 small yellow or white onion, halved and sliced ¼ inch thick

2 cloves garlic, coarsely chopped

1 tablespoon peeled and finely chopped fresh ginger

2 small fresh red chile peppers, preferably Thai or serrano, finely chopped,
    or ½ teaspoon red pepper flakes

2 tablespoons sake or Chinese rice wine

2 tablespoons low-sodium soy sauce

1½ teaspoons salt

½ teaspoon sugar

⅓ cup water

3 medium-size Yukon gold potatoes (about ¾ pound), cut into ¼-inch-thick rounds

4 scallions, trimmed and slivered lengthwise, for garnish

8 to 10 sprigs fresh cilantro, for garnish

1. Heat the oil in the pressure cooker over high heat until beginning to smoke. Add the beef and sauté over medium-high heat until lightly browned, about 2 minutes.

2. Add the onion, garlic, ginger, and chile peppers and stir to mix. Add the sake, soy sauce, salt, sugar, and water and stir to mix. Add the potato rounds but don't stir. Lock on the lid and bring to pressure over high heat, about 2 minutes. Cook over medium heat for 5 minutes. Remove from the heat and let sit for 8 minutes to finish cooking.

3. With the steam vent pointed away from your face, gently release any remaining pressure, remove the lid, and let sit for 5 minutes more. Top with the scallion slivers and cilantro and serve right away.

◇ Beef Bourguignon

Alice B. Toklas was my mentor for beef bourguignon, and a good lesson in being prepared was the first time I made it. In my enthusiasm, I had invited guests to share and began cooking in what seemed plenty of time before the appointed dinner hour. All went well until I got to the paragraph about how long to simmer the stew—three hours! It never occurred to me to read that far before embarking and never occurred to me that it would take such long simmering to develop the full flavor of the dish. I don't remember how impatiently the guests twiddled their fingers while the pot simmered. It was finally done in time for a fashionable Spanish-hour dinner, ten o'clock. Social embarrassment aside, it seemed worth the wait: Beef bourguignon is a classic. Since then, I've made many Burgundy-style beef stews, sometimes with nut-

Beef for Stews

While the pressure cooker is a dream machine for turning out beef stews with the deep flavor of long simmering in considerably less time, it can't turn stone into gold. For the most tender, richest broth and meat, choose boneless beef short ribs or cross-cut beef shanks, which are also my choices for stove-top or oven cooking such dishes.

meg (à la Alice B.), with or without brandy (that's a toss-up among cooks), sometimes with orange zest and sometimes without, but always with more aplomb than that first time.

Following is the rendition I like best, with flavorful, tender boneless beef short ribs, cooked one of the ways I like best, in the pressure cooker. To suit the yielding texture of a beef bourguignon, a sturdy counter-crunch of oven-roasted russet potato wedges or fried bread (see page 125) is called for.

Makes 4 to 6 servings

2 pounds trimmed boneless beef short ribs, cut into 2- to 3-inch pieces
½ cup brandy
4 large sprigs fresh thyme, or ½ teaspoon dried
6 large sprigs fresh flat-leaf parsley
1 bay leaf
Leaves from 1 rib celery
2 pieces orange zest
2 tablespoons butter
2½ ounces blanched salt pork (see Note page 70), diced
12 pearl or small boiling onions, parboiled for 1 minute and peeled
½ pound button mushrooms, stems trimmed
1 tablespoon all-purpose flour
2½ cups dry red wine
1 large clove garlic, smashed
Tiny pinch of ground nutmeg
1 teaspoon salt

1. Toss together the beef and brandy in a large bowl and set aside at room temperature.

2. Tie together the thyme, parsley, bay leaf, celery leaves, and orange zest with kitchen string to make an herb bundle. Set aside.

3. Melt the butter in the pressure cooker over medium-high heat. Add the salt pork and cook until softened, about 2 minutes. Transfer the salt pork pieces to a kitchen platter and set aside.

4. Add the onions to the pressure cooker and cook over medium-high heat until beginning to brown, about 1 minute. Transfer the onions to the platter with the salt pork. Add the mushrooms to the pressure cooker and sauté over medium-high heat until lightly browned, about 5 minutes. Transfer to the platter with the salt pork and onions and set aside.

5. Remove the beef chunks from the brandy marinade and add to the pressure cooker. Cook briefly over medium-high heat to brown on all sides, about 2 minutes. Sprinkle with the flour and stir to coat the beef. Add the wine, garlic, nutmeg, salt, and herb bundle. Stir to mix, lock on the lid, and bring to pressure over high heat, about 2 minutes. Reduce the heat to medium–low and cook for 40 minutes.

6. Remove from the heat and let sit for 15 minutes to finish cooking.

7. With the steam vent pointed away from your face, gently release any remaining pressure and remove the lid. Lift out the herb bundle and discard. With a slotted spoon, transfer the meat to a kitchen platter. Set aside.

8. Let the liquid in the pot rest for another 15 minutes for the fat to rise to the top. Skim off the fat. Add the onions, mushrooms, and salt pork and cook briskly over medium–high heat until the liquid is reduced to a rich red-brown color and the vegetables are tender, 7 to 10 minutes.

9. Return the meat to the pot to reheat briefly. Arrange the meat, onions, and mushrooms on the serving platter. Pour the sauce over all and serve right away.

Note: These days, salt pork usually comes not so salty because it has been rinsed and blanched before packaging. If you have the old-fashioned salt-coated kind, rinse it in several changes of cool water and parboil it for 5 minutes before dicing.

◇ ◇ ◇

Argentinian Beef Stew with Chimichurri Sauce

In Argentina, one of the New World's original cattle raising areas, beef is made into a succulent home-on-the-range stew that satisfies any yen for (far) south-of-the-border flavors.

Makes 4 to 5 servings

1½ to 1¾ pounds boneless beef short ribs, cut into 2-inch pieces
5 cloves garlic, smashed and coarsely chopped
1 small dried red chile pepper, finely chopped, or
    ½ teaspoon red pepper flakes
1 tablespoon chopped fresh marjoram, or 2 teaspoons dried
½ teaspoon dried green peppercorns, smashed
¼ teaspoon salt
1 tablespoon olive oil
1 cup dry red wine
1 cup Chimichurri Sauce (page 72), for serving

1. Combine the beef, garlic, chile pepper, marjoram, green peppercorns, and salt in a large dish and toss to coat. Set aside in the refrigerator for 1 to 2 hours.

2. Heat the oil in the pressure cooker over high heat until beginning to smoke. Brown the beef and seasonings in batches so as not to crowd the pot, 2 to 3 minutes per batch. Return all of the meat to the pressure cooker, add the wine, lock on the lid, and bring to pressure over high heat, 2 to 3 minutes. Reduce the heat to medium–low and cook for 40 minutes. Remove from the heat and set aside for 10 minutes to finish cooking.

3. With the steam vent pointed away from your face, gently release any remaining pressure, carefully remove the lid, and let sit for another 5 minutes. Serve with the sauce on the side.

Chimichurri Sauce *Chimichurri is an Argentinian green salsa. With a generous note of onion and a small bite of fresh green chile pepper, it extends the range of parsley sauce all the way to South America.*

Makes about 1 cup

½ cup finely chopped yellow or white onion
¼ cup chopped fresh flat-leaf parsley
1½ teaspoons finely chopped fresh serrano or jalapeño chile pepper
1 large clove garlic, finely chopped
1 tablespoon chopped fresh oregano, or 1 teaspoon dried
¼ cup extra virgin olive oil
2 tablespoons red wine vinegar
1 teaspoon salt

Combine all the ingredients in a small bowl and whisk to mix. Use right away or store in the refrigerator, covered, for up to 3 days.

◈ Pan-Asian Spicy Beef or Pork Curry with Eggplant and Mustard Greens

Setting out from India and traveling south through the lands of curries, you find the meat might be beef or pork, depending on the religious dietary rules of the household. The following curry is one that can serve any Asian table—for some, you make it with beef; for others, with pork. (See pages 160 and 161 for two shrimp curries.)

Makes 4 servings

2 tablespoons vegetable oil
6 large cloves garlic, finely chopped
2 tablespoons peeled and coarsely grated fresh ginger
1 teaspoon yellow mustard seeds
3 small dried cayenne or other red chile peppers, coarsely chopped
1¾ pounds beef or pork stew meat

3 Japanese, Italian, or Chinese eggplants, cut into 1-inch-thick rounds, or
    8 Thai eggplants, halved
2 tablespoons freshly squeezed lime juice
2 tablespoons fish sauce (*nam pla*)
2 cups water
1 teaspoon salt
4 cups coarsely chopped mustard greens, well washed and drained
¼ cup chopped fresh mint leaves, for garnish
½ cup unsweetened coconut flakes, lightly toasted (see Note), for garnish
Basic Steamed Rice (page 215), for serving

1. Heat the oil in the pressure cooker over medium-high heat. Stir in the garlic, ginger, mustard seeds, and chile peppers and cook until lightly toasted, about 1 minute. Add the meat, stir to mix, and cook until no longer red, about 2 minutes. Add the eggplants, lime juice, fish sauce, water, and salt and stir to mix. Set the mustard greens on top but don't stir in. Lock on the lid and bring to pressure over high heat, about 5 minutes. Reduce the heat to medium and cook for 5 minutes. Remove from the heat and let sit for 15 minutes to finish cooking.

2. With the steam vent pointed away from your face, gently release any remaining pressure. Sprinkle the mint and coconut over the top and serve right away with the steamed rice.

Note: You can toast the coconut in a microwave on high or in an ungreased skillet over medium-high heat for 3 to 4 minutes, until beginning to turn golden.

◈ Black Pepper Pot Steak with Shallots and Spicy Red Wine Gravy

Unbelievable as it may seem, a pressure-cooked rare steak can be had. The most important key is the cut. It must be tender—rib eye is best—and quite thick, at least two inches (see Note). The second key is the timing. The cooking must be less than for a pot roast, but long resting after cooking is essential to achieve a succulent dish. That leaves just the right amount of time to reduce the cooking liquid to a rich, gravy-like sauce.

Makes 4 servings

One 2-inch-thick boneless rib-eye steak (about 1¾ pounds)
1 tablespoon cracked black peppercorns
1 teaspoon salt
1 tablespoon olive oil
½ pound shallots, peeled
1 cup dry red wine
1 tablespoon tomato paste
1 large bay leaf, crumbled

1. Rub the steak all over with the pepper and salt. Set aside at room temperature for at least 30 minutes or refrigerate, covered, up to overnight.

2. Heat the oil in the pressure cooker over medium-high heat until beginning to smoke. Add the steak and brown on both sides, about 2 minutes total. Transfer the meat to a plate.

3. Reduce the heat to medium and add the shallots to the pressure cooker. Stir, then add the wine, tomato paste, and bay leaf. Return the meat to the pot, lock on the lid, and bring to pressure over high heat, 2 to 3 minutes. Reduce the heat to medium and cook for 10 minutes. Remove from the heat and let sit for 5 minutes to finish cooking.

4. With the steam vent pointed away from your face, gently reduce any remaining pressure and transfer the steak and shallots to a serving platter. Set aside in a warm place.

5. Meanwhile, simmer the liquid in the pressure cooker over medium-high heat until the color is a rich reddish brown and the liquid is as thick as gravy, 7 to 8 minutes. Pour over the steak and serve right away.

Note: The extra-thick rib eye may require a special order, but I've found most butchers, including those who work behind the scenes in supermarkets, are happy to accommodate. In a pinch, you can substitute trimmed boneless beef short ribs. Not quite as tender, this is still a tasty cut; reduce the cooking time to 5 minutes.

◇ Flank Steak Roulade Braised in Red Wine, Soy, and Ginger

Any stuffed and wrapped dish that gets braised or steam cooked is a candidate for quick pressure cooking. Here, flank steak is butterflied and rolled around spinach and grated carrot, then steam braised in its flavorful marinade. Sliced and sauced with a reduction of the marinade, the dish looks fancy on the plate even though the preparation is not particularly elaborate.

Makes 4 servings

1 flank steak (about 1½ pounds), butterflied and lightly pounded (see page 76)
1½ cups dry red wine
2 tablespoons freshly squeezed lemon juice
⅔ cup low-sodium soy sauce
¼ cup plus 1 tablespoon olive oil
1 tablespoon peeled and grated fresh ginger
4 large cloves garlic, chopped
1 bay leaf, crumbled
1 teaspoon chopped fresh oregano, or ½ teaspoon dried
1 medium-size carrot, coarsely grated
¾ to 1 pound spinach, tough stems removed, leaves well washed and drained
Salt and freshly ground black pepper to taste

1. Place the flank steak in a nonreactive dish large enough to hold it opened out flat. Add the wine, lemon juice, soy sauce, ¼ cup oil, ginger, garlic, bay leaf, and oregano and turn to mix and coat both sides of the steak. Set aside to marinate at room temperature for 15 to 30 minutes.

Butterflying a Flank Steak

The easiest way to butterfly a flank steak is to have the butcher do it for you. Otherwise, use a sharp chef's knife and carefully cut the meat in half through the flat surface without severing all the way through. Open out the 2 halves to look like a book being read or a butterfly with wings spread. Lightly pound the meat.

2. Lift the steak out of the marinade and pat it dry. Reserve the marinade. Spread the carrot and spinach leaves over the steak to within 1/2 inch of the edges. Roll up the steak lengthwise and, starting at the center, tie to secure at 1-inch intervals up to each end. Sprinkle salt and pepper all over the roulade.

3. Heat the remaining 1 tablespoon oil in the pressure cooker over high heat until beginning to smoke. Add the roulade and brown all around, about 1 minute. Add the marinade, lock on the lid, and bring to pressure over high heat, about 2 minutes. Reduce the heat to medium and cook for 10 minutes. Remove from the heat and let sit for 5 minutes to finish cooking.

4. With the steam vent pointed away from your face, release any remaining pressure and transfer the roulade to a kitchen platter. Set aside.

5. Boil the marinade in the pressure cooker over high heat until reduced and thickened, about 10 minutes.

6. Slice the roulade into 1½-inch-thick rounds, removing the strings as you go, and arrange the slices on a serving platter. Stir the juices from the kitchen platter into the reduced marinade and pour over the meat. Serve right away.

◈ Oxtail Stew with Wine Grapes and Fennel Seeds

I devised this lusty dish on a September day while sitting among the grapes at one of the Robert Mondavi Winery vineyards in California's Napa Valley. Looking upon row after row of lush, ripe, purple grapes, the cook in me could not resist imagining an oxtail stew to take the chill off an autumn evening, a stew perfumed with the fennel seeds falling to the ground in the wild part of my own backyard, all made ambrosial with some of those harvest grapes. Wine grapes are sometimes found in upscale produce markets, or table grape offerings, preferably purple ones for the color they lend to the sauce, will do.

Even with the aid of the pressure cooker to hasten the cooking time, to do this dish properly takes a certain amount of cooling and settling time. So plan accordingly.   Makes 4 servings

1 teaspoon olive oil
1 ounce salt pork, blanched (see Note page 70), and coarsely chopped
1 large clove garlic, finely chopped
1 medium-size yellow or white onion, finely chopped
1 carrot, peeled and finely chopped
¼ cup dry red wine
2½ pounds cut-up oxtails
1 bay leaf, crumbled
½ teaspoon fennel seeds
1 teaspoon chopped fresh thyme, or ½ teaspoon dried
¼ teaspoon freshly ground black pepper
1 pound purple grapes, preferably wine grapes,
   stemmed and rinsed
1½ cups Beef Broth (page 15) or Chicken Broth (page 18)
1 tablespoon balsamic vinegar
½ cup chopped fresh fennel fronds, if available (see Note page 78), or
   flat-leaf parsley, for garnish

1. Heat the oil in the pressure cooker over medium-high heat. Stir in the salt pork and cook, stirring occasionally, until beginning to turn translucent, about 2 minutes. Add the garlic, onion, and carrot. Stir, then add the wine.

2. Add the oxtails, bay leaf, fennel seeds, thyme, and pepper. Stir to mix. Finally, add the grapes, broth, and vinegar and stir again. Lock on the lid and bring to pressure over high heat, about 4 minutes. Reduce the heat to medium and cook for 40 minutes. Remove from the heat and let rest for 10 minutes to finish cooking.

3. With the steam vent pointed away from your face, gently release any remaining pressure and remove the lid. With a slotted spoon, transfer the oxtails to a large bowl and set aside to cool, then refrigerate until ready to use.

4. Strain the juices from the pressure cooker into a separate bowl. Set aside in the refrigerator until the fat rises to the top, at least 2 hours, or up to overnight. Remove the fat before continuing with the recipe.

5. When ready to serve, place the oxtails and defatted juices in a large pot. Set over medium heat until warm all the way through, about 10 minutes. Sprinkle the fennel fronds over the top and serve right away.

Note: Fresh fennel fronds can be cut from the tops of fennel bulbs, now widely available in produce stores and most supermarkets. If the tops have been trimmed away so there's not much left of the greens, the grocer may be able to supply you with a bunch from the back. Otherwise, flat-leaf parsley will do fine.

◇ Texas Chili

Texas chili means beef and kidney beans. Otherwise, it's not Texas chili. However, Texas being a very large place, there's always room to grow in a different direction, add a bit of this and that around the perimeter. The following keeps to tradition with the chili but innovates with the accompaniments. The recipe requires more advance prep steps than is usual for this book. For instance, I virtually never presoak beans for pressure cooking, but it's required here or the beans and meat won't cook in the same time. With the effort, though, what you get is a fabulous, not just a pedestrian, chili.

Makes 4 to 6 servings

1 cup dried red kidney beans (see Note, page 80)
4 cups water
2 large dried ancho or other red chile peppers
1 medium-size yellow or white onion, peeled
1 large clove garlic, peeled
1 cup coarsely chopped canned tomatoes, with juices

1½ teaspoons chopped fresh oregano, or ½ teaspoon dried

1 tablespoon vegetable oil

2 pounds boneless beef chuck, trimmed and cut into ½-inch pieces

1½ teaspoons ground cumin

2 tablespoons chili powder

⅛ teaspoon cayenne

Pinch of ground cinnamon

1½ tablespoons tomato paste

1 teaspoon salt

Warm flour tortillas (see page 280), for serving

An Out-of-the-Ordinary Assortment of Sides for Texas Chili

- A plate of blanched green beans with a ring of sliced nectarines, freshly ground black pepper, and a drizzle of olive oil over all
- A bowl of sour cream or Crème Fraîche (page 282)
- A small plate of pressed garlic chopped together with serrano chile peppers and salt

1. Place the beans and 2 cups of the water in the pressure cooker. Lock on the lid and bring to pressure over high heat. Reduce the heat to low and cook for 3 minutes. Remove from the heat and let sit for 4 minutes to finish cooking. With the steam vent pointed away from your face, gently release any remaining pressure and set aside without draining.

2. Meanwhile, remove the stems and seeds from the ancho chiles. Place them in a small saucepan and add 1 cup of the water. Bring to a boil, then turn off the heat and let sit for 5 minutes in the liquid to soften.

3. Combine the onion, garlic, tomatoes and their juices, oregano, and anchos and their liquid in a food processor. Puree as fine as possible and set aside.

4. Heat the oil in a large, heavy skillet over medium-high heat until beginning to smoke. Brown the meat on all sides in batches to avoid crowding, about 2 minutes per batch.

5. When all the meat is browned, add it to the pressure cooker with the soaked beans and their liquid. Stir in the cumin, chili powder, cayenne, and cinnamon. Add the pureed ancho mixture, tomato paste, salt, and remaining 1 cup water and stir to mix. Lock on the lid and bring to pressure over high heat, about 5 minutes. Reduce the heat to medium-high and cook for 15 minutes. Remove from the heat and let sit for 10 minutes to finish cooking.

6. With the steam vent pointed away from your face, gently release any remaining pressure. Set the lid ajar and set aside for at least 10 minutes (up to 30 minutes is better).

7. When ready to serve, reheat, if necessary. Ladle into bowls and accompany with warm tortillas and assorted sides (see page 79).

Note: Instead of "soaking" the beans in the pressure cooker, you can soak the beans overnight or use the ordinary quick-soak-on-the-stove-top method: Bring the beans and water to cover to a boil, boil for 2 minutes, and set aside to soak for 1 hour. If you choose one of these ways, the pressure cooker will be free to use for sautéing the meat.

A Brine in Time

Pickling brine used to be called corning brine when it was used in butcher shops to cure fresh ham in a barrel. The butcher's barrel brine also contained some saltpeter, a preservative, required by the USFDA, that is the best preventive of bacterial growth. It is also the agent that turns the ham, tongue, or corned beef a rosy pink; without it, the meat will be more of a foggy gray color. If you care to, you can simulate the coloring property of saltpeter by adding a chunk of cured ham to the brine. Powdered saltpeter is available in pharmacies.

The amount of brine in the following recipe is sufficient for 1 chicken or 2 or 3 trout (let soak for 24 hours) or 1 pork roast (let cure for 24 to 48 hours). For a beef brisket or tongue, make a double batch and let cure for 1 week. For a turkey, make a triple batch and let cure for 72 hours.

Makes 6 cups

6 cups water	½ tablespoon juniper berries, smashed
⅓ cup kosher salt	½ tablespoon black peppercorns, smashed
2 tablespoons sugar	2 bay leaves, torn up a bit
8 large cloves garlic, smashed	6 sprigs fresh thyme, or 2 teaspoons dried

Combine all the ingredients and stir to dissolve the salt and sugar. Add whatever you are going to brine and refrigerate for 24 hours, or up to 1 week, depending on what you are preparing.

◈ Brined Pork Shoulder Roast with Fennel and Dried Figs

Pork loin cuts, center to end, are priced as though they were the preferred choice for tasty pork meat. The shoulder (or butt) of pork is considered a second, albeit less expensive, selection. For pressure cooking, though, there's no doubt the shoulder is what works best. Taking the time to let the shoulder soak in an aromatic brine for one or two days settles any controversy with the first bite. Fennel and figs complement the pork beautifully, but there's plenty of room to reinterpret the recipe with alternatives of your choice, such as dried apricots, celery, and so on. Makes 6 to 8 servings

One 2½-pound boneless pork shoulder roast, soaked in brine for
    24 to 48 hours (see left)
1 large fennel bulb, fronds trimmed off and reserved,
    bulb sliced lengthwise ½ inch thick
12 dried golden (Calimyrna) figs, halved
1 cup water
½ cup dry white wine

1. Lift the pork roast out of the brine and rinse it.

2. Spread the fennel fronds on the bottom of the pressure cooker. Set the roast on top. Spread the fennel slices and figs over the roast. Pour in the water and wine, lock on the lid, and bring to pressure over high heat, about 5 minutes. Reduce the heat to medium to medium–high and cook for 45 minutes, adjusting the level so the pressure doesn't build up too high. Remove from the heat and let sit for 15 minutes to finish cooking.

3. With the steam vent pointed away from your face, gently release any remaining pressure. Let the roast rest for 10 minutes with the lid ajar.

4. Remove the roast, slice it ½ inch thick, and arrange the slices on a serving platter. Top with the fennel and figs from the pot. Remove and discard the fennel fronds, then spoon the juices over the roast and vegetables. Serve right away.

◎ Pork Picnic Shoulder Braised with Rhubarb and Celery Root

A whole picnic shoulder of pork, with a heft of six or seven pounds, might seem like nothing you would ever bring home to cook—too big and too unfamiliar, even though it is there for the taking in most supermarkets on a regular basis. But, with a large pressure cooker, 8- to 10-quart capacity, such a grand cut, which offers magnanimous flavors and generous helpings, can be the center of a home-cooked feast. The preparation calls for an unusual use of the pressure cooker: It serves both as the tub for marinating the meat and as the pot for cooking it—an attraction for those who hate doing dishes. Another attraction, this one for those who don't revel in prep work, is that since the ingredients for marinating the shoulder get strained before cooking, it doesn't matter how coarsely or how unprettily chopped they are.

Makes 8 to 12 servings

1 medium-size yellow or white onion, quartered
1 medium-size carrot, coarsely chopped
3 cloves garlic, halved
1 small leek, coarsely chopped, well washed, and drained
6 sprigs fresh flat-leaf parsley
1 large sprig fresh rosemary
1 teaspoon celery seeds
1 bay leaf
½ teaspoon coriander seeds, smashed
1 teaspoon black peppercorns, smashed
1 tablespoon salt
One 750 ml bottle dry red wine
½ cup red wine vinegar
1 pork picnic shoulder (about 6½ pounds)
¾ pound rhubarb stalks, ends trimmed and cut into 1-inch pieces
1 medium-size celery root (1 to 1¼ pounds), peeled (see page 37),
    quartered, and sliced 1 inch thick

6 medium-size new potatoes, red, white, or yellow, halved

1 cup fresh flat-leaf parsley, chopped, for garnish

1. Combine all the ingredients up to and including the wine vinegar in a large pressure cooker. Slide in the picnic shoulder and set a weight, such as a large can in a plastic zippered bag, on top to keep it submerged. Place in the refrigerator to marinate for 3 days.

2. When ready to cook, remove the pressure cooker from the refrigerator and let sit at room temperature for 1 hour. Remove the weight. Lift out the shoulder, rinse, and pat dry. Strain the liquid into a bowl, wipe out the pot, and return the strained liquid to the pot. Return the shoulder to the pot, skin side up, and spread the rhubarb and celery root over the top.

3. Lock on the lid and bring to pressure over high heat, 9 to 10 minutes. Reduce the heat to medium and cook for 1 hour. Remove from the heat and let sit for 15 minutes to finish cooking.

4. With the steam vent pointed away from your face, gently release any remaining pressure and remove the lid. Let sit, uncovered, for at least 30 minutes, or up to 2 hours.

5. Transfer the shoulder to a platter and set aside. Pour the juices into a bowl and let sit for 15 minutes. Skim off the fat and return the juices to the pressure cooker.

6. Add the potatoes to the pressure cooker, lock on the lid, and bring to pressure over high heat, 5 to 6 minutes. Reduce the heat to medium and cook for 5 minutes. Remove from the heat and let sit to finish cooking while carving the meat.

7. Carve the meat into slices and arrange them on a large serving platter. With the steam vent pointed away from your face, gently release any remaining pressure from the pressure cooker and transfer the potatoes to the platter with the meat. Spoon the liquid from the pot over all, including any pieces of rhubarb or celery root. Sprinkle the parsley over the top and serve.

Baby Back Ribs in Apricot Preserve, Garlic, and Szechwan Pepper Marinade

Baby back ribs were once considered the toss-away of boning out the good part, pork loin, with not enough meat left on them to bother. Then, as small vegetables and small bites became part of upscale American cuisine, the baby back ribs grew in price and diminished in availability. Even so, they're not so expensive as to prohibit serving them occasionally. The apricot, garlic, and Szechwan pepper marinade brings together pork, fruit, and spice in a traditional flavor combination made lively with a turn in the pressure cooker. It's one of my favorite recipes in this volume.

Makes 4 servings

2 pounds pork baby back ribs, cut into 4 sections
1 cup Apricot Preserve, Garlic, and Szechwan Pepper Marinade
  (recipe follows)
10 to 12 sprigs fresh cilantro, for garnish

1. Combine the ribs and marinade in a large dish and turn to coat the ribs all around. Cover and set aside in the refrigerator to marinate for at least 3 hours, or up to overnight.

2. To cook, transfer the ribs and marinade to the pressure cooker. Lock on the lid and bring to pressure over high heat, about 3 minutes. Reduce the heat to medium and cook for 11 minutes. Remove from the heat and let sit for 5 minutes to finish cooking.

3. With the steam vent pointed away from your face, gently release any remaining pressure. Set the lid ajar and let rest for 5 minutes.

4. Arrange the ribs on a serving platter and spoon the marinade juices over the top. Garnish with the cilantro sprigs and serve.

Apricot Preserve, Garlic, and Szechwan Pepper Marinade

Makes about 1 cup

½ cup chunky apricot preserves
8 cloves garlic, slivered
¼ teaspoon Szechwan pepper (see Note)
¼ cup freshly squeezed lime juice
¼ cup dry white wine
1 tablespoon low-sodium soy sauce

Combine all the ingredients in a small bowl and stir to mix. Use right away or refrigerate, covered, for up to 3 days.

Note: Szechwan pepper, sometimes called brown pepper, is not a pepper at all but a spicy berry used dry in Chinese cooking, much like true peppercorns. White peppercorns make a good substitute.

◈ Pork and Clams Portuguese Style

Such an esoteric combination as pork and clams would probably not have occurred to me out of the clear blue sky. But when my friend and sometimes co-author, Susanna Hoffman, visited Portugal one year, she introduced the notion. At first a reluctant disbeliever, I became a convert as we worked up a recipe, somewhat different from the one here, that was eventually published in our Well-Filled Microwave Cookbook. What I love about this dish is that once the pork has been rubbed and marinated with the seasonings, there's not a lot more prep to do—just add a dollop of tomato paste, stir, and pressure cook for 15 minutes, counting start-up and cool-down time. Add the clams, heat for a wink more, and you're done. Serve with hunks of olive-oiled, garlicked, and warmed country bread and dinner's on.

Makes 6 servings

1 pound boneless country-style pork spareribs, cut into 1½-inch pieces

2 large cloves garlic, pressed or minced

1 small yellow or white onion, finely chopped

1 bay leaf, crumbled

1 teaspoon mild paprika

1 teaspoon salt

¾ cup dry white wine

2 tablespoons olive oil

2 tablespoons tomato paste

1 pound Manila clams, rinsed

6 very thinly sliced lemon rounds, for garnish

12 sprigs fresh cilantro or flat-leaf parsley, for garnish

1. Combine the pork, garlic, onion, bay leaf, paprika, salt, wine, and 1 tablespoon of the olive oil in a large dish or bowl. Set aside in the refrigerator, covered with plastic wrap, to marinate at least overnight, or up to 2 days. Remove from the refrigerator 1 hour before cooking.

2. When ready to cook, heat the remaining 1 tablespoon oil in the pressure cooker over medium-high heat until beginning to smoke. Brown the pork for 2 minutes, then add the marinade to the pot. Add the tomato paste and stir to mix. Lock on the lid and bring to pressure over high heat, about 2 minutes. Reduce the heat to medium-high and cook for 8 minutes. Remove from the heat and let sit for 5 minutes to finish cooking.

3. With the steam vent pointed away from your face, gently release any remaining pressure. Add the clams to the pot, cover without locking on the lid, and cook over high heat for 2 minutes. Discard any clams that haven't opened by the end of the cooking time. Garnish with the lemon and cilantro and serve.

◇ ◇ ◇

◇ Chilied Pork with Golden Raisins

Warm, not hot, dried red chile peppers; punchy, but not acrid, fresh garlic; sweet raisins; heady cumin; fragrant oregano; tart cider vinegar. Such a seemingly disparate chorus of strong flavors is pure harmony when played as background music to tender, inviting pork. For the ancho chile paste, I prefer to keep the seeds: In dried chile peppers their heat is not objectionable, and I like the mottled look they give to the sauce.

Makes 4 to 6 servings

2 dried ancho chile peppers (see Note page 88)
6 large cloves garlic, coarsely chopped
1½ cups water
1½ pounds boneless country-style pork spareribs or pork butt steaks,
    cut into 1½-inch-wide strips
1 tablespoon chopped fresh oregano, or 1½ teaspoons dried
1 teaspoon ground cumin
1½ tablespoons cider vinegar
¾ teaspoon salt
1 tablespoon olive oil
⅔ cup golden raisins
10 to 12 sprigs fresh cilantro, for garnish

1. Tear the anchos into 3 or 4 large pieces each and combine them with the garlic and water in a small saucepan. Bring to a boil, reduce the heat, and simmer briskly for 5 minutes. Set aside until cool enough to handle. Then, puree the anchos and garlic with ½ cup of the cooking water to make a paste.

2. Place the pork strips in a large nonreactive dish. Add the ancho paste, oregano, cumin, vinegar, and salt and toss to mix. Cover and marinate in the refrigerator for at least 3 hours (overnight is better).

3. Heat the oil in the pressure cooker over high heat and brown the pork in 2 batches, about 4 minutes per batch. Stir in the raisins and the marinade and lock on the lid. Bring to pressure over high heat, about 2 minutes. Reduce the heat to medium-high and cook for 15 minutes. Remove from the heat and let sit for 10 minutes to finish cooking.

4. With the steam vent pointed away from your face, gently release any remaining pressure. Set the lid ajar and let rest for 10 minutes. Serve with the cilantro sprigs strewn across the top.

Note: You can substitute dried pasilla chile peppers or dried New Mexico chile peppers for the anchos, though neither has as full a flavor as the anchos.

◇ Chile Verde

Boneless, country-style pork ribs need only to be cut into strips. Canned green chiles also need only to be cut into strips. The food processor does the job of chopping the onions and garlic; the pressure cooker does the job of simmering; and there you have it—a slow-cooked dish that takes advantage of modern conveniences and is ready for the table in one third the time of the classic stove-top version.

Makes 6 to 8 servings

2 tablespoons peanut oil
4 pounds boneless country-style pork spareribs, trimmed and cut crosswise into
    ½-inch pieces (see top right)
2 medium-size yellow or white onions, finely chopped
5 large cloves garlic, finely chopped
2 small fresh green chile peppers, finely chopped
1½ cups Beef Broth (page 15)
3 cups water
2 teaspoons salt
One 11-ounce can roasted and peeled green chiles (see top right),
    cut into ¼-inch-wide strips
Warm corn or flour tortillas (see page 280), for serving

1. Heat the oil in the pressure cooker over high heat until beginning to smoke. Brown the pork over medium-high heat in batches, about 2 minutes per batch, removing each to a platter when done.

2. Add the onions, garlic, and fresh chile peppers and stir to coat with the oil. Return the meat to the pot and add the broth, water, and salt. Stir to mix, add the canned chiles, and stir to mix again. Lock on the lid and bring to pressure over high heat, 11 to 12 minutes. Reduce the heat to medium and cook for 35 minutes. Remove from the heat and let sit for 10 minutes to finish cooking.

3. With the steam vent pointed away from your face, gently release any remaining pressure, carefully remove the lid, and let sit for 15 minutes more. Spoon off the fat that has risen to the top and serve with a basket of warm corn or flour tortillas.

Italian Fresh Pork Sausage with Lima Beans Cotechino, zampone. *They sound like words from an Italian movie, maybe with some rough characters. Actually, they're large fresh Italian sausages, slightly dried. If you live in a metropolitan area with an Italian population, you can find these sausages, or the equivalent in a different casing, in Italian delis during the winter holidays. They are traditionally eaten together with lentils on New Year's Day to bring good luck throughout the coming year. Reminiscent of the black-eye peas and ham hocks that are de rigueur for New Year's luck in the American South, the Italian dish brings, if not lot-*

tery-level fortune, at least happiness and good cheer at the table. Fresh Italian sausage, the kind you find in most butcher and deli counters, makes a good substitute, though a less impressive show.

Makes 4 servings

1 *cotechino* sausage (about ¾ pound)
1 cup dried lima beans
3 cups water
Salt to taste
¼ cup chopped fresh flat-leaf parsley, for garnish
Dijon mustard, for serving

1. Place the sausage, limas, and water in the pressure cooker. Lock on the lid and bring to pressure over high heat, about 6 minutes. Reduce the heat to medium and cook for 20 minutes. Remove from the heat and let sit for 10 minutes to finish cooking.

2. With the steam vent pointed away from your face, gently release any remaining pressure. Remove the sausage and slice it into ½-inch-thick rounds. Season the limas with salt and transfer them to a high-lipped serving platter. Arrange the sausage slices over the beans and pour the juices from the pot over all. Sprinkle with the parsley and serve with mustard on the side.

Other Scenarios for *Cotechino* Sausage

Cotechino sausage cooked on its own, without the limas, can be served the more traditional way, with lentils, as they do in Emilia-Romagna, or less traditionally, with black-eyed peas. *Cotechino* is also a traditional, and special, element in a *bollito misto* (see page 118). Thin slices of *cotechino* make a notable addition to a charcuterie platter or as a topping for bruschetta. Thinly sliced and slivered, *cotechino* adds definition to a lusty salad of arugula, pickled red onion, fennel, and cheese croutons. It also makes a memorable pasta dish of fusilli and fresh fava beans tossed with extra virgin olive oil and freshly grated parmesan cheese.

◈ Ham Shanks, Creamer Potatoes, and Endives in Madeira Cream

Ham appears with Madeira or cream in many guises in French cooking, notably as jambon au madère *or* jambon à la crème. *Putting Madeira, cream, and ham together makes a delectable threesome, and the Belgian endive is just the right foil to keep the combination from being cloying. As with osso buco (see page 103) and lamb shanks (see page 92), the pressure cooker truly shines at turning out succulent shank meat in no time flat.*

Makes 4 servings

4 pieces smoked ham shanks (½ pound each)
6 juniper berries, smashed, or 1 tablespoon gin
1 medium-size yellow or white onion, coarsely chopped
Tops of 2 ribs celery
4 cups water
4 creamer potatoes, preferably red, halved
4 large Belgian endives (about ¾ pound), halved lengthwise
2 tablespoons Madeira
¾ cup heavy cream

1. Combine the ham, juniper berries, onion, celery tops, and water in the pressure cooker and stir to mix. Lock on the lid and bring to pressure over high heat, about 6 minutes. Reduce the heat to medium and cook for 20 minutes. Remove from the heat and let sit for 10 minutes to finish cooking.

2. With the steam vent pointed away from your face, gently release any remaining pressure. Transfer the shanks to a platter and set aside. Strain the juices into a bowl and set aside for 20 minutes for the fat to rise to the top.

3. Spoon off the fat and return the juices to the pressure cooker. Add the potatoes and bring to a boil. Cook over medium-high heat, boiling hard to reduce the juices, for about 10 minutes. With a slotted spoon, transfer the potatoes to the platter with the shanks.

4. Add the endives to the juices in the pressure cooker and cook over medium-high heat for 4 minutes. Lift out the endives and add to the platter with the shanks and potatoes.

5. Stir the Madeira into the juices in the pressure cooker. Add the cream. Boil hard for 3 minutes to reduce.

6. Pour the cream sauce over the shanks, potatoes, and endives and serve on the platter.

◒ Lamb Shanks Braised with Garlic, Rosemary, and White Wine
Pressure cooking lamb shanks is the only way I've found to equal a long, slow cook in the oven and turn an otherwise forbidding hunk of meat and bone into a dish that practically rolls over and purrs on your plate. If you're serving family style, the garlic cloves don't need peeling; add them to the pot unpeeled and let each person enjoy them on a peel-as-you-go basis.

Makes 4 servings

1½ tablespoons olive oil
2 large lamb shanks (2½ pounds), each cut crosswise into 3 pieces
3 heads garlic, cloves separated and peeled (see headnote)
¾ cup dry white wine
2 medium-size tomatoes, coarsely chopped
2 teaspoons chopped fresh rosemary, or ½ teaspoon dried
Salt and freshly ground black pepper to taste
Several sprigs fresh rosemary or fresh lemon leaves (optional), for garnish
¼ cup chopped lemon zest, for garnish

1. Heat the oil in the pressure cooker over medium-high heat until beginning to smoke. Add the lamb and garlic and brown the lamb all around, 4 to 5 minutes. Pour in the wine and stir to deglaze the bottom of the pot. Add the tomatoes and chopped rosemary and sprinkle liberally with salt and pepper. Lock on the lid and bring to

The Zestiest Zest

There are two excellent reasons to seek out unsprayed citrus—orange, lime, or lemon—especially if the recipe calls for zest. First, the taste difference is astounding: Organic or unsprayed citrus has the flavor of the fruit pure and unadulterated, whereas ordinary supermarket lemons have been sprayed with chemicals and the zest in particular retains that flavor. Second, for health reasons alone, unsprayed citrus is better for you. If all you have available is sprayed citrus, scrub the skins well with soap and water before using. Or, omit the zest and substitute another garnish.

pressure over high heat, about 5 minutes. Reduce the heat to medium-high and cook for 20 minutes. Remove from the heat and let sit for 10 minutes to finish cooking.

2. With the steam vent pointed away from your face, gently release any remaining pressure. Arrange the rosemary sprigs, if using, on a serving platter. Transfer the shanks to the platter and spoon the juices over the top. Sprinkle on the zest and serve right away.

◈ Lamb Daube à la Elizabeth David   *The combination of lamb with other meats, sometimes beef or rabbit but especially pork, is particularly French. In an Avignon-style daube, generous-size cubes of leg of lamb, a somewhat lean meat, are long cooked with salt pork to make a stew of sublime depth and richness. The following rendition is fairly true to Elizabeth David's recipe, except that I added anchovy and subtracted carrot; the pressure cooker reduced the time by almost 75 percent. As with many a long-cooking meat stew, the flavor is enhanced if made the day before. Elizabeth David suggests serving the daube with white haricot beans or flageolets (see page 272). Boiled potatoes or egg noodles also suit the savory, homey spirit of the dish.*

Makes 4 to 6 servings

2-pound trimmed boneless leg of lamb, cut into approximately
  $2\frac{1}{2} \times 2\frac{1}{2} \times 1\frac{1}{2}$-inch pieces
1 recipe Aromatic Red Wine Marinade (recipe follows)
2 tablespoons olive oil
2 ounces blanched salt pork (see Note page 70), cut into $\frac{1}{2} \times 1$-inch pieces
1 large yellow or white onion, coarsely chopped
4 large cloves garlic, coarsely chopped
2 wide strips orange zest (removed with a vegetable peeler)
4 anchovy fillets, chopped

1. Combine the lamb and marinade in a large nonreactive dish, such as an enameled pot, a glazed or unglazed clay baking dish, a glass baking dish, or a stainless steel roasting pan. Toss to mix, cover, and set aside in the refrigerator to marinate for at least 4 hours, or up to overnight. When ready to cook, remove from the refrigerator for 30 minutes or so to take off the chill.

2. Heat the oil in the pressure cooker over medium-high heat. Add the salt pork and cook, stirring, until turning translucent, about 2 minutes. Add the lamb and sauté until slightly browned, about 5 minutes.

3. Add the onion, garlic, orange peel, and anchovies. Stir to mix and lock on the lid. Bring to pressure over high heat, 4 to 5 minutes. Reduce the heat to medium-high and cook for 45 minutes. Remove from the heat and let sit for 10 minutes to finish cooking.

4. With the steam vent pointed away from your face, gently release any remaining pressure. Set aside with the lid ajar to rest for another 10 minutes. Serve right away.

◇ ◇ ◇

Aromatic Red Wine Marinade *With a mound of aromatic vegetables and herbs and a generous soupçon of brandy, half a bottle of red wine becomes a multipurpose, but never ordinary, marinade for lamb, beef, squabs, game hens, or quail.*

Makes enough for 2 pounds cut-up meat, 4 squabs or game hens, or 8 quail

2 ribs celery, very coarsely chopped
1 carrot, very coarsely chopped
1 small yellow or white onion, very coarsely chopped
3 large cloves garlic, smashed
10 to 12 sprigs fresh flat-leaf parsley
6 to 8 sprigs fresh thyme, or 1 teaspoon dried
1 large bay leaf, crumbled
1 teaspoon freshly ground black pepper
2½ cups dry red wine
½ cup brandy

Combine all the ingredients in a medium-size bowl. Use right away.

◈ **Mediterranean Lamb and Green Bean Stew** *All around the Mediterranean, lamb is paired with green beans and tomatoes in a rustic potage to serve as filling, but special, family fare. In my childhood, the dish was certain to appear on the table soon after a leg of lamb, usually prepared as shish kebab, because the bones and trim of the leg provided material for the lamb broth base. Lamb neck or bone-in lamb stew meat substitutes perfectly for the leg trim. For the best flavor, the green beans should be fresh, not difficult to find most of the year these days. Armenian Pilaf and Cucumbers in Yogurt are must accompaniments.*

Makes 4 servings

2 tablespoons olive oil

1 small leek, trimmed, thinly sliced, well washed, and drained

2 large cloves garlic, coarsely chopped

1 teaspoon chopped fresh oregano, or ½ teaspoon dried

3 medium-size fresh tomatoes, peeled (see page 24) and coarsely chopped,
  or an equivalent amount of canned tomatoes

1 teaspoon salt

½ teaspoon Aleppo pepper (see page 232), or ⅛ teaspoon cayenne

2 pounds bone-in lamb stew meat

1 pound green beans, ends trimmed and cut into 1- to 1½-inch pieces

2 cups water

3 cups Armenian Pilaf (page 227), warm, for serving

2 cups Cucumbers in Yogurt (recipe follows), for serving

1. Heat the oil in the pressure cooker over medium-high heat until beginning to smoke. Add the leek, garlic, and oregano and cook, stirring occasionally, over medium heat until wilted, about 2 minutes.

2. Add the tomatoes, salt, and Aleppo pepper and cook, stirring occasionally, until the tomatoes wilt, about 1 minute. Add the lamb, green beans, and water. Lock on the lid and bring to pressure over high heat, about 5 minutes. Reduce the heat to medium and

It's in the Look

Presentation enhances a dish almost as much as the cooking. It's true that a well-conceived dish, lovingly assembled and well tended during cooking, will undoubtedly be delicious to eat. But if the dish is served up with attention to eye appeal also, it's almost guaranteed to taste even better. Almost any kind of edible fresh greenery does the trick. For instance, you can glamorize the platter with edible flowers or a confetti of very finely minced red bell pepper or carrot. In the same vein, to make the most of a lemon zest garnish, cut it into very fine long shreds, a labor of love that makes a spectacular finishing touch.

cook for 10 minutes. Remove from the heat and let sit for 8 minutes to finish cooking.

3. With the steam vent pointed away from your face, gently release any remaining pressure with the lid ajar and let sit for at least 15 minutes, or up to 1 hour. Serve hot, reheating if necessary, with the pilaf and cucumbers on the side.

Cucumbers in Yogurt *Around the Mediterranean, a dish of cucumbers in yogurt is considered both sauce and side salad. Sometimes mint or dill is included, or often, as here, garlic, which takes the sauce in a Greek direction. Kirby (pickling) cucumbers are the best to use. Regular cucumbers are also good as long as any large seeds are removed. English, or hothouse, cucumbers don't work: They are too mild and fade into the background when enveloped in the yogurt.*

Makes 2 cups

2 cloves garlic, peeled
½ teaspoon salt
1½ cups plain yogurt
1 teaspoon chopped fresh dill (optional)
4 large pickling cucumbers or 2 medium-size regular cucumbers, peeled

Finely chop the garlic and salt together. Transfer to a bowl and add the yogurt and dill, if using. Seed the cucumbers, if necessary. Cut them lengthwise into quarters, then crosswise into ¼-inch-thick pieces. Add to the yogurt and stir to mix. Serve right away or refrigerate and serve chilled.

◈ Scotch-Style Lamb and Pearl Barley Stew with Turnips, Carrots, and Cabbage
It seems that at first the meat was beef, but by the last half of the eighteenth century, mutton had become as regular a choice, and now modern British cookbooks call for either/or. Pearl barley, turnips, carrots, and cabbage are almost always included, and sometimes there's celery. The sprinkle of dill on top is my addition, as is serving the

dish as a one-plate stew rather than serving the broth first, then the meat and vegetables after. If you'd like to vary the stew a step further, you can use wheat berries instead of pearl barley; the cooking time is the same. Makes 4 to 6 servings

2 large lamb shanks (2½ pounds), each cut crosswise into 2 pieces
½ cup pearl barley, well rinsed
1 medium-size carrot, peeled and cut into 1-inch-thick diagonal slices
½ small yellow or white onion, halved
2 whole cloves, stuck into the onion pieces
1 bay leaf
1 teaspoon salt
Freshly ground black pepper to taste
6 cups water
Pinch of ground nutmeg
2 medium-size turnips, halved and each half cut into thirds
½ small green cabbage, halved, cored, and each half cut into thirds
2 medium-size leeks (white and light green parts only), chopped, well washed, and drained
2 tablespoons chopped fresh dill, for garnish

1. Place the lamb, pearl barley, carrot, clove–stuck onion pieces, bay leaf, salt, pepper, and water in the pressure cooker. Lock on the lid and bring to pressure over high heat, about 7 minutes. Reduce the heat to medium and cook for 10 minutes. Remove from the heat and let sit for 10 minutes to cool down.

2. With the steam vent pointed away from your face, gently release any remaining pressure and carefully remove the lid. Remove and discard the onion pieces.

3. Sprinkle the nutmeg over the meat and set the turnips, cabbage, and leeks on top. Without stirring, lock on the lid and bring to pressure over high heat, about 5 minutes. Remove from the heat and let sit for 10 minutes to finish cooking.

4. With the steam vent pointed away from your face, gently release any remaining pressure. Remove and discard the bay leaf. Dish the meat, vegetables, and barley into large individual bowls or a large, high-lipped serving platter. Spoon the juices over the top, sprinkle with the dill, and serve.

Note: Before dishing up the stew, you can pour off the juices into a bowl and let them settle for 15 minutes. Then skim off the fat layer and proceed.

◇ Lamb Tagine with Quinces and Three Condiments

There's nothing obscure about tagines besides their name: They are the North African, especially Moroccan, version of stew. Often, tagines are served with the tiny beads of semolina pasta called couscous. Then, the dish is called couscous. When the stew is served without the couscous, tagine is the way it's described here, and it may be accompanied by many grain alternatives, from a bulgur pilaf (pages 230 to 231) to nut- or seed-flavored country-style bread from the bakery. For the quinces, you must seize the opportunity: Late fall to early winter is their season. Otherwise, substitute slightly underripe tart apples, such as Pippins.

Makes 4 servings

2 tablespoons peanut oil
2 pounds bone-in lamb stew meat
1 medium-size yellow or white onion, halved and sliced ¼ inch thick
¾ teaspoon ground ginger
½ teaspoon ground turmeric
One 2-inch piece cinnamon stick
⅛ teaspoon cayenne
½ cup chopped fresh cilantro
2 small quinces (about ¾ pound), unpeeled, quartered, and cored
¼ cup water
½ cups sliced almonds, lightly toasted (see page 41), for garnish
¼ cup Harissa (page 100), for serving
1 recipe Minted Yogurt Balls (page 101), for serving

1. Heat the oil in the pressure cooker over medium–high heat until beginning to smoke. Brown the lamb in two batches, about 1 minute per batch.

2. Add the onion and stir to mix. Add the ginger, turmeric, cinnamon stick, cayenne, and cilantro and stir to mix. Put the quince quarters on the top and pour in the water. Lock on the lid and bring to pressure over high heat, about 2 minutes. Reduce the heat to medium–high and cook for 15 minutes. Remove from the heat and let sit for 10 minutes to finish cooking.

3. With the steam vent pointed away from your face, gently release any remaining pressure. Transfer the stew to a platter, sprinkle with the toasted almonds, and serve with the harissa and yogurt balls.

Harissa *I prefer harissa fresh and bright, like pesto and salsa, before it mellows with standing for two or three days. On the other hand, I sometimes double or triple the recipe, as I do with pesto and salsa, to have some on hand in the refrigerator.* Makes ¼ cup

> 4 small fresh red chile peppers, such as serrano or cayenne, seeded and
>   coarsely chopped, or ¼ cup red pepper flakes
> 4 large cloves garlic, pressed
> 1 teaspoon caraway seeds
> ½ teaspoon salt
> 3 tablespoons peanut oil

Place the chiles, garlic, and caraway seeds on a cutting surface. Sprinkle the salt over the top and chop together into a coarse paste. Transfer to a small bowl and stir in the oil. Let sit for 30 minutes or so, then use. The harissa will keep in the refrigerator, covered with plastic wrap, for up to 1 week.

Minted Yogurt Balls *Yogurt drained long enough goes from thick to thicker, and eventually becomes firm enough to form into loose balls. Yogurt balls are delicate; they will keep in the refrigerator for up to five days, not longer.*

Makes about ten 1-inch balls

2 cups plain yogurt
1 tablespoon chopped fresh mint
½ teaspoon salt
½ teaspoon thinly shredded fresh mint
½ teaspoon red pepper flakes
Cracked black peppercorns to taste
¼ cup olive oil

1. Line a colander with a damp kitchen towel or a triple layer of cheesecloth, making sure the cloth extends over the sides of the colander. Set the colander over a bowl narrow enough and deep enough to hold the colander well away from the bottom. Put the yogurt in the colander, cover with plastic wrap, and set the whole contraption in the refrigerator to drain overnight. Periodically check the level of whey drained off the yogurt; if it has reached the bottom of the colander, pour it off.

2. Transfer the drained yogurt to a medium-size bowl. Add the chopped mint and salt and whisk to smooth. Refrigerate until firm, about 30 minutes.

3. In 2-tablespoon amounts, roll the yogurt mixture between the palms of your hands to make balls. As you go, set the balls in a lipped dish large enough to hold them in a single layer. Sprinkle the balls with the shredded mint, red pepper flakes, and cracked peppercorns. Pour the oil over all and serve. Or, refrigerate, covered with plastic wrap, for up to 5 days.

Lamb Tongues with Yukon Gold Potatoes and Mustard Sauce

Lamb tongue is highly regarded in lands where sheep provide the main meat of the diet. Rich and tender, lamb tongue takes well to pairing with soft, not-quite-mealy potatoes and nippy Dijon mustard. A good handful of parsley stirred into the sauce at the end adds the right touch to remind us it's spring.

Makes 4 servings

1 pound (4 to 5) lamb tongues
1 teaspoon salt
1 bay leaf, crumbled
2 tablespoons olive oil
½ pound Yukon gold potatoes, cut into ½-inch-thick rounds
¼ cup freshly squeezed lemon juice
¼ cup water
1 clove garlic, minced or pressed
1 tablespoon Dijon mustard
¼ cup chopped fresh flat-leaf parsley

1. Toss the tongues with the salt and bay leaf in a medium-size bowl. Set aside in the refrigerator, covered with plastic wrap, for at least 2 hours, or up to overnight.

2. Heat the oil in the pressure cooker over medium-high heat until beginning to smoke. Add the potatoes and cook, stirring, until they begin to turn golden, about 3 minutes. Add the tongues, lemon juice, water, and garlic and stir to coat. Lock on the lid and bring to pressure over high heat, about 2 minutes. Reduce the heat to medium-high and cook for 10 minutes. Remove from the heat and let sit for 10 minutes to finish cooking.

3. With the steam vent pointed away from your face, gently release any remaining pressure. Lift out the tongues and set aside for a few minutes until cool enough to handle.

4. Peel off the skins of the tongues and cut them crosswise into ¼- to ½-inch-thick slices. Arrange the slices on a serving platter. Lift out the potatoes and arrange them around the tongue slices.

5. Stir the mustard into the juices in the pot, whisking to mix well. Whisk in the parsley, pour over the tongue slices and potatoes on the platter, and serve.

◈ Osso Buco with Salted Lemon Gremolata

The pressure cooker lifts osso buco, a classic slow food, into the realm of timely possibility. The classic gremolata topping, made here with salted lemon, lifts it into the realm of food for the gods, a fitting status for what has become a rather pricey dish.

Makes 4 servings

2 tablespoons olive oil
Four 2½-inch-thick pieces veal shank
All-purpose flour, for coating the meat
½ medium-size carrot
½ medium-size yellow or white onion, peeled
1 rib celery
1 clove garlic, peeled
½ cup dry white wine
½ cup Chicken Broth (page 18)
1 cup peeled (see page 24), seeded, and coarsely chopped tomatoes, with juices
3 large sprigs fresh thyme, or ½ teaspoon dried
1 bay leaf
2 strips lemon peel (removed with a vegetable peeler)
½ teaspoon salt
¼ teaspoon freshly ground black pepper
⅓ cup Salted Lemon Gremolata (page 104), for garnish

1. Heat the oil in the pressure cooker over medium-high heat until beginning to smoke. Sprinkle the veal shanks with flour and brown on both sides, 4 to 5 minutes. Add the carrot, onion, celery, and garlic and cook over medium heat, stirring occasionally, until the onion is slightly wilted, about 2 minutes.

2. Add the wine, broth, tomatoes and their juices, thyme, bay leaf, lemon peel, salt, and pepper. Stir to mix, lock on the lid, and bring to pressure over high heat, about 3 minutes. Reduce the heat to medium-high and cook for 30 minutes. Remove from the heat and let sit for 10 minutes to finish cooking.

3. With the steam vent pointed away from your face, gently release any remaining pressure. Set the lid ajar and let rest for at least 10 minutes (see Note). Remove the lemon peel and bay leaf, sprinkle the gremolata over the top, and serve.

Note: If possible, let the osso buco rest for 1 hour or so, then reheat gently before serving.

Salted Lemon Gremolata *Salted lemon adds an out-of-the-ordinary zing to the gremolata mixture and takes but a few minutes to prepare. Though I often press garlic, for gremolata it must be minced.*

Makes about ⅓ cup

3 large cloves garlic, minced
¼ cup chopped fresh flat-leaf parsley
2 tablespoons chopped salted lemon rind (see page 40)

Combine the ingredients in a small bowl. Use right away or within several hours; gremolata doesn't keep, even overnight.

◌ ◌ ◌

Bacon Considerations

Pancetta is a peppery, Italian-style bacon that is salt-cured but not smoked. It is softer and milder than American-style bacon and works particularly well where bacon is wanted in the recipe but its flavor should be subtle, not overpowering. A thinly sliced, mildly smoked bacon is an option, but it should first be blanched for 1 minute to temper its flavor.

◇ Pancetta-Wrapped Veal Birds with Arugula and Shiitake Mushroom Stuffing

My first memory of veal birds is of my mother bending over the oven, turning them to make sure they cooked evenly all around. When I asked, I found out they were called birds because the bacon wrap with freely flapping ends made the rolls look like birds without heads. (She was always quick to tell a good story when a child needed attention as she continued to attend to what she was doing.) It was a lasting image, but how those birds have flown: from veal to beef to chicken as the wrap. From bacon to pancetta girdle, from no stuffing at all to arugula and shiitake mushroom stuffing, and then to sauce! This version is a contemporary telling of an old story, deliciously rendered in the pressure cooker.

Makes 3 servings

3 veal scaloppine cutlets (about 1 pound)
Salt and freshly ground black pepper to taste
3 tablespoons freshly grated parmesan cheese
1 cup shredded arugula leaves
3 medium-size fresh shiitake mushrooms, stemmed and thinly sliced
Olive oil, for moistening the filling
3 slices pancetta
1 tablespoon olive oil
1½ cups Beef Broth (page 15) or Chicken Broth (page 18)
1 tablespoon freshly squeezed lemon juice
1 tablespoon chopped fresh dill, or 1 teaspoon dried

1. One at a time, place the cutlets between 2 pieces of waxed paper or plastic wrap and pound with a mallet into a thin 7 × 10-inch rectangle, $\frac{1}{16}$ inch thick.

2. Sprinkle each cutlet with salt and pepper and then with 1 tablespoon cheese. Spread one third of the arugula over the cheese. Arrange one third of the mushroom slices down the center, going the short way. Moisten with olive oil and roll up the cutlets, enclosing the arugula and mushrooms, to make rolls about 7 inches long and 2 inches thick. Wrap each roll with a slice of pancetta around the middle.

3. Heat the 1 tablespoon olive oil in the pressure cooker over medium-high heat until beginning to smoke. Add the veal rolls and brown all around, about 2 minutes.

4. Pour the broth into the pot, lock on the lid, and bring to pressure over high heat, about 2 minutes. Reduce the heat to medium and cook for 2 minutes. Remove from the heat and let sit for 5 minutes to finish cooking.

5. With the steam vent pointed away from your face, gently release any remaining pressure. Lift the rolls onto a serving platter and set aside in a warm place. Bring the liquid in the pot to a boil and cook over high heat until thickened and saucy and reduced by half, about 5 minutes.

6. Stir in the lemon juice and dill. Pour over the rolls and serve right away.

Mushroom Considerations

The veal bird recipe calls for shiitake mushrooms because those are the ones I use most often in recipes that call for fresh mushrooms. Portobellos are more commonly called for these days, but I reserve them to serve as a plate of their own, especially as breaded and fried whole caps, where their meaty brawn is showcased. If I need to use dried mushrooms, I choose porcinis over dried shiitakes for most recipes, unless the dish is of Asian essence.

◇ Veal Breast Niçoise Stuffed with Sweet Italian Sausage, Spinach, and Olives

I think of stuffed veal breast as panache without price because it makes an impressive picture on the platter yet it's quite inexpensive, especially as veal goes. You probably have to order the breast from the butcher; as long as you're at it, have the butcher open the pocket. Fill it with the sausage, which you can purchase if mixing your own is one too many steps to do, set it in the pressure cooker with the usual aromatic seasonings, and steam away.

Makes 6 to 8 servings as an entrée,
or 12 to 15 servings as a buffet or picnic dish

1½ pounds Sweet Italian Sausage (page 108)
2 cups chopped fresh spinach leaves, washed, drained, and wilted
    for 5 minutes in the microwave or on the stove top
¼ cup chopped pitted black olives, preferably Niçoise or mild oil-cured olives
1 veal breast (about 2½ pounds) meat section separated away
    from bones (see Note page 108)
2 tablespoons olive oil
1 small carrot, peeled and coarsely chopped
1 small yellow or white onion, coarsely chopped
2 ribs celery, coarsely chopped
2 cups dry white wine
2 cups water
Dijon mustard, for serving
French bread, for serving

1. Mix together the sausage, spinach, and olives in a medium-size bowl.

2. Spread the sausage mixture between the bones and meat flap of the veal breast. Enclose the stuffing by stretching the flap over the bones and secure with a needle and thread or skewers, as you would to truss a turkey to hold in the dressing. Wrap a length of kitchen string across and around the breast, like tying a package, to further truss it and also to make a handle for lifting the meat out of the pressure cooker.

3. Heat the oil in the pressure cooker over high heat until beginning to smoke. Set the stuffed breast in the pot, meat side down, and brown for 2 minutes. Without turning it over, add the carrot, onion, celery, wine, and water. Lock on the lid and bring to pressure over high heat, about 4 minutes. Reduce the heat to medium and cook for 50 minutes, taking care to make adjustments along the way, if necessary, to keep the pressure up but not so high that there will be spillover. Remove from the heat and let sit for 10 minutes to finish cooking.

4. With the steam vent pointed away from your face, gently release any remaining pressure and let sit for 10 minutes more with the lid ajar.

5. If serving warm, transfer the breast to a platter. Discard the vegetables and juices. Remove the string or skewers from the breast and slice into "chops." Arrange the chops on a serving platter.

If serving chilled, let the breast cool in the cooking liquid, then store in the refrigerator overnight. When ready to serve, slice into chops and arrange on a platter. Serve with Dijon mustard and French bread.

Note: It's not difficult to open the pocket yourself with a boning or curved paring knife. Insert the knife into the large end of the breast close to the bones. Work the knife along the bones almost, but not quite, to the other end.

Sweet Italian Sausage

The "sweet" in sweet Italian sausage refers to the fennel seeds. Adding spinach and olives makes it Niçoise. Italian or Niçoise, it's a sausage you can use in many a dish or form into patties and fry or grill on their own. Makes 1½ pounds

1½ pounds ground pork
1 large clove garlic, minced
1 tablespoon chopped fresh flat-leaf parsley
2 teaspoons chopped fresh oregano, or ¾ teaspoon dried
1 teaspoon chopped fresh thyme, or ½ teaspoon dried

1 teaspoon fennel seeds

⅛ teaspoon cayenne

¼ teaspoon freshly ground black pepper

1 teaspoon salt

⅓ cup dry white wine

Combine all the ingredients in a medium-size bowl and mix with your hands until well blended. Use right away or, preferably, cover and set aside in the refrigerator overnight for the flavors to blend.

◇ ◇ ◇

Two Meat Loaves

Meat loaf in the pressure cooker makes sense. Of whatever nationality, a meat loaf needs moist heat, but not too much, which the pressure cooker provides. It needs even, all around cooking, which the pressure cooker provides. It needs gentle cooking so it melts into succulence without becoming desiccated, which the pressure cooker provides. Just don't expect a grand 3-pound loaf to set in the middle of the table for a warm main course or to make wide slices for a picnic presentation. You'll have to settle instead for two smaller, narrower ones, unless, of course, a manufacturer comes out with a pressure cooker of twice the diameter. In the meantime, you can also settle for a round loaf cooked in a 1-quart soufflé dish. It looks larger than the smaller, 1½-pound rectangular loaves even though, ounce for ounce, it's not much more.

◇ American All-Beef Meat Loaf

Meat loaf holds a place somewhere between humble fare and exemplar of the best home cooking. It seems just about everyone likes it. But, while it's no trouble to mix up, it conventionally takes one and a half hours to cook. The pressure cooker cuts that time by half with no sacrifice of quality, making it feasible to have this comfort food even in a too-busy-to-cook household.

Makes one 1½-pound loaf, or about 4 servings

1 pound lean ground beef

1 small russet potato (4 ounces), peeled and coarsely grated

½ medium-size yellow or white onion, finely chopped

1 large clove garlic, finely chopped

½ cup chopped fresh flat-leaf parsley

1 large egg

¼ cup heavy cream

1½ teaspoons salt

½ teaspoon freshly ground black pepper

1 tablespoon tomato paste

1 bay leaf

1. Combine all the ingredients except the tomato paste and bay leaf in a medium-size bowl and mix well. Pat the mixture into a 1-quart loaf pan or soufflé dish. Spread the tomato paste over the top and set the bay leaf in the center.

2. Place the loaf pan on a trivet in the pressure cooker. Pour in 2 cups water. Lock on the lid and bring to pressure over high heat, about 3 minutes. Reduce the heat to medium and cook for 25 minutes. Remove from the heat and let sit for 10 minutes.

3. With the steam vent pointed away from your face, gently release any remaining pressure. Let cool for 20 minutes, then serve.

◇ Terrine of Pork and Veal   *A terrine needs resting time for the flavors to mingle, so, if you are serving this as a warm loaf, let it sit at room temperature for two to three hours and reheat it briefly in the microwave or oven. If it is to be served as a pâté loaf, let it cool, then refrigerate it overnight, or up to one week. Instead of the carrots, you can make the middle layer of wilted spinach, sautéed mushrooms, blanched veal sweetbreads, or sautéed chicken livers. Accompany the warm terrine with a puree of potatoes and celery root. If cold, accompany it with Dijon mustard, sour gherkins (cornichons), and warm French bread.*

This recipe makes two terrines, but both loaves won't fit into the pressure cooker at the same time, so you'll have to cook them in two rounds.

Makes two 1½-pound loaves, or about 8 servings

1 medium-size carrot, peeled and cut into ¼-inch-thick diagonal slices

2 pounds ground pork

1 pound ground veal

3 large shallots, minced

2 large cloves garlic, minced

1 teaspoon chopped fresh thyme, or ½ teaspoon dried

1 teaspoon chopped fresh sage, or ½ teaspoon dried

1 large egg

½ cup dry white wine

1½ teaspoons salt

½ teaspoon freshly ground black pepper

8 slices bacon

2 bay leaves

1. Blanch the carrot slices in a pot of boiling salted water for 3 minutes. Drain, rinse with cool water, and set aside.

2. Combine the pork, veal, shallots, garlic, thyme, sage, egg, wine, salt, and pepper in a medium-size bowl. Mix well with your hands.

3. Place 2 slices of bacon on the bottom of each of two 1-quart loaf pans. Pat one quarter of the meat mixture over the bacon in each pan, making sure to spread it all the way to the corners of the pan. Arrange the carrots down the center of each pan and pat the remaining meat mixture over them. Cover with 2 slices of bacon and top with a bay leaf.

4. Place a metal trivet in the pressure cooker and set one of the loaves on top of it. Pour 3 cups water into the pressure cooker around, but not into, the loaf pan. Lock on the lid and bring to pressure over high heat, about 2 minutes. Reduce the heat to medium and cook for 35 minutes. Remove from the heat and let sit for 10 minutes to finish cooking.

5. With the steam vent pointed away from your face, gently release any remaining pressure. If serving warm, let sit with the lid ajar for 2 to 3 hours, then lift the loaf out of the juices and slice. If serving cold, cool completely and refrigerate in the container for up to 1 week. Scrape away the layer of fat around the edges, then slice.

Note: The terrines may be prepared (but not cooked) a day in advance and set aside in the refrigerator. Remove from the refrigerator and let sit at room temperature for 1 hour before cooking.

◈ Rabbit Braised with Fresh Bacon, Onion, and White Wine

This recipe and the next are two of my favorite recipes in this entire book. Fresh bacon is salt pork that hasn't been salted, or bacon that hasn't been brined or smoked. You can find it in butcher shops that cater to a Southern or Chinese clientele. Blanched salt pork can be substituted, but then omit the salt until the dish is done so you can taste the sauce before adding any salt.   Makes 4 servings

½ tablespoon olive oil
4 ounces fresh bacon or blanched salt pork (see Note page 70),
     cut into ½ × 1-inch pieces
1 rabbit (about 2½ pounds), cut into 6 pieces
1 medium-size white onion, halved and sliced ¾ inch thick
1 carrot, peeled and cut into ½-inch-thick diagonal slices
1 teaspoon chopped fresh thyme, or ½ teaspoon dried
½ teaspoon salt (optional)
½ cup dry white wine
2 tablespoons Dijon mustard
¼ cup water
2 tablespoons chopped fresh flat-leaf parsley, for garnish

1. Heat the oil in the pressure cooker over medium-high heat. Add the bacon and cook, stirring occasionally, until beginning to soften, 4 to 5 minutes.

2. Add the rabbit pieces and sauté until beginning to turn golden, about 5 minutes.

3. Stir in the onion, carrot, thyme, and salt, if using. Add the wine, mustard, and water and stir to mix well. Lock on the lid and bring to pressure over high heat, about 2 minutes. Reduce the heat to medium-high and cook for 10 minutes. Remove from the heat and let sit for 10 minutes to finish cooking.

4. With the steam vent pointed away from your face, gently release any remaining pressure. Arrange the rabbit, bacon, and vegetables on a serving platter. Taste the sauce, adjust the salt, and pour the sauce over the rabbit and vegetables. Sprinkle the parsley over the top and serve right away.

◇ Rabbit with Fennel Seeds, Parsnips, and Prunes in Brandy Cream

Rubbing rabbit with salt and spices and letting it sit for a day before cooking is akin to brining it, as for pork shoulder (see page 82). Either method elevates the meat to a tastier, more succulent level. In a pinch, you can just go ahead without the rub and still have a fine, aromatic, and creamy rabbit stew.

Makes 4 servings

1 rabbit (about 2½ pounds), cut into 6 pieces
2 tablespoons Aromatic Salt (page 114)
1 tablespoon butter
1 tablespoon olive oil
6 pitted prunes, coarsely chopped
2 medium-size parsnips, peeled and cut into ½-inch-thick rounds
1 medium-size yellow or white onion, halved and sliced ½ inch thick
2 teaspoons powdered mustard
1 cup Chicken Broth (page 18)
2 tablespoons brandy
1 cup heavy cream
¼ cup chopped fresh flat-leaf parsley, for garnish

1. Place the rabbit pieces in a large dish and pat the salt rub over both sides of each piece. Cover with plastic wrap and refrigerate overnight.

2. Wipe the salt and spices off the rabbit pieces but don't rinse them. Heat the butter and oil in the pressure cooker over medium-high heat until the butter melts. Add the rabbit and brown on all sides, about 2 minutes. Stir in the prunes, parsnips, and onion. Stir in the mustard, broth, and brandy, turning to mix well.

3. Lock on the lid and bring to pressure over high heat, about 1 minute. Reduce the heat to medium and cook for 10 minutes. Remove from the heat and let sit for 2 minutes to finish cooking.

4. With the steam vent pointed away from your face, gently release any remaining pressure. Let sit with the lid ajar for at least 15 minutes, or up to 1 hour.

5. When ready to serve, lift the rabbit, prunes, and vegetables out of the pressure cooker and place on a serving platter. Set aside in a warm place. Bring the juices in the pot to a boil and stir in the cream. Simmer briskly for a minute or two until thickened, then pour onto the serving platter. Garnish with the parsley and serve.

Aromatic Salt

Before it became trendy to pat and rub all manner of herbs and spices into meat and poultry before cooking, salt, usually with some aromatics, was used in the same way, but with a more expansive purpose in mind. A salt rub, if left long enough, serves to preserve the meat, an important consideration before the days of year-round, indoor refrigeration. If left for even a short time, it tenderizes and seasons, enhancing the texture and flavor of chicken, duck, goose, and pork. You can tailor the herbs to suit.

Makes 2½ tablespoons

3 bay leaves, coarsely crumbled	1 tablespoon kosher salt
2 teaspoons fennel seeds	2 teaspoons black peppercorns, smashed

Combine all the ingredients in a small bowl.

Poultry Under Pressure

According to modern belief, the pressure cooker is terrific for chicken soup. But where to go from there? I set out to explore world paths, some of which I had already traversed, some I hadn't traveled except from an armchair. I wound up with what I think is a wonderful compilation of recipes for pressure cooking poultry. Some are for quick, weeknight family fare, some are for occasions. Some are for a whole chicken cut up, some for breasts only or leg/thigh sections only. Two are for a whole chicken and one is for the ever popular wings. Game hens and duck you might not have thought of cooking and pheasant that will expand your horizons about how good a game bird can be have all found a place in my pressure cooker.

Poultry Under Pressure

◈ Sunday Chicken Poached Belgian Style, with Leeks, Celery, and Bread Crumbs

Waterzooi. That's the name of the dish in Flemish, and there's a story to be told about it. Waterzooi was originally made with fish from the waters of the meandering streams that wend their way through the landscape around Ghent. Later, as the fish supply diminished in the march of time, chicken became the main ingredient, I think with equal success. Waterzooi with chicken is a bright star in the shining constellation of Belgian cuisine. A note: Carrot is always included in waterzooi, *and it's true the dish looks brighter with a touch of color from the orange spectrum. However, I find that the carrot adds too sweet a taste to the sauce. As a solution to that dilemma, I set the carrot on top of the chicken, where it can steam separately, or else I cook it separately and add it to the vegetables when serving.*

Makes 4 servings

1 bunch celery, tough outer ribs removed, inner ribs peeled with a vegetable peeler and cut into 3-inch chunks

2 medium-size leeks, trimmed, well washed, drained, and cut into 1-inch pieces

4 sprigs fresh thyme, or ¾ teaspoon dried

Salt to taste

One 4- to 4½-pound chicken, excess fat removed

1 large carrot, peeled and cut into 1-inch-thick slices

½ cup Chicken Broth (page 18)

¼ cup dry white wine

3 tablespoons butter

2 cups very coarse bread crumbs (see page 187)

⅓ cup chopped fresh flat-leaf parsley, for garnish

1. Place the celery, leeks, and thyme in the pressure cooker. Rub salt all around the outside and the cavity of the chicken. Set the chicken, breast side down, on top of the vegetables. Arrange the carrot pieces over the chicken and pour in the broth and wine.

2. Lock on the lid and bring to pressure over high heat, about 4 minutes. Reduce the heat to medium-high and cook for 20 minutes. Remove from the heat and let sit for 5 minutes to finish cooking. With the steam vent pointed away from your face, gently release any remaining pressure. Set aside to rest.

3. Meanwhile, melt the butter in a large skillet over medium heat. Add the bread crumbs and cook, stirring, until turning golden, 4 to 5 minutes. Remove from the heat.

4. Lift the chicken out of the pot onto a high-lipped serving dish and cut it into sections. Using a slotted spoon, lift out the vegetables and arrange them around the chicken. Spread the toasted bread crumbs over the top. Spoon the cooking juices overall, sprinkle with parsley, and serve.

◈ Bollito of Chicken and Sausage with Two Sauces *In the full-up version of* bollito misto, *there's also beef tongue, beef brisket, veal breast or shank, and perhaps a calf's foot. In other words, it's a grand dinner of mixed boiled meats. Two sauces are* de rigueur: *tomato sauce and green sauce, and, if available, a fruity, spicy, sweet condiment,* mostarda di Cremona. *Sometimes horseradish sauce replaces the green sauce. This recipe is simplified to suit a pressure-cooked meal for a Sunday or company dinner. Hot and Sweet Grape Mostarda (page 306) is a perfect substitute for the Italian* mostarda di Cremona.

Makes 4 to 6 servings

½ medium-size yellow or white onion, coarsely chopped
1 small carrot, coarsely chopped
¼ medium-size red bell pepper, seeded and coarsely chopped
Tops of 2 ribs celery

4 sprigs fresh thyme, or ¾ teaspoon dried

3 ounces pancetta, finely chopped

One 3½- to 4-pound chicken (including giblets)

4 cups water

1 teaspoon salt

2 fresh Italian sausages (about ¼ pound each)

¾ cup Piquant Green Sauce (page 120), for serving

2 cups Simmered Chunky Tomato Sauce (page 120), warm, for serving

1. Place the onion, carrot, red bell pepper, celery tops, thyme, and pancetta in the pressure cooker. Place the chicken, breast side down, on top of the vegetables and add the giblets around the chicken. Pour in the water, sprinkle the salt over the back of the chicken, and tuck in the sausages. Lock on the lid and bring to pressure over high heat, about 10 minutes. Reduce the heat to medium-high and cook for 10 minutes. Remove from the heat and let sit for 10 minutes to finish cooking.

2. With the steam vent pointed away from your face, gently release any remaining pressure. Remove the lid and let sit with the lid ajar for at least 30 minutes, or up to 1½ hours (see Note).

3. Lift out the chicken and sausages, set them on a kitchen platter, and set the platter aside in a warm place. Strain the liquid into a bowl and let sit for 15 minutes or so for the fat to rise to the top. Skim off the fat and return the liquid to the pressure cooker.

4. When ready to serve, cut the chicken into leg, thigh, and breast pieces and place them in a deep serving platter. Cut the sausages into 1-inch-thick rounds and arrange them around the chicken. Reheat the liquid and spoon half of it over the chicken and sausages, reserving the remaining half for another use. Serve right away with the sauces on the side.

Note: The dish can be cooled, covered, and refrigerated overnight without removing the chicken and sausages. In this case, the next day, lift off and discard the fat that has risen to the top and reheat the dish before slicing the chicken and sausages and straining the sauce.

Piquant Green Sauce *In Italy, a piquant green sauce almost invariably accompanies a bollito misto. I find the same sauce excellent with lots of other foods, for instance grilled pork chops, poached or steamed fish, or sautéed chicken breasts.* Makes ¾ cup

8 anchovy fillets
10 sour gherkin pickles (cornichons)
1 cup fresh flat-leaf parsley
1 clove garlic, peeled
1 teaspoon white wine vinegar
⅓ cup extra virgin olive oil

Combine all the ingredients in a food processor and process until finely chopped and the oil is emulsified. Or finely chop the anchovies, gherkins, parsley, and garlic and combine with the vinegar and oil, beating together vigorously with a fork until the oil is emulsified. Use right away or store in the refrigerator, covered, for up to 3 days.

Simmered Chunky Tomato Sauce *In northern Italian–style tomato sauce, there's no olive oil, no oregano, no garlic! Often the sauce, which I prefer chunky, is pureed. If opting for that version, a food mill or fine-mesh sieve will render the smoothest version.* Makes 1½ cups

3 tablespoons butter
2 ounces pancetta, finely chopped
1 medium-size yellow or white onion, finely chopped
4 medium-size tomatoes, peeled (see page 24), seeded, and
    finely chopped, with juices
1 teaspoon chopped fresh thyme, or ½ teaspoon dried
1 bay leaf
¼ teaspoon sugar
½ teaspoon salt
½ teaspoon freshly ground black pepper
¼ cup water, if the tomatoes are not juicy

1. Melt 1 tablespoon of the butter in the pressure cooker over medium-high heat. Add the pancetta and cook, stirring occasionally, until wilted, 2 minutes. Stir in the onion and continue cooking, stirring occasionally, until wilted but not browned, about 3 minutes.

2. Stir in the tomatoes and their juices, thyme, bay leaf, sugar, salt, pepper, and water, if needed. Lock on the lid and bring to pressure over high heat, about 2 minutes. Reduce the heat to medium–low and cook for 10 minutes. Remove from the heat and let sit for 5 minutes to finish cooking.

3. With the steam vent pointed away from your face, remove the lid and stir in the remaining 2 tablespoons butter. Use right away or cool and store in the refrigerator, covered, for up to 1 week, and reheat before serving.

◇ Chicken Avgolemono   Avgolemono—*egg and lemon sauce—hardly needs an introduction to anyone fond of Greek cooking, and the rendition of chicken* avgolemono *here is fairly traditional. Making the dish in the pressure cooker is, however, an innovation, and including carrots is definitely out of the ordinary, but good and colorful.*   Makes 4 servings

4 skinless chicken leg/thigh pieces
Salt to taste
1 tablespoon olive oil
½ teaspoon freshly ground black pepper
1 bay leaf
1½ cups Chicken Broth (page 18)
2 medium-size carrots, peeled and cut into 2-inch chunks
3 large eggs
¼ cup freshly squeezed lemon juice
1 tablespoon chopped lemon zest, for garnish
1 tablespoon chopped fresh chives, for garnish

1. Sprinkle the chicken pieces with salt. Add the oil to the pressure cooker and set over medium–high heat. Add the chicken and cook, turning to brown all around, about 5 minutes.

2. Add the pepper, bay leaf, and broth. Place the carrots on top of the chicken. Lock on the lid and bring to pressure over high heat, about 3 minutes. Reduce the heat to medium-high and cook for 5 minutes. Remove from the heat and let sit for 5 minutes to finish cooking.

3. With the steam vent pointed away from your face, gently release any remaining pressure. Remove the lid and transfer the chicken and carrots to a serving platter. Set aside in a warm place.

4. In a small bowl, whisk the eggs and lemon juice together until frothy. If necessary, reheat the broth slightly in the pressure cooker. Whisk ½ cup of the broth into the lemon-egg mixture, then right away whisk the mixture back into the broth in the pressure cooker. Cook, stirring, over medium heat without boiling until thickened, about 5 minutes.

5. Pour over the chicken and carrots on the platter. Garnish with the zest and chives and serve right away.

◇ **Coq au Vin** *Under any other name coq au vin would not be recognizable. It might not even taste as good without the romance of the French moniker. Julia Child, among others, made sure of that in the 1970s, when French cuisine took American cooking by storm and everyone from home cooks to novice chefs acquired a taste for gourmet. Eventually the lust for such dishes faded as fresh, seasonal, regional became the credo of the new American style in the 1980s and 1990s. Fast-forwarding to the next millennium, meaning now, the pressure cooker provides a marvelous way to re-enact the original enthusiasm with practicality for today. Not only does the pressure cooker reduce the cooking time, it also serves triple yeoman duty as sauté pan for browning the ingredients, cocotte for stewing, and saucepan for reducing the juices. I can't recall a richer wine sauce for the coq than this one.* Makes 6 servings

2 tablespoons butter

8 ounces blanched salt pork (see Note page 70),
   cut into $\frac{1}{2} \times$ 1-inch pieces

12 small boiling onions, parboiled for 2 minutes and peeled

4 large fresh shiitake mushrooms, stemmed and quartered

One 5- to 6-pound chicken, cut into 10 pieces,
   breasts halved crosswise

3 cups dry red wine

2 cloves garlic, pressed or minced

1 bay leaf

3 sprigs fresh thyme, or $\frac{1}{2}$ teaspoon dried

$\frac{1}{4}$ teaspoon freshly ground black pepper

18 fried bread rounds (see page 125), for garnish

$\frac{1}{4}$ cup chopped fresh flat-leaf parsley, for garnish

1. Melt the butter in the pressure cooker over medium-high heat. Add the salt pork and cook, stirring occasionally, until turning golden, about 4 minutes. Remove and set aside. Add the onions and mushrooms to the pressure cooker and cook, stirring occasionally, over medium heat until sweating, about 3 minutes. Transfer the onions and mushrooms to a platter and set aside.

2. Add the chicken, wine, garlic, bay leaf, thyme, pepper, and salt pork to the pot. Lock on the lid and bring to pressure over high heat, about 5 minutes. Reduce the heat to medium and cook for 10 minutes. Remove from the heat and let sit for 10 minutes to finish cooking.

3. With the steam vent pointed away from your face, gently release any remaining pressure. Remove the lid, set the pot over high heat, and boil briskly for 5 minutes. Add the onions and mushrooms and continue cooking briskly until the sauce is thickened, 5 minutes more. Let sit off the heat for at least 30 minutes.

4. To serve, gently reheat the stew. Arrange the chicken, onions, and mushrooms on a serving platter. Ladle the sauce over the top, surround with the bread rounds, and sprinkle with the parsley.

◑ Chicken Marengo with Porcini-Topped Fried Bread Rounds

Originally, chicken Marengo was an on-the-spot concoction made of chicken, tomatoes, maybe some shellfish (tales differ here) gathered from domiciles around the countryside where Napoleon bivouacked on the plain near the town of Marengo in Spain to rest and feed the troops after a victorious expedition. Then, Parisian chefs got hold of it—Napoleon dined first upon it, after all, so it came with a certain cachet. So chicken Marengo remained for years, with many tiers of embellishment added by the garnish-loving grand chefs of the nineteenth century. In this twenty-first-century version, the dish returns to its plain origins, with the added pizzazz of a porcini toast garnish. And it's perfect for the pressure cooker.   Makes 6 servings

One 4½- to 5-pound chicken, cut into 10 pieces,
   breasts halved crosswise
Salt and freshly ground black pepper to taste
All-purpose flour, for coating the chicken
1½ tablespoons olive oil
2 large shallots, chopped
1 large clove garlic, smashed
3 medium-size tomatoes, peeled (page 24), seeded, and chopped, with
   juices, or 1 cup canned tomatoes, seeded and chopped, with juices
½ cup dry white wine
½ cup water
1 bouquet garni of 6 sprigs fresh parsley, 1 bay leaf, and
   top of 1 rib celery (see Note)
Porcini-Topped Fried Bread Rounds (recipe follows), for garnish
2 tablespoons chopped fresh flat-leaf parsley, for garnish

1. Rinse and pat dry the chicken pieces. Sprinkle them generously with salt, pepper, and flour, turning to coat all around.

2. Heat the oil in the pressure cooker over medium-high heat until beginning to smoke. In 2 batches, sauté the chicken pieces all around until lightly golden, 4 to 5 minutes, transferring to a plate after each batch.

3. Stir the shallots and garlic into the oil, then add the tomatoes and their juices and set the chicken pieces on top, along with any collected juices. Pour in the wine and water and tuck in the bouquet garni. Lock on the lid and bring to pressure over high heat, 2 to 3 minutes. Reduce the heat to medium and cook for 10 minutes. Remove from the heat and let sit for 10 minutes.

4. With the steam vent pointed away from your face, gently release any remaining pressure. Remove the lid and let sit for 10 to 20 minutes more for the juices to settle.

5. To serve, remove and discard the bouquet garni and arrange the chicken pieces on a serving platter. Spoon the liquid from the pot over the chicken and garnish with the porcini-topped fried bread. Sprinkle the parsley over all and serve right away.

Note: To make a bouquet garni, place the herbs on a small piece of cheesecloth, gather up the sides, and tie the bundle closed with kitchen string.

Porcini-Topped Fried Bread Rounds *Without the porcini mushroom topping, the recipe is a basic one for fried bread rounds to garnish many dishes. A sprinkle of chopped fresh thyme or marjoram, a spread of soft chèvre, or a rub of garlic and tomato are also excellent toppings for the rounds.*

Makes 18 rounds

2 tablespoons butter
¼ ounce dried porcini mushrooms (about ¼ cup), soaked in ½ cup
   warm water for 30 minutes
1 clove garlic, pressed or minced
¼ cup chopped fresh flat-leaf parsley
Pinch of salt
Olive oil, for frying
Eighteen 1-inch slices baguette

1. Melt the butter in a medium-size saucepan over medium-high heat. Squeeze dry the porcini mushrooms and add them to the pan along with the garlic, parsley, and salt. Cook, stirring occasionally, until soft, 1 to 2 minutes. Set aside.

2. Pour the olive oil to a depth of $\frac{1}{4}$ inch in a sauté pan and set over medium-high heat until beginning to smoke. Add as many slices of bread as will fit in 1 uncrowded layer and fry, turning once, until golden on both sides, less than 1 minute altogether. Remove to paper towels to drain. Continue in batches until all the bread is fried.

3. Spread some of the sautéed porcini mushrooms on each slice.

◎ West African Chicken Stew in Peanut and Tomato Sauce

When cutting up a chicken, most often I reserve the backbone and wing tips for making stock. For West African chicken and peanut stew, however, these parts are essential for the flavor and feel of the dish. If you purchase a whole chicken already cut up, cut the backbone in half crosswise and use it in the dish. The optional Cilantro Mint Chutney and Silken Yam Puree make for a festive full table, but to simplify a family dinner, you can serve the stew with rice alone. Makes 4 to 6 servings

One 4- to 5-pound chicken
1 tablespoon salt
1 tablespoon ground ginger
2 tablespoons peanut oil
1 medium-size yellow or white onion, finely chopped
1 clove garlic, finely chopped
1 cup canned crushed tomatoes
2 tablespoons tomato paste
$\frac{1}{2}$ teaspoon peeled and finely chopped fresh ginger
$\frac{1}{2}$ teaspoon Aleppo pepper (see page 232) or hot paprika
$\frac{1}{2}$ teaspoon white pepper, preferably freshly ground
$\frac{3}{4}$ cup smooth peanut butter

1¾ cups water

¾ cup coarsely chopped peanuts, toasted (see page 41), for serving

Cilantro Mint Chutney (optional, page 267), for serving

Silken Yam Puree (optional, page 190), for serving

1. Cut the chicken into 12 pieces: 2 legs, 2 thighs, 4 breast pieces, 2 wings, and the backbone cut in half. Rub the pieces with the salt and ground ginger.

2. Heat the oil in the pressure cooker over medium–high heat until beginning to smoke. Brown the chicken pieces a few at a time for 4 to 5 minutes, removing them to a kitchen platter as you go.

3. Stir in the onion and garlic and cook until wilted, about 1 minute. Add the tomatoes, tomato paste, fresh ginger, Aleppo pepper, white pepper, peanut butter, and ¾ cup of the water and whisk to mix. Return the chicken pieces and any collected juices to the pot and add the remaining 1 cup water.

4. Lock on the lid and bring to pressure over high heat, about 6 minutes. Reduce the heat to medium and cook for 15 minutes. Remove from the heat and let sit for 10 minutes to finish cooking.

5. With the steam vent pointed away from your face, gently release any remaining pressure and remove the lid. Let sit for 10 to 15 minutes for the juices to settle.

6. When ready to serve, arrange the chicken pieces on a large serving platter. Strain the sauce through a fine-mesh sieve over the chicken. Accompany with the roasted peanuts, chutney (if using), and yams (if using) in separate side dishes.

Chicken with Kohlrabi and Salt Pork *Together with an odd (to American cooking) vegetable, kohlrabi, the old reliable flavor enhancer salt pork, and caraway, a favorite spice of eastern European cooking, chicken leg and thigh pieces turn into a delicious and unusual stew*

with a minimal number of ingredients. The recommended mostarda *completes the round of flavors and is worth the small effort to make if grapes are in season.*   Makes 4 servings

1 tablespoon butter
2½ ounces blanched salt pork (see Note page 70), cut
    into ½ × 1-inch pieces
2 small kohlrabies (1¼ pounds), leaves cut off, chopped, and set aside;
    bottoms peeled, quartered, and sliced ½ inch thick
4 chicken leg/thigh pieces
4 cups Chicken Broth (page 18)
½ teaspoon caraway seeds
1½ cups Hot and Sweet Grape Mostarda (optional, page 306), for serving

1. Melt the butter in the pressure cooker over medium heat. Add the salt pork and cook, stirring occasionally, until well browned, 5 to 7 minutes.

2. Add the kohlrabi leaves and slices and stir to mix. Place the chicken pieces on top and add the broth and caraway seeds. Lock on the lid and bring to pressure over high heat, 5 to 7 minutes. Reduce the heat to medium and cook for 10 minutes. Remove from the heat and let sit for 10 minutes to finish cooking.

3. With the steam vent pointed away from your face, gently release any remaining pressure and let cool enough to handle.

4. Cut the chicken pieces in half at the joint between the leg and thigh. Arrange the pieces on a serving platter. Spread the kohlrabi slices and salt pork over the top. Spoon the liquid over all and serve right away with the *mostarda*, if using.

◌ ◌ ◌

◈ Paprika Chicken with Two Hungarian Side Salads

Where but in the land of the Magyars, namely Hungary, would you find a meal of velvety chicken sauced with paprika-spiked sour cream and accompanied by two vegetable side salads? The combination works in a way peculiar to the cuisine, as full of surprises as its people. The pressure-cooked paprika chicken is a delight; the side salads add a gay note if you'd like to complete the picture in a multicolored way.

Makes 4 servings

1 tablespoon vegetable oil
One 3½- to 4-pound chicken, backbone removed, quartered,
   and skinned (see Note page 130)
1 small yellow or white onion, finely chopped
2 teaspoons hot paprika, preferably Hungarian
½ cup Chicken Broth (page 18)
1 medium-size tomato, peeled (see page 24) and coarsely chopped
1 teaspoon salt
½ cup sour cream
6 ounces extra-wide egg noodles, cooked, drained, buttered and kept warm
Hungarian Cucumbers (optional, page 130)
Hungarian Green Bean Salad (optional, page 130)

1. Heat the oil in the pressure cooker over medium-high heat until beginning to smoke. Add the chicken pieces and cook until golden all around, 4 to 5 minutes. Transfer to a plate. Add the onion, paprika, and broth and stir to mix. Return the chicken to the pot and add the tomato, but don't stir it in. Add the salt. Lock on the lid and bring to pressure over high heat, 4 to 5 minutes. Reduce the heat to medium and cook for 5 minutes. Remove from the heat and let sit for 5 minutes to finish cooking.

2. With the steam vent pointed away from your face, gently release any remaining pressure and transfer the chicken to a plate. Set aside in a warm place while the liquid cooks in the pot for 15 minutes.

3. Whisk the sour cream in a small bowl until smooth. Add ¼ cup of the liquid from the pot and whisk until smooth. Pour the sour cream mixture into the pot and whisk to mix. Return the chicken pieces and any accumulated juices to the pot. Reheat briefly without boiling.

4. Spread the warm egg noodles on a serving platter. Arrange the chicken over the noodles and pour the sauce over all. Accompany with the cucumber salad and green bean salad, if desired.

Note: Don't be tempted to substitute chicken parts for the chicken quarters because the timing is not the same and the parts don't come out as succulent as the quarters. Also, removing the backbone and skinning the quarters makes for a lower-fat, more svelte sauce.

Hungarian Cucumbers

A sweet/tart cucumber salad puts in a regular appearance on many central and eastern European tables, not just in Hungary. From Germany to Austria and beyond, it is obligatory for any meal-starter salad array and often sits beside the entrée for the main meal. Note that the recipe amount is hard to gauge: What looks like a huge pile of sliced cucumbers wilts down as it rests in the dressing.

Makes about 2 cups

10 large pickling cucumbers or 2 large regular cucumbers,
    seeds removed if large
¼ cup cider vinegar
¼ cup water
1 teaspoon sugar
¼ teaspoon salt

Slice the cucumbers as thinly as possible. Place them in a medium-size bowl and toss together with the remaining ingredients. Let sit for at least 30 minutes, or up to 2 hours, before serving.

Hungarian Green Bean Salad

Makes about 2 cups

1 pound green beans
1 shallot, minced

¼ cup chopped fresh flat-leaf parsley

1½ tablespoons sherry wine vinegar

3 tablespoons extra virgin olive oil

Salt and freshly ground black pepper to taste

1. Pinch off the stem ends of the green beans. If the beans are very small, leave them whole. If larger, cut them lengthwise into 2 or 3 pieces. Blanch the beans in boiling water for 4 to 8 minutes, depending on their age, until quite limp and tender but still bright green. Drain in a colander and set aside to drip-dry and cool for 15 minutes or so.

2. Toss together the green beans and remaining ingredients in a medium-size bowl. Let marinate for 1 hour at room temperature before serving. The salad will keep in the refrigerator for up to 2 days.

◈ Ginger and Sesame Steamed Chicken *Steam cooking with Asian flavors is almost a sure bet. From wok to pressure cooker, the translation of technique doesn't skip a beat.*

Makes 4 servings

One 3½- to 4-pound chicken, quartered

Salt to taste

2 tablespoons peeled and coarsely chopped fresh ginger

2 cloves garlic, slivered

1 small fresh red or green chile pepper, thinly sliced

2 tablespoons low-sodium soy sauce

1 tablespoon sesame oil

3 scallions (white and light green parts only), trimmed and
   cut lengthwise into thin strips

2 tablespoons dry sherry

1 teaspoon sesame seeds, lightly toasted (see page 41), for garnish

6 sprigs fresh cilantro, for garnish

1. Rub the chicken quarters generously with salt and set aside.

2. Combine the ginger, garlic, chile pepper, soy sauce, and sesame oil in the pressure cooker. Place a trivet or steamer basket in the pot and set the chicken quarters on top. Spread the scallions over the chicken and pour the sherry over all.

3. Lock on the lid and bring to pressure over high heat, 3 to 4 minutes. Reduce the heat to medium and cook for 10 minutes. Remove from the heat and let sit for 7 minutes to finish cooking.

4. With the steam vent pointed away from your face, gently release any remaining pressure and let sit for 5 minutes more.

5. Arrange the chicken pieces and scallions on a serving platter. Pour the juices over all. Sprinkle the sesame seeds over the top, garnish with the cilantro, and serve.

◎ Quick Chicken with Garlic, Tarragon, and Red Wine

A dish with a history always attracts my attention. This one does, certainly, because it's one from my own history beginning with my second cookbook, Good and Plenty: America's New Home Cooking, *which I co-authored with Susanna Hoffman. At first we called it Desperation Chicken because it was what she made when kids needed feeding, very right now. It was quick off the stove top, and she devised many variations to keep them, their friends, and herself interested as the dish got turned out over and over again, but always with a new twist. From there to the microwave version that we developed for our* Well-Filled Microwave Cookbook, *and now to the pressure cooker, the dish remains a winner for when you desperately need dinner sooner rather than later.*

Makes 4 servings

2 tablespoons olive oil
8 boneless chicken thighs

Salt and freshly ground black pepper to taste

12 large cloves garlic, halved

2 teaspoons chopped fresh tarragon, or ½ teaspoon dried,
  plus extra for garnish

1 cup dry red wine

2 tablespoons butter

1. Heat the oil in the pressure cooker over high heat until beginning to smoke. Add the thighs, sprinkle with salt and pepper, and turn to coat. Add the garlic, tarragon, and red wine. Lock on the lid and bring to pressure over high heat, about 2 minutes. Reduce the heat to medium and cook for 2 minutes. Remove from the heat and let sit for 2 minutes to finish cooking.

2. With the steam vent pointed away from your face, gently release any remaining pressure. Transfer the thighs to a serving platter and set aside in a warm place.

3. Reduce the juices left in the pot over high heat for 2 minutes. Swirl in the butter and pour over the thighs. Garnish with extra tarragon and serve.

Neo–Nero Wolfe Chicken in Red Sauce with Chopped Egg, Parsley, and Lemon Zest

From the list of ingredients, we can see Nero was as generous about seasoning his dishes as he was self-indulgent about eating them. Bold as his silhouette, expansive as his figure, they comprise a lusty dish. Of course, Nero had Archie, his able assistant, to give direction to Fritz, his more-than-able cook, so he could attend to his solarium of orchids and contemplate how to solve the latest mystery while the chicken cooked. For those in a less privileged situation, it's a chicken stew easy enough to turn out with the aid of a pressure cooker. The components are quickly assembled from a well-stocked cupboard plus a short trip to the supermarket for the chicken, egg, and chorizo sausage.

Makes 4 servings

1½ tablespoons olive oil

4 skinless chicken leg/thigh pieces or 2 game hens, quartered

Salt to taste

One 2-inch piece chorizo sausage

2 cups water

1 medium-size carrot, cut into 2-inch chunks

1 small yellow or white onion, halved

2 whole cloves, stuck into the onion halves

1 rib celery, cut into 2-inch chunks

1 bay leaf

Pinch of cayenne

One 1-inch piece cinnamon stick

½ cup dry sherry

1 tablespoon freshly squeezed lemon juice

1 large egg, hard-boiled and coarsely chopped, for garnish

2 tablespoons chopped fresh flat-leaf parsley, for garnish

2 teaspoons chopped lemon zest, for garnish

¼ cup sliced almonds, lightly toasted (see page 41), for garnish

1. Heat the oil in the pressure cooker over high heat. Add the chicken pieces, lightly salt them, and sauté over medium-high heat

Nero Wolfe and the Pressure Cooker

Nero Wolfe and the pressure cooker might never have come together except for my friend and some-times co-author, Susanna Hoffman. As a single mother raising two children who were always ready to eat even before she'd had a chance to consider that step of the day, she swore by the pressure cooker for a meal-in-a-minute solution to the "let's eat now" cry. Chicken stew or soup was a main-stay. She also has always been an avid late-night reader of not-too-heavy-but-interesting literature. Rex Stout's Nero Wolfe mysteries were and are a favorite, and when the food and recipes from the collected stories were published in a volume, I received a copy as a present for my thirty-eighth birthday. Together we adapted Nero's shad roe recipe for our *Well-Filled Microwave Cookbook*. Here, I adapted his Chicken in Curdled Egg Sauce for the pressure cooker.

to brown lightly, 2 to 3 minutes. Remove to a platter. Add the chorizo and brown lightly, about 1 minute. Return the chicken to the pot. Add the water, carrot, onion, celery, bay leaf, cayenne, and cinnamon stick. Return the chicken to the pot. Lock on the lid and bring to pressure over high heat, 4 to 5 minutes. Reduce the heat to medium-high and cook for 5 minutes. Remove from the heat and let sit for 10 minutes to finish cooking.

2. With the steam vent pointed away from your face, gently release any remaining pressure. Remove the lid and let sit for 10 minutes more.

3. With kitchen tongs, remove and discard the cinnamon stick, carrot, onion, celery, bay leaf, and sausage (see Note). Lift out the chicken pieces, arrange them on a serving platter, and set aside in a warm place.

4. Add the sherry to the liquid in the pot and bring to a boil over medium heat. Simmer for 2 to 3 minutes, until no longer raw tasting. Stir in the lemon juice and ladle the sauce over the chicken on the platter. Garnish with the chopped egg, parsley, zest, and almonds.

Note: The chorizo is for color and flavor in the sauce. If you'd like, you can slice it and add it to the dish when serving. If you can't find it, substitute 1 tablespoon hot Hungarian paprika.

Chicken Breasts in Yogurt Turmeric Sauce with Green Peas

With fresh green peas, my preference, chicken breasts slathered in a sauce made bright yellow with turmeric is a dish for late spring to early summer. With frozen green peas, it's a dish for fall when the fresh peas have come and gone and the chickens have grown a bit plumper in the breast. Marinating the breasts before cooking adds to the velvety texture because yogurt, as Middle Eastern cooks know, is a natural tenderizer.

Makes 4 servings

1 cup plain yogurt

1 teaspoon ground turmeric

1 teaspoon ground cumin

1 teaspoon yellow mustard seeds

1 teaspoon salt

½ teaspoon freshly ground white pepper

4 boneless, skinless chicken breast halves

1 tablespoon butter

1 large russet potato, cut into ¼-inch-thick rounds

1 cup shelled fresh peas or frozen peas

¼ cup chopped fresh cilantro

1. Mix together the yogurt, turmeric, cumin, mustard seeds, salt, and pepper in a dish large enough to hold the breasts in 1 layer. Add the breasts and turn to coat. Cover with plastic wrap and marinate in the refrigerator for 2 to 4 hours.

2. Melt the butter in the pressure cooker over medium heat. Layer the potatoes across the bottom, then add the chicken and yogurt mixture. Without stirring, lock on the lid and bring to pressure over high heat, 2 to 3 minutes. Reduce the heat to medium-high and cook for 8 minutes. Remove from the heat and let sit for 3 minutes to finish cooking.

3. With the steam vent pointed away from your face, gently release any remaining pressure. Transfer the breasts and potatoes to a

Fresh Turmeric: A Treasure for the Cook's Palette

Like ginger, turmeric is a rhizome. And, like ginger, it's one to have fresh in your kitchen. If you find it, bring it home and grate it into any dish that needs a color boost. Though it's scintillatingly vivid to the eye, its flavor is mellow, and you can use it to tint any dish or sauce that would benefit from a sparkle of bright, deep yellow.

serving platter and set aside in a warm place. Cook the sauce over high heat until reduced and slightly thickened, 2 to 3 minutes.

4. Stir in the peas and cilantro. Spoon over the chicken and serve right away.

◇ Chinese Chicken Wings

At my deli, Pig-by-the-Tail, we processed what seemed like a ton of chicken per week for our sausages, galantines, terrines, and salads. The cut-away parts—bones, giblets, wings, wing tips—were cooked up into chicken stock for many dishes. But, at a certain point, there was enough stock to float the world; we needed no more. What to do? That's when we began making Chinese chicken wings. They've stayed on my restaurant and cookbook menus from then on. Imagine my delight when I discovered how good they are pressure cooked. Instead of more than 2 hours in the oven, once marinated, the pressure cooker does the job in 25 minutes, start to finish.

Makes 8 to 12 appetizer servings

24 chicken wings
¼ cup low-sodium soy sauce
¼ cup hot-and-sweet mustard
1 tablespoon dry white wine, Chinese rice wine, or sake
¼ teaspoon red pepper flakes
1 teaspoon sesame seeds (optional), lightly toasted (see page 41), for garnish
Several sprigs fresh cilantro, for garnish

1. Rinse and pat dry the wings. If desired, cut off the wing tips and reserve for stock.

2. Combine the soy sauce, mustard, wine, and pepper flakes in a large bowl. Add the wings, toss to coat, and refrigerate to marinate for at least 30 minutes (overnight is best).

3. Place the wings and sauce in the pressure cooker. Lock on the lid and bring to pressure over high heat, 3 to 5 minutes, depending on how cold the wings are. Reduce the heat to medium–high and cook for 15 minutes. Remove from the heat and let sit for 5 minutes to finish cooking.

4. With the steam vent pointed away from your face, gently release any remaining pressure. Arrange the wings on a platter and pour the sauce over them. Sprinkle with the sesame seeds, if using, and top with the cilantro sprigs.

Note: If marinating overnight, toss 2 or 3 times to remix so all the pieces get the benefit of the marinade.

◇ ◇ ◇

Buffalo Wings

Prepare the wings as described in Step 1 for the Chinese wings, cutting off the wing tips and severing the wings in half at the joint. For the marinade, combine $\frac{1}{3}$ cup Tabasco or other hot pepper sauce, a pinch of cayenne, and $\frac{1}{4}$ teaspoon salt. Add the wings to the marinade, toss to coat, and refrigerate for 30 minutes, or up to overnight. Cook as described in Step 3 and serve with Blue Cheese Dipping Sauce and celery sticks on the side.

Blue Cheese Dipping Sauce

Makes 1$\frac{1}{2}$ cups

1 cup plain yogurt	2 teaspoons cider vinegar
$\frac{1}{4}$ cup mayonnaise	$\frac{1}{2}$ cup crumbled blue cheese

Combine the yogurt, mayonnaise, and vinegar in a small bowl and whisk to smooth. Stir in the cheese and use right away or refrigerate, covered, for up to 1 week.

Game Hens Aplenty

Game hens, sometimes called Cornish hens, are just right for the pressure cooker—the right size, the right ease of cutting up, the right delicacy to remain succulent under pressure cooking. I often opt for them in lieu of cut-up chicken when I want a more tender texture and richer, dark-meat flavor. Look for fresh game hens, now widely available in supermarkets; they are far superior to those that have been frozen. In addition to the following three recipes, other recipes in this chapter where you can use game hens rather than the called-for chicken are:

Quick Chicken with Garlic, Tarragon, and Red Wine (page 132)
Chicken Marengo with Porcini-Topped Fried Bread Rounds (page 124)
Chicken Avgolemono (page 121)
Neo–Nero Wolfe Chicken in Red Sauce with Chopped Egg, Parsley, and Lemon Zest (page 133)

Or in place of duck:

Duck with Green Olives, Turnips, and Turnip Greens (page 142)
Duck Gumbo (page 143)

◈ Game Hens with Fig, Orange Zest, and Herb Couscous Stuffing in Honey Almond Glaze
Game hens plumped out with couscous stuffing, and glazed with flower-scented honey, and a fragrance of orange wafting around and about leads me straight to the Casbah. Or, maybe to the table on a warm evening in July.

Makes 4 servings

2 game hens
2¼ cups Fig, Orange Zest, and Herb Couscous Stuffing (page 140)
¼ cup honey, preferably flower scented
½ teaspoon ground turmeric
¼ teaspoon almond extract
½ cup water

1. Rinse and pat dry the game hens. Stuff them as full as possible with the couscous stuffing, reserving the extra stuffing on the side.

2. Combine the honey, turmeric, almond extract, and water in the pressure cooker and bring to a boil over medium-high heat. Add the game hens and turn to coat.

3. Bring to a boil, lock on the lid, and bring to pressure over high heat, 1 to 2 minutes. Reduce the heat to medium and cook for 20 minutes. Remove from the heat and let sit for 5 minutes to finish cooking.

4. With the steam vent pointed away from your face, gently release any remaining pressure. Remove the lid and let sit, uncovered, for 5 minutes.

5. Reheat the reserved stuffing on the stove top or in the microwave. Spread it on a large serving platter. Cut the game hens into quarters, set them on top of the couscous bed, and spoon the sauce over the top. Serve right away.

Fig, Orange Zest, and Herb Couscous Stuffing

Makes 2¼ cups

1 tablespoon butter
6 dried golden (Calimyrna) figs, quartered
1 small yellow or white onion, finely chopped
1 small dried red chile pepper
1 tablespoon chopped orange zest
¼ cup chopped fresh mint
¼ cup chopped fresh flat-leaf parsley
½ teaspoon salt
¾ cup couscous
1 cup water

1. Melt the butter in a large sauté pan over medium-high heat. Add the figs, onion, chile pepper, orange zest, mint, parsley, and salt and stir to mix.

2. Add the couscous and water and stir to mix. Set aside for 10 minutes, or until the couscous is rehydrated and plumped up. Remove and discard the chile pepper. Use right away or cool and store in the refrigerator, covered, for up to 2 days.

Game Hens Bistro Style, in Vinegar Tomato Sauce with Farro

In her Bistro Cooking cookbook, Patricia Wells offers a recipe for a chicken dish with ingredients as elementary as those of any country bistro or farmhouse kitchen. In my pressure-cooked adaptation, here served over farro, or spelt, the spirit of the Italian countryside or a bistro atmosphere is presented at your own table.

Makes 4 servings

1 tablespoon butter
1 tablespoon olive oil
2 game hens, backbones removed and halved
½ cup drained and chopped oil-packed sun-dried tomatoes
1 tablespoon tomato paste
½ cup good-quality red wine vinegar
½ cup Chicken Broth (page 18)
2 cups cooked Farro (page 245), warm

1. Heat the butter and oil together in the pressure cooker over medium-high heat until the butter melts. Add 2 of the game hen halves, skin side down, and cook until browned, without turning, about 5 minutes. Transfer to a plate and brown the remaining 2 halves in the same way. Do not remove them from the pot.

2. Add the sun-dried tomatoes, tomato paste, vinegar, and broth to the pot, along with the 2 game hen halves from the first batch. Turn to mix, lock on the lid, and bring to pressure over high heat, about 2 minutes. Reduce the heat to medium-high and cook for 10 minutes. Remove from the heat and let sit for 10 minutes to finish cooking.

3. With the steam vent pointed away from your face, gently release any remaining pressure, remove the lid, and let sit, uncovered, for 5 minutes.

4. Transfer the game hen halves to a plate and set aside in a warm place. Cook the sauce in the pot over high heat until reduced and thickened, 4 to 5 minutes.

5. Mound the warm farro on a large serving platter. Arrange the game hen pieces around the farro and ladle the sauce over all. Serve right away.

◈ Duck with Green Olives, Turnips, and Turnip Greens

When combining long-cooking meats or poultry with quick-cooking vegetables, do them separately and combine at the end. For instance, here the baby turnips are pressure cooked in advance, then the greens are spread over the top to steam wilt while the duck finishes stewing. At the last minute the turnips and greens are arranged on the serving platter as a bed for the piping hot duck and juices. The result is a stew where each ingredient shines forth, cooked to perfection.

Makes 4 servings

2 bunches baby turnips
2 tablespoons butter
½ cup water
1 tablespoon olive oil
One 5- to 5½-pound duck, backbone removed and quartered
Salt and freshly ground black pepper to taste
1 cup Beef Broth (page 15) or Chicken Broth (page 18)
2 cups mild green olives, such as picholine or lightly cured Sicilian olives
4 sprigs fresh thyme, or 1 teaspoon dried
1 tablespoon tomato paste
4 Duck Liver Crostini (optional, see Sidebar, right)

Duck Liver Crostini

Duck liver should not be discarded even though it's not included in stock. Sauté the duck liver in a little bit of butter seasoned with sage, salt, and pepper over medium-high heat until firm but still pink in the middle, 6 to 8 minutes. Mince the liver and spread it over thin slices of lightly toasted and buttered baguette. Serve as a before-dinner tidbit or use it to garnish the duck with olives and turnips.

1. To prepare the turnips, cut off the tops, leaving a little bit of green stem on the bulbs. Cut the greens into ½-inch-wide shreds. Wash and drain them and set aside. Cut the turnips in half and place them in the pressure cooker with the butter and water. Lock on the lid and bring to pressure over high heat, about 2 minutes. Remove from the heat and let sit for 3 minutes to finish cooking. With the steam vent pointed away from your face, gently release any remaining pressure and spread the greens over the top without mixing them in. Transfer to a warm plate and set aside in a warm place.

2. Heat the oil in the pressure cooker over medium-high heat until beginning to smoke. Add the duck pieces, sprinkle them with salt and pepper, and lightly brown on both sides, 2 to 3 minutes total.

3. Stir in the broth, olives, and thyme. Lock on the lid and bring to pressure over high heat, about 3 minutes. Reduce the heat to medium and cook for 20 minutes. Remove from the heat and let sit for 10 minutes to finish cooking.

4. With the steam vent pointed away from your face, gently release any remaining pressure. Pour the juices into a 2-cup measuring cup or small bowl. Let sit for at least 15 minutes for the fat to rise to the top.

5. Skim off the fat and stir the tomato paste into the juices. Pour the juices back into the pot with the duck and reheat briefly. Spread the turnips and greens on a serving platter. Arrange the duck and olives over the top and pour the juices over all. Serve right away, accompanied by the Duck Liver Crostini, if using.

◇ Duck Gumbo *When chef Paul Prudhomme was giving a new spin to Cajun cooking and making the New Orleans restaurant Commander's Palace famous, duck filé gumbo turned up with wild mushrooms in the dish. I've adapted and streamlined his marvelous recipe for home cooking*

and, to suit my own taste, omitted the brown roux and the mushrooms and exchanged the gumbo filé for okra as thickener and seasoning. Serve this over white rice.   Makes 6 servings

½ pound young okra pods, tops trimmed off
¼ cup distilled white or cider vinegar
Salt to taste
1 tablespoon vegetable oil
One 5- to 5½-pound duck, backbone and wings removed, quartered, and skinned
All-purpose flour, for coating the duck
1 medium-size yellow or white onion, cut into ¼-inch dice
2 ribs celery, cut into ¼-inch dice
1 medium-size green bell pepper, seeded and cut into ¼-inch dice
3 large cloves garlic, coarsely chopped
1 bay leaf, crumbled
½ teaspoon dried oregano
1 teaspoon dried thyme
⅛ teaspoon cayenne
1 cup coarsely chopped tomatoes, with juices
5 cups Duck Broth (left) or Chicken Broth (page 18), or a mixture
½ pound Cajun andouille or other smoked sausage, cut into 2-inch pieces

Duck Broth

To make duck broth for gumbo, use the backbone, wings, and giblets, except the liver, plus ½ medium-size yellow or white onion, ½ small carrot, 1 rib celery with top, 1 clove garlic, and 4 cups water. Pressure cook for 20 minutes or simmer on the stove top for 1 hour. Strain, cool, and skim the fat off the top. Yields about 3½ cups.

1. Combine the okra, vinegar, and a liberal sprinkling of salt in a medium-size bowl. Set aside for 30 to 45 minutes. Rinse the okra before adding it to the pressure cooker.

2. Heat the oil in the pressure cooker over medium-high heat. Lightly coat the duck pieces with flour and add them to the pot. Brown on both sides, 2 to 3 minutes total, and transfer to a plate.

3. Add the onion, celery, bell pepper, garlic, bay leaf, oregano, thyme, and cayenne to the pot. Sauté over medium heat until well wilted, about 10 minutes.

4. Return the duck and collected juices to the pot. Add the tomatoes and their juices and the broth, lock on the lid, and bring to pressure over high heat, about 5 minutes. Reduce the heat to medium-low and cook for 15 minutes. Reduce the heat to low and cook for

Gumbos Galore

The word "gumbo" is derived from the name of the vegetable okra, called *ngumbo* in its native Africa. In the American South, "gumbo" came to mean the soup-stew that often contains okra. To confuse matters, the seasoning, gumbo filé, is not okra at all, but the ground young leaves of the sassafras tree. It is used like okra, though, as both flavoring and thickener. And most confusing, there are authentic gumbos that include neither okra nor gumbo filé. To vary duck gumbo in old and new ways, you can:

- Add wild mushrooms, as in the original Commander's Palace recipe (see headnote page 143)
- Use gumbo filé, sprinkled over the top, in place of the okra
- Omit the okra and add fresh oysters, stirred in at the very last minute
- Replace the duck with chicken or game hen
- Replace the duck with shrimp, crab, or oysters, or a mixture

25 minutes more. Remove from the heat and let sit for 5 minutes to finish cooking.

5. With the steam vent pointed away from your face, gently release any remaining pressure. Add the okra and sausage and simmer briskly with the lid ajar for 10 minutes. Serve hot.

Note: If you don't care to eat around the bones, you can lift out the duck before adding the okra and sausage and remove the bones while the gumbo finishes cooking.

◇ Pheasant Braised with Walnuts and Shallots

For years I danced around the notion of cooking pheasant for a romantic meal. But I never could get quite the tango (me and the pheasant) I was imagining until a hunter friend brought me a pheasant when I was in the process of writing this book. I tried a whole new rendition—what are friends for, after all, but to spur you on. It was so good, I look forward with the eye and nose of a hound to the next pheasant season. Served on a bed of pressure-steamed cabbages, there's not a better fall meal for two. Farm-raised pheasant also works well.

Makes 2 servings

6 slices bacon
One 1½- to 2-pound pheasant, plucked and dressed
1 tablespoon olive oil
6 large shallots, halved lengthwise
½ cup walnut pieces
6 sprigs fresh thyme, or ¾ teaspoon dried
1 bay leaf
1 blade mace
¼ teaspoon freshly ground black pepper
¼ cup brandy
¾ cup Chicken Broth (page 18)
Steamed Cabbage (page 184), warm, for serving

1. Wrap the bacon slices around the pheasant and secure with toothpicks.

2. Heat the oil in the pressure cooker over high heat until beginning to smoke. Add the pheasant and turn to brown all around, about 2 minutes.

3. Reduce the heat to medium–high and add the shallots, walnuts, thyme, bay leaf, mace, pepper, brandy, and broth. Stir to mix, winding up with the pheasant breast side up. Lock on the lid and bring to pressure over high heat, about 2 minutes. Reduce the heat to medium–high and cook for 20 minutes. Remove from the heat and let sit for 5 minutes to finish cooking.

4. With the steam vent pointed away from your face, gently release any remaining pressure. Set aside with the lid ajar for 10 minutes.

5. When ready to serve, spread the cabbage on a serving platter. Set the pheasant on top, along with the shallots and walnuts from the pot. Remove the thyme, bay leaf, and mace blade. Spoon the juices over the top and serve.

Seafood:
Simple to Sublime

was reluctant at first to approach cooking seafood in the pressure cooker. "Won't everything turn out tough and overcooked?" I worried. Nonetheless, I pressed on out of curiosity. The results of my forays were eye-opening. A lively bowl of bistro-style mussels; trout steamed pure and simple and modestly dressed with a parsley sauce; exotic shrimp curries; a Spanish mixed seafood *zarzuela* made earthy with a bread crumb and pulverized almond thickening all convinced me that pressure cooking is a way to bring fresh, bright seafood, fancy or plain, to the dinner table, not only in good time, but also pristinely. It's true, seafood cooks quickly on the stove top. But, pressure cooked, there's not the clean-up of stir-frying, or the extra oil needed for pan-frying, and grand dishes like salmon roast poached in a water bath can be done in half the time. And, there's more. The following pages offer a veritable treasure table of jewels from the world's waters that the pressure cooker brings to perfection.

Seafood: Simple to Sublime

◈ Trout à la Vapeur with Toasted Almonds and Parsley Sauce

Cooking under steam, or à la vapeur, is a technique particularly well suited to seafood. Especially with trout and other whole, delicate, small fish, the method results in firm flesh and intense flavor undiluted by a poaching liquid or unmodified by frying oil. If cooking and serving the fish with the heads on is a bother for you, you can remove them. But try to purchase the fish that way so you can see if the eyes are clear, the best sign of freshness. Sandwiching the fish between two layers of lettuce leaves helps concentrate the steam for quicker cooking.

Makes 4 servings

4 very fresh river trout, boned (about ½ pound each)

Salt to taste

Distilled white vinegar to taste

4 cups torn outer lettuce leaves

½ cup water

½ cup Parsley Sauce (page 150)

2 tablespoons sliced almonds, tossed with 1 teaspoon peanut oil and
   toasted (see page 41), for garnish

1. Sprinkle the trout with salt and vinegar inside and out. Place 3 cups of the lettuce in the pressure cooker. Set the trout on top and cover with the remaining lettuce. Pour in the water and lock on the lid. Bring to pressure over high heat, about 3 minutes. Immediately remove from the heat and let sit for 3 minutes to finish cooking.

2. With the steam vent pointed away from your face, gently release any remaining pressure. Lift the trout onto a plate and peel away the skin from both sides using your fingers and a table knife. Remove the heads, if desired.

3. Set the peeled trout on a serving platter. Spread a tablespoon or so of the sauce over the top of each and sprinkle the almonds over the sauce. Serve right away with the remaining sauce.

Parsley Sauce *Water as an ingredient makes a refreshing, moist sauce without too much vinegar or any oil at all.*

Makes ½ cup

1 cup packed fresh flat-leaf parsley leaves, minced
1 large shallot, minced
Pinch of salt
1 teaspoon champagne vinegar or other white wine vinegar
2 tablespoons water

Combine all the ingredients in a small bowl and mix with a fork. Use right away or set aside for up to 1 hour, but not longer, or the parsley will lose its sparkle.

Halibut with Black Olive Butter Sauce

Halibut's mild white flesh takes well to aromatic pressure steaming, which preserves its firm, flaky texture and unassertive flavor. Butter swirled with lime and dotted with dill and black olives adds enrichment and color at the same time. Sea bass, salmon, or bluenose steaks or fillets will also do for the fish, but for the sauce, the butter must be butter—margarine won't turn out a smooth blend because it doesn't bind well with the lime.

Makes 4 servings

Two 1- to 1½-inch-thick halibut steaks or fillets (about 1 pound each)
Salt to taste
12 sprigs dill
½ white onion, sliced ¼ inch thick
¾ cup dry white wine
¾ cup water
½ cup Black Olive Butter Sauce (recipe follows)

1. Sprinkle the fish with salt. Place a trivet in the pressure cooker and spread half of the dill sprigs and onion slices on it. Set the fish on top and cover with the remaining dill sprigs and onion slices. Pour in the wine and water, lock on the lid, and bring to pressure over high heat, about 4 minutes. Remove from the heat right away and let sit for 5 minutes to finish cooking.

2. With the steam vent pointed away from your face, gently release any remaining pressure. Transfer the fish to a serving platter, leaving behind the dill sprigs and onion slices and reserving the cooking liquid. Set the fish aside in a warm place and prepare the sauce.

3. Pour the sauce over the top and serve.

Black Olive Butter Sauce

Makes about ½ cup

6 tablespoons (¾ stick) butter
1½ tablespoons freshly squeezed lime juice
1 tablespoon reserved cooking liquid from halibut
1 tablespoon chopped fresh dill
8 black olives, such as Kalamata, pitted and coarsely chopped

Heat the butter in a small saucepan over medium heat until melted but not foaming. Whisk in the lime juice and cooking liquid, stirring until smooth. Swirl in the dill and olives. Use right away.

Pacific White Fish Fillets Simmered in Coconut Milk with Green Papaya and Fried Garlic Salad *Most Pacific white fish,*

such as red snapper, escolar, black sea bass, or flounder, slip smoothly into a seasoned coconut bath. After the fish is simmered, the liquid is turned into a sauce of thickened coconut milk warmed with chile pepper to flavor the fish on the plate.

Makes 4 servings

2½ cups unsweetened coconut milk, drained for 30 minutes, liquid reserved
¼ cup freshly squeezed lime juice
1 stalk lemongrass, coarsely chopped
One 2-inch piece fresh ginger, cut into ½-inch-thick slices
2 jalapeño chile peppers, preferably 1 green and 1 red for color,
    seeded and slivered (see Note)
1 teaspoon salt
1½ pounds thick white fish fillets (see headnote), cut into 4 equal pieces
¼ cup chopped fresh cilantro, for garnish
¼ cup unsweetened coconut flakes, lightly
    toasted (see page 218), for garnish
Green Papaya and Fried Garlic Salad (recipe follows)

1. Pour the reserved liquid from draining the coconut milk into the pressure cooker. Add the lime juice, lemongrass, and ginger and bring to a boil. Cook briskly over medium-high heat until reduced to ⅓ cup, about 8 minutes. With a slotted spoon, lift out and discard the lemongrass and ginger pieces.

2. Whisk in the thick, drained coconut milk. Add the jalapeño slivers, salt, and fish pieces. Lock on the lid and bring to pressure over high heat, 1 to 2 minutes. Immediately remove from the heat and let sit for 3 minutes to finish cooking.

3. With the steam vent pointed away from your face, gently release any remaining pressure. Transfer the fish to individual high-lipped plates or large, shallow bowls. Divide the sauce in the cooker among them and garnish each with cilantro and toasted coconut. Accompany with the salad on the side.

Note: I usually don't bother to seed small fresh chile peppers because I like their extra bite. But when the look of the dish needs to be a little more refined, I scrape away the seeds before cutting the peppers into neat slivers.

◌ ◌ ◌

Green Papaya and Fried Garlic Salad *Green papaya is not at all like ripe papaya, though it is the same fruit. Rather than soft and sweet and very aromatic, green papaya tastes and feels more like a cucumber or jicama. It is used in fresh preparations around the eastern Pacific Rim, but the combination with golden fried garlic is one particular to Cambodian cuisine.*

Makes 4 to 6 side dish servings

1 green papaya (about 1 pound)
2 tablespoons peanut oil
6 large cloves garlic, thinly sliced
2 tablespoons freshly squeezed lime juice
Several sprigs fresh cilantro, for garnish

1. Peel the papaya with a vegetable peeler. Cut it in half and scoop out the seeds. Cut each half into thin slices and arrange on a small platter. Set aside.

2. Heat the oil in a small skillet until beginning to smoke. Add the garlic and cook, stirring, over medium-high heat until golden all around, no more than 2 minutes. Transfer to paper towels to drain.

3. Sprinkle the lime juice over the papaya. Scatter the garlic over the top. Garnish with the cilantro and serve.

Catfish Steamed in Banana Leaves with Papaya and Green Chiles

Banana leaves are the green wrap of many Mexican, Caribbean, and Pacific Rim steamed dishes. They add a fragrance that calls to mind those tropical climes. You can find banana leaves in Asian or Latin markets, sometimes in the fresh section, sometimes in the freezer section. Corn husks make a good substitute. Catfish, a fish native to the river waters throughout Indochina, together with papaya, green chiles, and ginger, is a Burmese take on a banana leaf surprise package. For a change, halibut, an equally firm-fleshed ocean fish,

will also do, and the papaya can be steamed alone for a side dish (see below).

Makes 8 packets, or 4 to 8 servings

Just Papaya

For an exotic side dish, you can wrap slices of firm papaya with grated fresh ginger, mint leaves, and lime juice in banana leaves and steam them as in the catfish recipe to serve alongside poultry or grain dishes. The timing is the same.

2 teaspoons minced lemongrass (tender white part only)

1 jalapeño chile pepper, seeded and slivered

1 tablespoon peeled and grated fresh ginger

4 thinly-sliced red onion rounds, rings separated

1 teaspoon hot paprika

1 teaspoon salt

1½ tablespoons peanut oil

1½ pounds catfish fillets, cut into 1½-inch chunks

8 to 10 banana leaf squares (see below), about 10 × 10 inches

½ firm papaya, peeled, seeded, and cut crosswise into ½-inch-thick slices

1 cup fresh cilantro sprigs, for serving

2 limes, quartered, for serving

1. Toss together the lemongrass, jalapeño, ginger, onion rings, paprika, salt, and oil in a large bowl. Add the fish and turn to coat.

2. Lay a banana leaf square on the counter and mound some of the fish mixture in the center. Place 2 or 3 papaya slices on top and fold up the leaf, corner to corner and corner to corner again, to make a neat packet. Continue until the fish mixture is used up. You should have 8 to 10 packets.

Working with Banana Leaves

Banana leaves are not as supple as grape leaves, corn husks, or cabbage leaves. That means they tend to crack and split as you fold them. So make sure you have extra for patching as you go along. The leaves soften in the steaming and look just fine when the packets are served up. Any extras can be frozen for future use.

3. Arrange the packets in 2 layers in a bamboo steamer or similar device that will hold them above the water as they cook (see page 8). Pour in 2 cups water, lock on the lid, and bring to pressure over high heat, about 3 minutes. Reduce the heat to medium-high and cook for 10 minutes. Remove from the heat and let sit for 3 minutes to finish cooking.

4. With the steam vent pointed away from your face, gently release any remaining pressure. Remove the lid and let sit until cool enough to handle.

5. Transfer the packets to a serving platter or individual plates and serve, accompanied with the cilantro and lime wedges on the side. Each person opens a packet, tops the contents with some cilantro, and squeezes on some lime juice just before eating.

◇ Atlantic Salmon Roast Poached in Red Wine Court Bouillon with Arugula Pesto

Atlantic salmon is my fish of choice for poaching for three reasons: It has just the right fat content to cook up succulently and tenderly; the poaching liquid, court bouillon, infuses the flesh without overpowering it; and its large bones are few and very easy to see and remove as you eat. A roast of two to three pounds cut from the center of the fish will cook most evenly, though you may prefer a cut from the fattier head end that includes the very tasty collar bone meat prized by Japanese cooks. Very thick salmon steaks also poach beautifully, but the time is much less; they're done as soon as the pot comes to pressure and sits off the heat for 10 minutes, with no intermediate cooking.

Makes 6 servings

One 2½-pound salmon roast, preferably a center cut
5 cups Red Wine Court Bouillon (page 156)
2 cups Arugula Pesto (page 157)
12 thinly sliced lemon rounds, for garnish

1. Wrap the salmon roast in a length of cheesecloth long enough to extend about 3 inches from either end. (This ensures that you can lift the salmon roast out of the court bouillon and off the trivet intact.)

2. Heat the court bouillon in the pressure cooker over medium-high heat until almost, but not quite, boiling. Set a trivet in the pot. Using the ends of the cheesecloth as handles, lower the salmon onto the trivet. Lock on the lid and bring to pressure over high heat, about 6 minutes. Reduce the heat to medium and cook for 12 minutes for medium-rare, 16 minutes for more well done. Remove from the heat and let sit for 20 minutes to finish cooking.

3. With the steam vent pointed away from your face, gently release any remaining pressure. Using the ends of the cheesecloth as handles, transfer the salmon to the sink to drain. When cool enough to handle, about 5 minutes, carefully unwrap the cheesecloth and peel away the skin with your fingers and a paring knife. With 2 wide spatulas and perhaps an extra pair of hands, transfer the salmon to a serving platter. Spread a thin layer of the pesto across the top and garnish the plate with the lemon rounds. Serve with the remaining pesto on the side.

Red Wine Court Bouillon *This recipe is a basic court bouillon for poaching fish. Red wine for salmon enhances the salmon's orange tones, but if poaching a white fish, such as halibut, use white wine.*

Makes 5 cups

1 yellow or white onion, quartered

2 whole cloves

1 rib celery, very coarsely chopped

1 bay leaf

2 sprigs fresh thyme, or ½ teaspoon dried

3½ cups water

2 cups dry red wine

2 tablespoons red wine vinegar

2 teaspoons salt

½ teaspoon black peppercorns

1. Combine all the ingredients in the pressure cooker. Lock on the lid and bring to pressure over high heat, about 5 minutes. Reduce the heat to medium and cook for 10 minutes. Remove from the heat and let sit for 15 minutes to finish cooking.

2. With the steam vent pointed away from your face, gently release any remaining pressure. Use right away or strain, cool completely, and store, covered, in the refrigerator for up to 3 days.

Arugula Pesto

Makes 2 cups

Pesto, Not Prosaic

You can spin many a leafy green into a delicious pesto. For instance:

- Use cilantro in place of the arugula and parsley, adding a jalapeño chile pepper and replacing the sherry wine vinegar with lime juice.
- Use a mixture of greens, such as spinach, watercress, and young kale leaves, instead of the arugula and replace the shallot with garlic.
- Use mostly parsley with ¼ cup fresh oregano, omit the sherry wine vinegar, and be sure to include the grated parmesan cheese.

½ cup pine nuts
2 cups coarsely chopped arugula leaves
1 cup fresh flat-leaf parsley
1 large shallot, coarsely chopped
¾ teaspoon salt
2 teaspoons sherry wine vinegar
½ cup extra virgin olive oil
½ cup freshly grated parmesan cheese (optional)
¼ to ½ cup water, if necessary

Pulverize the pine nuts in a food processor. Add the remaining ingredients except the water and process as fine as possible. If the mixture is too thick to spoon, thin it with the water, starting with ¼ cup and adding more if necessary. Use right away or store in the refrigerator, covered, for up to 1 week.

◻ ◻ ◻

◈ Ken Hom's Steamed Scallops

When I was writing The Gardeners' Community Cookbook, *my friend, famed chef, cookbook writer, and BBC television personality Ken Hom offered his recipe for steamed scallops with words of description that fit precisely into the spirit of this volume. "Fresh scallops are sweet and rich. Perhaps one of the best methods featuring their qualities is the Chinese method of steaming. Using hot wet vapors, this technique brings out the succulent texture of the scallops without overcooking them. Their briny seafood taste and flavors are emphasized. And the bonus is that it is very simple to prepare and takes literally minutes to cook— ideal for a quick and easy, healthful meal." I couldn't possibly expand on his remarks except to say that for steaming, the pressure cooker is the right tool.*

Makes 4 servings

1 pound large sea scallops
2 small fresh red chile peppers, seeded and chopped
1 tablespoon thinly sliced young ginger, unpeeled, or 2 teaspoons peeled
    and coarsely chopped regular ginger
1 medium-size leek (white and light green parts only), cut into
    3-inch-long slivers, well washed, and drained
1 cup chopped fresh cilantro
2 thick slices prosciutto, torn into ½-inch-wide strips
1 tablespoon low-sodium soy sauce
1 tablespoon dry sherry
¼ teaspoon salt
Pinch of freshly ground black pepper
⅓ cup water
6 lime wedges, for garnish

1. Place the scallops on a bamboo steamer or trivet in the pressure cooker. Arrange the chiles, ginger, leek, cilantro, and prosciutto over the top. In a small bowl, mix together the soy sauce, sherry, salt, pepper, and water. Pour over the scallops and aromatics. Lock on the lid and bring to pressure over high heat, about 4 minutes. Immediately remove from the heat and let sit for 3 minutes.

2. With the steam vent pointed away from your face, gently release any remaining pressure. Transfer the scallops and aromatics to a serving platter. Pour the juices from the pot over them. Serve right away, garnished with the lime wedges.

◇ French Bistro Mussels
Mussels evoke sea breezes and clear seawater. Fruit of the sea, they are also the stuff of easy, romantic dining in an intimate bistro in Normandy or Burgundy while waiting for the ferry to London. Or the occasion for adventure, traipsing the rocks of the northern California Pacific coast at low tide to pluck the farthest-out ones, the freshest because they're almost always under water in their whirling, cleansing saline Jacuzzi spa. New Zealand mussels, green-lipped they're called, are also a delight, though I've only had them from the fish market. Mussels from the pressure cooker shimmer as though plucked fresh from their rocks. There's no need to complicate matters: Some garlic, a bit of diced tomato, a soupçon of white wine, and a garnish of parsley add up to bistro mussels for any coast. Makes 4 servings

4 small tomatoes, peeled (see page 24), seeded, and coarsely chopped
6 large cloves garlic, coarsely chopped
½ cup dry white wine
2 tablespoons butter
2 pounds mussels, rinsed
¼ cup chopped flat-leaf parsley, for garnish
Eight 1-inch slices baguette, fried in butter and olive oil
    over medium heat until golden, for garnish

1. Combine the tomatoes, garlic, wine, and butter in the pressure cooker and stir to mix. Mound the mussels on top. Lock on the lid and bring to pressure over high heat, 3 to 4 minutes. Reduce the heat to medium and cook for 3 minutes. Remove from the heat and let sit for 2 minutes to finish cooking.

2. With the steam vent pointed away from your face, gently release any remaining pressure. Transfer the mussels to a serving bowl and pour the juices over them. Sprinkle the parsley over the top and arrange the fried bread around the edges. Serve right away.

Indian-Style Shrimp Curry with Potatoes and Tomatoes

Cauliflower instead of potatoes would make an equally authentic Indian-style curry, but peeling the tomatoes would not! They are cooked with the skins on in Indian cuisine. Makes 4 servings

1½ tablespoons vegetable oil
1 medium-size yellow or white onion, cut into ¼-inch dice
¾ teaspoon cumin seeds
2 teaspoons grated fresh turmeric (see page 136), or 1 teaspoon ground
1½ teaspoons chili powder
1½ teaspoons salt
4 medium-size tomatoes, coarsely chopped, with juices
2 medium-size Yukon gold or White Rose potatoes (about ½ pound), cut into ¾-inch dice
1 tablespoon freshly squeezed lemon juice
¼ cup water
1 pound medium-size shrimp, shelled, deveined if necessary, and tails removed
¾ pound medium-size or large shrimp, shelled, deveined if necessary, and tails left intact
12 sprigs fresh cilantro, for garnish
Steamed basmati rice (see page 215), for serving

1. Heat the oil in the pressure cooker over medium-high heat until beginning to smoke. Add the onion and cook, stirring occasionally, until beginning to wilt, about 1 minute. Stir in the cumin seeds, turmeric, chili powder, and salt and continue cooking until the spices become fragrant, about 2 minutes.

2. Add the tomatoes and their juices, the potatoes, lemon juice, and water. Stir and bring to a boil. Add the shrimp, toss to coat, and

lock on the lid. Bring to pressure over high heat, about 3 minutes. Immediately remove from the heat and let sit for 7 minutes to finish cooking.

3. With the steam vent pointed away from your face, gently release any remaining pressure. Garnish with the cilantro sprigs and serve with the steamed rice.

◎ Thai-Style Shrimp Curry with Long Beans and Coconut Milk
Pairing long beans with shrimp and coconut milk in a mild curry is a typical Thai concoction. If long beans are not available, use regular green beans, also cut up, or the small haricots verts, left whole. Leaving half the shrimp with tails intact creates an interesting visual effect in the dish, and the tails also add flavor to the sauce. Rice is a must accompaniment, preferably jasmine rice for Thai dishes.

Makes 4 servings

1½ tablespoons vegetable oil

2 large cloves garlic, finely chopped

2 large shallots, finely chopped

2 tablespoons peeled and coarsely grated fresh ginger

1 to 2 small fresh green chile peppers, such as Thai or serrano, finely chopped

½ cup coarsely chopped fresh cilantro, leaves and stems

¾ pound long beans, cut into 1-inch pieces

1 pound medium-size shrimp, shelled, deveined if necessary, and tails removed

¾ pound medium-size or large shrimp, shelled, deveined if necessary, and tails left intact

1 stalk lemongrass (tender white and light green parts only), cut into 2-inch pieces

One 14-ounce can unsweetened coconut milk

1 tablespoon fish sauce (*nam pla*)

4 scallions, trimmed and cut lengthwise into 2-inch-long slivers, for garnish

1 lime, quartered, for serving

Steamed jasmine rice (see page 215), for serving

1. Heat the oil in the pressure cooker over medium–high heat. Stir in the garlic and shallots and cook until beginning to wilt, about 1 minute.

2. Add the ginger, chile pepper, cilantro, and beans and stir to mix. Add the shrimp and stir to mix. Add the lemongrass, coconut milk, and fish sauce, stir again, and lock on the lid. Bring to pressure over high heat, 3 to 4 minutes. Remove from the heat and let sit for 7 minutes to finish cooking.

3. With the steam vent pointed away from your face, gently release any remaining pressure. Remove and discard the lemongrass. Garnish the curry with the scallion slivers and serve with the lime wedges and steamed rice.

◇ In-House Clambake Steamed Under Seaweed

Culinary triumph and native dish both, the clambake has earned a place in any account of American seafood cookery. Except for some minor details, the ingredients are agreed upon: clams from the beach nearby, corn from the field nearby, likewise potatoes, freshly dug; all put together in a hot rock sand pit and covered with seaweed, then a wet-down canvas tarp, and finally another layer of hot rocks. Recipes and opinions vary about whether or not to include extras—a bit of lobster, sausage, or sweet potatoes. According to the great food writer Raymond Sokolov, at the most renowned of all clambakes, the Allen's Neck Clambake festival (near Dartmouth, Massachusetts) held in August every year since 1888, white fish and tripe are part of the composition, no two ways about it. Basically the technique is steaming. And this can be nicely done in the pressure cooker. If you can order fresh seaweed from an accommodating fish market, so much the better, but the husks from freshly shucked corn can substitute. So can fresh cuttings from a nearby pine or spruce tree.

½ pound fresh seaweed (optional, see headnote)

4 small potatoes, such as baby Yukon gold or red or white creamer,
    or 1 large sweet potato, or a mixture, cut into 1- to 1½-inch chunks
    or left whole if small

2 pounds clams, such as Manila or cherrystone, rinsed

2 small ears fresh corn, husks and silks removed, and cobs cut
    crosswise into 1-inch-thick rounds

¼ pound fresh garlic sausage, cut into 4 pieces

1 small live lobster (¾ pound) or 8 giant shrimp (optional)

1 loaf warm French bread, for serving

½ cup (1 stick) butter, melted, for serving

1. Set a trivet in the pressure cooker. Spread half of the seaweed on the trivet. Layer the remaining ingredients over the seaweed, starting with the potatoes, then the clams, the corn, the sausage, and the lobster, if using. Cover with the other half of the seaweed and pour in ½ cup water. Lock on the lid and bring to pressure over high heat, 6 to 8 minutes.

2. Reduce the heat to medium-high and cook for 5 minutes. Remove from the heat and let sit for 10 minutes to finish cooking.

3. With the steam vent pointed away from your face, gently release any remaining pressure and carefully remove the lid. Taking care to avoid escaping steam, lift off and discard the top layer of seaweed. Transfer the lobster, if included, to a platter, let cool enough to handle, and divide into parts.

4. Place the pot on the table and dish out from it, lifting the ingredients off the seaweed bed and making sure everyone has a bit of everything. Using tongs, remove the remaining bottom layer of seaweed and the trivet to a kitchen bowl. Ladle some of the juices over each serving. Serve the lobster, if using, on the side and accompany all with warm bread and melted butter.

Note: If you prefer a less informal way of serving, you can arrange the ingredients on a serving platter, discard the seaweed, and remove the trivet. Then, pour the juices over the dish and serve.

◈ Pressure-Steamed Dungeness Crab

Alaska has its own, king crab and snow crab; Maryland and Louisiana have their own, blue crab; Hawaii has its own, Kona crab. But the true crab crown goes to the Dungeness crab of northern Pacific waters between Baja California and southern Alaska, and especially to those of San Francisco Bay. Their tender, not stringy, flesh and sea-fresh taste are matched by no other. If you have the opportunity to purchase and cook one live, I guarantee it will be a crab eating experience never to forget. Having the advantage of living in the San Francisco Bay area, I often cook crab, and pressure cooking is my method of choice. Once you've cooked the crab, San Francisco style is an obvious way to serve it—pretty much fresh from the pot and cracked as soon as it's cool enough to handle, accompanied by warm French bread (sourdough to be authentic), melted butter, lemon wedges, and lots of napkins so there's no shyness about digging in. Or, you can turn to the other side of the Pacific, the Orient, and serve the crab in a Chinese style (see the following recipe). One crab generously serves two, or maybe three, so if you're making a party of it, cook two or more consecutively.

Makes 2 to 3 servings

1½ cups water
1 live Dungeness crab (about 3 pounds)

1. Pour the water into the pressure cooker. Add the crab (see right), lock on the lid, and bring to pressure over high heat,

No two ways about it—the crab will wiggle and squirm and try to pinch you as you lift it into the pot. There's a way to do it without harm. The secret is this: The crab's front claws, the pincers, can't reach behind, and the back claws, though active, have no pincers. So, use long-handled tongs and grasp the crab at the back end, place it in the pot, and quickly put on the lid.

about 5 minutes. Reduce the heat to medium-high and cook for 2 minutes. Remove from the heat and let sit for 3 minutes to finish cooking.

2. With the steam vent pointed away from your face, gently release any remaining pressure. Carefully drain into the sink and let cool enough to handle. Then, clean and crack it as described below. Serve either San Francisco style or Chinese style.

Cleaning and Cracking the Crab

You've watched the fishmonger do it dozens of times, and so swiftly. Now, you've taken the giant leap to cook the crab at home. How to clean it? Three easy steps get you there.

1. When the crab is cool enough to handle, snap off its claws and legs and set them aside.

2. Turn the body shell side down and pry loose the pointed flap at the back end. Pull the body away from the shell, taking care not to spill the juices left in the shell. Divide the body into 2 or 4 pieces, depending on how many you are serving. Set the pieces on a serving platter.

3. At this point, you can arrange the claws and legs around the platter and serve with crab cracker tools, so people can crack their own as they eat. Or, you can do the job in the kitchen: Using a mallet or hammer, crack each section of each leg and claw just hard enough to open the shell without splintering it. If desired, serve the crab juices from inside the shell, reserving the green liver, the white marrow, and the pink-orange coral to serve in separate small bowls, if desired.

◈ Dungeness Crab Chinese Style, on a Bed of Dinosaur Kale and Black Beans

Crab paired with black beans is a classic of Chinese cooking. Dinosaur kale is a curly leaf green—like regular kale that got a permanent at the hairdresser's. In appearance it resembles seaweed as much as a land plant can. The two come together in an easy way to make a bed for crab that sings of the Orient, looks beautiful, and tastes fabulous.

Makes 2 to 4 servings

3 cups Dinosaur Kale (recipe follows)
1 cup Chinese fermented black beans (see below)
1 Pressure-Steamed Dungeness Crab (page 164)
Lemon wedges, for garnish
Basic Steamed Rice (page 215), for serving

Spread the kale on a serving platter. Sprinkle the black beans over the kale. Arrange the crab over all, garnish with the lemon wedges, and serve. Accompany with a bowl of the marrow and juices from the crab (see page 166) and the rice.

Black Beans: Turtle or Soy?

The black beans familiar to Western cooks are often called turtle beans; I've never figured out why. They're a staple of southern Mexican cooking, especially around Oaxaca, where they're used as a tamale filling (see page 250). The black beans of Asian cooking are an Old World legume, a soybean. They come cooked and ready to go in packages described as salted black beans, available in Asian markets and health food stores. Oddly, however, the black turtle beans can substitute for the Asian black soybeans in the Chinese crab recipe, albeit with a softer texture.

Dinosaur Kale *A new darling of kitchen gardeners, dinosaur kale tastes pretty much like regular kale when it's full grown, past the baby stage you'd use for salad greens. It makes a lusty but not strident leafy green on which to bed pork, poultry, or crab, or to serve as a side dish on its own. It's recently become available as seedlings in garden centers and as seed in mail-order catalogs, and it's easy to grow in the ground or in a pot.*

Makes 3 cups

½ pound dinosaur kale, tough stems removed, tops shredded
   ½ inch wide, well washed, and drained
½ cup water

1. Put the still moist kale in the pressure cooker and pour in the water. Lock on the lid and bring to pressure over high heat, about 2 minutes. Reduce the heat to medium and cook for 2 minutes. Remove from the heat and let sit for 2 minutes to finish cooking.

2. With the steam vent pointed away from your face, gently release any remaining pressure. Drain and use right away.

◇ Squid Stewed in Red Wine

Squid has an odd characteristic in that it must be either flash cooked a mere minute or two or slow cooked for 30 minutes to 45 minutes (less in the pressure cooker). In between, it becomes rubbery and remains that way until coaxed back into suppleness with longer cooking. Tempting as it is to take advantage of the convenient ready-for-cooking squid available these days, don't. In the commercial cleaning, too much of the flavor is washed away, especially the taste and aroma of deep, clear seawater, which is the mark of fresh squid.

Makes 4 servings

Fresh octopus, should you
have access to it, is especially delicious cooked in
this way. Cut the tentacles
into 1-inch lengths and the
head into 1-inch-wide
strips. Cook as for the squid
except add 10 minutes to
the cooking time after
reaching pressure and 5
minutes to the sitting time.

3 pounds fresh squid

¼ cup olive oil

1 small yellow or white onion, finely chopped

2 large cloves garlic, minced

2 tablespoons tomato paste

1¼ cups dry red wine

12 small green olives, such as picholine

½ teaspoon salt

1 teaspoon chopped fresh thyme, or ½ teaspoon dried, for garnish

¼ cup chopped fresh flat-leaf parsley, for garnish

4 thick slices country-style bread, toasted and buttered, for garnish

1. Clean the squid (see below).

2. Heat the oil in the pressure cooker over medium-high heat until it begins to smoke. Add the onion and garlic and cook, stirring, over medium heat until they begin to turn golden, about 2 minutes.

How to Clean Squid the Easy Way

Cleaning squid need not be a laborious process if you don't mind not having circles. The form certainly doesn't affect the taste and, for most dishes, doesn't matter for the look. Cleaning squid is a messy job, however, so here are some tips and techniques to streamline both the prep and the clean-up:

Use a counter that is suitable for cutting on and that is situated adjacent to the sink. Line the counter and the sink with several layers of newspaper. Set a colander in the sink on top of the newspapers.

With a paring knife, cut off the tentacles, press out the hard ball in the middle, and discard onto the papers in the sink. Place the tentacles in the colander. Slit open the body lengthwise and, with the paring knife, scrape off the innards into the sink. Add the body to the colander with the tentacles.

Gather up and discard the newspapers from the counter and sink. Give the squid parts in the colander a brief rinse. Place the colander over a bowl to catch the drips and set aside in the refrigerator until ready to use, up to 6 hours, but not longer.

3. Stir in the tomato paste, then the wine, olives, salt, and squid. Lock on the lid and bring to pressure over high heat, about 3 minutes. Reduce the heat to medium and cook for 10 minutes. Remove from the heat and let sit for 10 minutes to finish cooking.

4. With the steam vent pointed away from your face, gently release any remaining pressure. Sprinkle the thyme and parsley over the top, garnish with the toast slices, and serve right away.

Zarzuela

An onomatopoetic name if ever there was one, zarzuela *describes a fandango of shellfish in the pot. The almonds and homemade bread crumbs add the very Spanish finishing touch. Stirring the parsley into the dish while it cooks rather than saving it for garnish takes the herb in a different direction: cooked leafy green element instead of fresh herb topping. The mixture of seafood can be flexible, depending on what's very fresh in the market and economically priced that day.*

Makes 4 servings

1½ tablespoons olive oil
1 medium-size yellow or white onion, finely chopped
1 tablespoon brandy
1 tablespoon tomato paste
½ cup dry white wine
1 large clove garlic, coarsely chopped
1 tablespoon chopped fresh flat-leaf parsley
½ teaspoon salt
1 pound sea bass fillets, cut into equal pieces
2 pounds squid, cleaned (see left), and cut in half
1 pound Manila clams or mussels, or a mixture, rinsed
½ pound medium-size to large shrimp, deveined if necessary,
    shells and tails left intact
¼ cup slivered almonds
One 2-inch-thick slice very stale or lightly toasted baguette, broken up

1. Heat the oil in the pressure cooker over medium–high heat until beginning to smoke. Add the onion and cook, stirring occasionally, until well wilted, 5 minutes. Stir in the brandy and raise the heat to high. Stir in the tomato paste, wine, garlic, parsley, and salt and bring to a boil.

2. Layer the sea bass, squid, clams, and shrimp in the pot. Lock on the lid and bring to pressure over high heat, about 5 minutes. Immediately remove from the heat and let sit for 5 minutes to finish cooking.

3. Meanwhile, pulverize the almonds and bread together in a food processor. Set aside.

4. With the steam vent pointed away from your face, gently release any remaining pressure from the cooker. Transfer the seafood and sauce to a serving platter and sprinkle the almond and bread crumb mixture over the top. Serve right away.

Vegetables:

Quick and Creative

t seems the quiet exhortation from Mom to "eat your vegetables" has turned into a din echoed throughout the culture, no longer to be ignored. That's good. In fact, I'm not sure where the notion arose in our culture that eating vegetables was a travail in the first place. This is a nation of immense agricultural output, in a land that cradled some of the most cherished native foods and indigenous cultures that knew how to use them well. Happily, fresh vegetables have become a good sell in modern times and are becoming more so each year, as testified to by the mounting number of vegetarian cookbooks and advocates who claim to be vegetarian, if only fair-weatherly so.

There's very little the pressure cooker can't do to expedite your fresh vegetable cooking. Braised carrots, gratinéed cauliflower, mashed potatoes, beautiful beets, stuffed peppers, broccoli any way, all come out with aplomb. Of course, there are limits. The pressure cooker's range doesn't stretch to quick wilting, as for fresh spinach you want to remain bright green or summer squash you want to stay somewhat *al dente*. It also doesn't suit cooking large globe artichokes (baby ones are okay) or green beans unless in a long-simmered soup. Mostly it steams, braises, stews, and simmers vegetables—to perfection. Following is a large sampler, but by no means an exhaustive one, of quick and creative vegetable recipes that you can have for dinner tonight.

Vegetables: Quick and Creative

Asparagus with Shallot, Lemon, and Olive Oil Dressing

In ancient Rome, there was a way of cooking asparagus in a pressure cooker! That means there was a way of cooking under pressure way back then. I have no idea what they thought a perfectly done asparagus was, nor what their pressure cooking apparatus was, but I do know I like the pressure cooker for the way, in almost no time flat, the spears come out bright green and cooked to the just-beyond al dente stage, where you can savor them from top to bottom without any raw aftertaste.

Makes 4 servings

1½ pounds large asparagus spears, peeled
½ cup water
2 tablespoons finely chopped shallot or white onion
¼ cup freshly squeezed lemon juice
½ teaspoon salt
¼ teaspoon ground white pepper
1 tablespoon extra virgin olive oil

1. Lay the asparagus spears down flat in the pressure cooker. Pour in the water, lock on the lid, and bring to pressure over high heat, 2 to 3 minutes. Immediately remove from the heat and let sit for 2 minutes to finish cooking.

2. With the steam vent pointed away from your face, gently release any remaining pressure. Remove the lid and let sit for 2 to 3 minutes, until the steam subsides. Transfer the spears to a serving platter.

3. Combine the onion, lemon juice, salt, pepper, and olive oil in a small bowl. Whisk to mix and pour over the asparagus. Serve right away or let sit at room temperature for up to 3 hours.

The Artichoke and Potato Anomaly

In cooking artichokes and potatoes, the done-just-right point is when they may seem overdone, on the verge of disintegrating. That's the anomaly. The secret is to ever so gently drain them and then leave them undisturbed until cooled down. In the process, they re-collect themselves into tender-all-the-way-through but not mushy bites. Cook them less and you'll have underdone, squeaky-leaf artichokes or *al dente* potatoes.

◎ Baby Artichokes and Two Sauces

When artichokes are cooked on the stove top, lemon juice is often squeezed into the water, not only to keep the color bright, which doesn't work, but also to add a hint of citrus flavor, which does work a bit. In the pressure cooker, the artichokes turn out their same cooked-artichoke color, but the steaming lemon water imbues the leaves with far more lemon taste than in stove-top cooking. Keep in mind, the artichokes must be baby ones; larger chokes won't do for pressure cooking.

Makes 4 to 6 side dish servings, or 12 appetizer servings

¼ cup freshly squeezed lemon juice

3 cups water

24 baby artichokes (about 2 pounds), outer leaves removed and tops
    cut off to the light green part

½ cup Lemon Garlic Butter (recipe follows) or ¾ cup Soft Garlic
    Anchovy Oil (page 176)

1. Pour the lemon juice and water into the pressure cooker. Set a trivet or steamer basket on the bottom and place the artichokes on top (they don't need to be in a single layer). Lock on the lid and bring to pressure over high heat, 5 to 6 minutes. Reduce the heat to medium-high and cook for 2 minutes. Remove from the heat and let sit for 10 minutes for soft artichokes or 6 minutes if you prefer them firmer.

2. With the steam vent pointed away from your face, gently release any remaining pressure. When the steam subsides, pour off the liquid, taking care not to break the artichokes apart. Set aside without disturbing until cool enough to handle.

3. When ready to serve, arrange the artichokes in a serving dish and pour the sauce over them. If using the butter sauce, serve right away while still warm. If using the flavored oil sauce, the dish may sit and marinate for up to several hours.

Lemon Garlic Butter

Makes ½ cup

3 tablespoons freshly squeezed lemon juice
2 cloves garlic, minced
½ cup (1 stick) butter, at room temperature

Heat the lemon juice and garlic together in a small saucepan over medium heat until beginning to steam. Whisk in the butter 1 tablespoon at a time, making sure each addition is incorporated before continuing, until you have a smooth sauce. Serve right away, or set aside in a warm spot for up to 30 minutes and whisk to smooth before serving.

Artichoke Alternatives

Here are some other sauces in this book to pair with artichokes:

Yogurt Garlic Dressing (page 275)

Creamy Horseradish Sauce (page 65)

Blue Cheese Dipping Sauce (page 138)

Parsley Sauce (page 150)

Black Olive Butter Sauce (page 151)

Soft Garlic Anchovy Oil

Makes ¾ cup

8 large cloves garlic, halved
⅔ cup water
8 oil-packed anchovy fillets, minced
1 tablespoon freshly squeezed lemon juice
½ cup extra virgin olive oil
2 teaspoons finely chopped lemon zest

1. Place the garlic and water in a small saucepan. Bring to a boil, then reduce the heat and cook over medium-high heat until the garlic is soft but not mushy, about 5 minutes. Drain and cool.

2. Mince the garlic and combine it with the anchovies in a small bowl. Whisk in the lemon juice and oil. Stir in the zest and use right away or set aside for up to several hours.

◇ ◇ ◇

Beet Tips

The best way to keep cooked beets is to store them in the refrigerator in their cooking water. They'll last this way for up to 10 days.

The beet cooking water can also be used as the base for a beet soup, as the base for a brine for pickled beets, and as a restoring tea.

Unlike potatoes, beets are done when a fork easily pierces them about one third of the way through and then meets resistance. Timing the cooking is a little tricky for beets because it varies according to the size and freshness. I prefer to err on the underdone side—it's easy enough to boil them a little longer—than to have them irreversibly too soft or mushy.

◈ Beets, Beautiful Beets

Along with carrots and turnips, beets are a constant in my garden, for somewhat the same reasons: Their tops are pretty and, in the case of turnips and beets, tasty; their bottoms are a prize of the earth; and they grow easily. In a warm winter climate, they'll nestle in and develop underground, awaiting a spring or early summer harvest. In a cold winter climate, they'll keep without withering or going woody in the root cellar. No wonder there are so many ways to prepare beets—roasted, boiled, steamed, sautéed, grated, or pureed into soup, sliced for salad, or pickled. Following is a basic recipe. The sugar is optional—I find beets plenty dulcet on their own, but some cooks like to heighten the natural sweetness with a touch of sugar.

Makes 4 to 6 servings

Easy Peeling

Beets and tomatoes are the only vegetables I know that you can peel by just pushing off their skins with your fingers when they're still warm. This means that even if you are not using the beets or tomatoes right away, you should be sure to peel them before cooling them completely or chilling them because then it takes a knife and a bit of paring to remove the peel.

6 medium-size beets (about 2 pounds)
6 cups water, or enough almost to cover
2 tablespoons butter
½ teaspoon freshly ground black pepper
½ teaspoon sugar (optional)
1 tablespoon balsamic vinegar
2 tablespoons chopped fresh herbs, such as tarragon, cilantro,
    parsley, dill, or chervil, for garnish

1. Combine the beets and water in the pressure cooker, lock on the lid, and bring to pressure over high heat, about 8 minutes. Reduce the heat to medium and cook for 6 minutes. Remove from the heat and let sit for 10 minutes to finish cooking.

2. With the steam vent pointed away from your face, gently release any remaining pressure. Lift the beets out of the cooking liquid with a slotted spoon and place them in a colander. Reserve the cooking liquid (see left).

3. When cool enough to handle, peel the beets by slipping off the skins and cut them into rounds, half rounds, or wedges, as you like.

4. Melt the butter in a sauté pan over medium heat. Add the beets, pepper, and sugar, if using, and cook, stirring occasionally, until heated through, about 5 minutes. Stir in the vinegar and transfer to a serving bowl. Sprinkle with the herbs and serve.

◊ ◊ ◊

And More Beets

Day-Glo Beet Salad

Coarsely grate 2 cooked and peeled beets. Spread them on a small serving platter. Moisten with a splash of balsamic or red wine vinegar and dust with freshly ground black pepper. Garnish with a line of sieved hard-boiled egg yolk down the center and a handful of whole fresh cilantro leaves. Serve without tossing.

Pickled Beets

Quarter cooked and peeled beets and place them in a large glass jar or heavy plastic container. Pour 1 cup of the beet cooking water, $\frac{1}{2}$ cup red wine vinegar, and $\frac{1}{2}$ cup dry red wine into a medium-size saucepan. Add 1 bay leaf, 2 whole cloves, and 1 teaspoon salt and bring to a boil. Reduce the heat and simmer for 2 minutes, then pour over the beets. Cool completely, cover, and refrigerate for at least 3 days before using.

Sturdy Greens

Turnip, collard, and mustard greens call to mind Southern cooking. Dandelion calls up images of Greek spring. Chard evokes northern Europe. Bok choy speaks of Asia, and kale travels everywhere. These are but a handful of the sturdy greens available to bolster a dish, fulfill the meal, or, when picked tiny, add a tender nip to a spring salad. See also page 167 for how to cook dinosaur kale.

Chard with Garlic and Black Olives *So enjoyed is this dish in my house, and so versatile, that it has appeared in one way or another in almost every one of my cookbooks. The pressure cooker does justice to the favorite green that always grows in my garden.*

Makes 4 servings

7 cups coarsely shredded chard leaves (see page 180), well washed and drained
1 tablespoon olive oil
1 small clove garlic, pressed or minced
3 Kalamata olives, pitted and coarsely chopped

1. Combine the still moist chard, oil, garlic, and olives in the pressure cooker. Without mixing, lock on the lid and bring to pressure over high heat, about 3 minutes. Reduce the heat to medium and cook for 2 minutes. Remove from the heat and let sit for 5 minutes to finish cooking.

2. With the steam vent pointed away from your face, gently release any remaining pressure. Transfer to a serving platter and serve right away.

Chard Choices

Yellow, red, white, and all colors in between are the ways chard comes these days. Good and delicious they all are. However, for the kitchen, there are some details to consider. Basically, the beautiful, rainbow-colored chards are gorgeous in the garden, but only their leaves are glorious in the pot; the stems are not succulent. The white-ribbed Swiss chard is the one to grow for savoring from the top to the bottom of the rib.

◇ Collard or Dandelion Greens with Slab Bacon, Pecans, and Malt Vinegar

Collards are the signature green of Southern cooking. Outside that realm, you might not think of having them, or dandelion greens, a more Mediterranean sturdy leaf, either. In both cuisines, the leaves picked at midsummer, when they need some coaxing to end up tender on the plate, are softened with fresh-cooked bacon, spiced with vinegar, and here, given a crunch with toasted pecans. The malt vinegar is a rustic perk that I like to use sometimes in place of cider or red wine vinegar.

Makes 4 servings

1 tablespoon olive oil
2 ounces fresh slab bacon (see headnote on page 112), finely chopped
1 small yellow or white onion, chopped
9 cups collard or dandelion greens cut into 1-inch-wide strips,
    well washed and drained
½ cup water
⅓ cup pecan halves, toasted (see page 41)
1 teaspoon malt vinegar
Salt to taste

1. Heat the oil in the pressure cooker over medium-high heat until beginning to smoke. Add the bacon and cook, stirring occasionally, until beginning to turn golden, about 2 minutes. Stir in the onion, then add the greens, stirring to mix them down. Add the water, lock on the lid, and bring to pressure over high heat, about 2 minutes.

2. Reduce the heat to medium-low and cook for 5 minutes. Remove from the heat and let sit for 5 minutes to finish cooking.

3. With the steam vent pointed away from your face, gently release any remaining pressure. Remove the lid and let the steam subside. Transfer the greens to a serving platter and toss with the pecans, vinegar, and salt. Serve right away.

Turnip Greens with Pine Nuts and Olive Oil *Sometimes, the simplest of things can combine to make the richest of flavors. Like blending esters for perfume, it's always a mystery, but when it's there, there's no doubt about it. That's how I think of turnip greens with pine nuts and olive oil.*

Makes 4 servings

10 cups shredded turnip greens, well washed and drained
½ cup water
½ cup pine nuts, lightly toasted (see page 41), for garnish
2 teaspoons extra virgin olive oil, for drizzling

1. Place the still moist greens in the pressure cooker. Add the water, lock on the lid, and bring to pressure over high heat, about 1 minute. Immediately remove from the heat and let sit for 2 minutes to finish cooking.

2. With the steam vent pointed away from your face, gently release any remaining pressure. Transfer the greens to a serving platter. Sprinkle on the pine nuts, then drizzle the oil over the top. Serve right away.

◐ Bok Choy with Mustard Miso Dressing *The news has been out for some time now—brassicas are good for you. That means cabbage, broccoli, mustard greens, and their numerous relatives in that large family of plants. Among them are the ones you might have seen in Asian markets in half a dozen or so varieties, some with broccoli-like tips, some with little yellow flowers, some bulbous shaped and leafy, like bok choy. Mostly, these vegetables are stir-fried in combination with other ingredients or steamed solo. Any choy can be steamed to perfection in the pressure cooker, and the Mustard Miso Dressing suits them all.*

Makes 4 to 6 servings

¾ pound bok choy
½ cup water
¾ cup Mustard Miso Dressing (recipe follows)

1. If the bok choy are baby, leave them whole; if larger, cut them lengthwise into quarters. Place in the pressure cooker and pour in the water. Lock on the lid and bring to pressure over high heat, about 3 minutes. Reduce the heat to medium and cook for 2 minutes. Remove from the heat and let sit for 3 minutes to finish cooking.

2. With the steam vent pointed away from your face, gently release any remaining pressure. Arrange the choy on a serving platter and pour the dressing over the top. Serve warm, at room temperature, or chilled.

Mustard Miso Dressing *The tongue-tingling combination of mustard with miso is a classic dressing for cooked green vegetables in Japanese cuisine, particularly for the choys. It translates well to vegetables not commonly used in Japan, such as asparagus, green beans, braised celery (see page 192), and salads of crunchy lettuce leaves like romaine or iceberg. Miso and mirin can be found in Asian food markets and better supermarkets that cater to an international clientele. Store leftover miso in the refrigerator, covered, for up to 3 months.* Makes ¾ cup

1½ teaspoons powdered mustard
3 tablespoons plus 2 teaspoons water
⅓ cup white miso
1½ tablespoons unseasoned mirin, sake,
    or Chinese rice wine

1. Stir together the mustard and 2 teaspoons water in a small cup and set aside until thickened to a paste, about 5 minutes.

2. In a small bowl, whisk together the mustard paste, miso, mirin, and remaining 3 tablespoons water. Use right away or within a few hours before the mustard flavor fades.

Baby Savoy Cabbages with Walnuts and Chèvre

Enchanted by the cute, baby red and green Savoy cabbages being sold at my local market as "salad Savoys," I couldn't resist bringing a few home (although regular-size Savoy cabbage, cored and cut into eighths, also works here). The walnuts in this recipe must be walnut halves because that's what makes them a main element, not just a sprinkle. Makes 2 to 3 servings

1 tablespoon butter
⅓ cup walnut halves
2 baby Savoy cabbages (about 2 ounces each), hard stems cut away,
    rinsed, and drained
¼ cup water
2 tablespoons soft chèvre, at room temperature

1. Melt the butter in the pressure cooker over medium–high heat. Stir in the walnuts and cook, stirring occasionally, until toasted, about 2 minutes. Add the cabbage, stir, and then add the water. Lock on the lid and bring to pressure over high heat, 1 to 2 minutes. Remove from the heat and let sit for 5 minutes to finish cooking.

2. With the steam vent pointed away from your face, gently release any remaining pressure. Transfer to a serving platter and dot with the chèvre. Serve right away.

◌ Steamed Cabbage *Cabbage and the pressure cooker are a food-meets-pot match not possible to better. In every way, from plain to chestnut-bejeweled to meat-and-rice-filled, the stiff leaves soften and comply with whatever the cook has dictated. Good-for-you, simple steamed cabbage might become a weekly staple; it's easier than blanching and requires no fat as in sautéing. Serve it in a bowl alone or as a bed on a platter of poultry, pork, or game.*

Makes 4 to 6 servings

6 cups shredded cabbage (¼ to ½ inch thick)
1 teaspoon salt
¾ cup water
¼ cup (½ stick) butter
Freshly ground black or white pepper to taste
Chopped fresh flat-leaf parsley or dill to taste

1. Place the cabbage in the pressure cooker, sprinkle on the salt, and toss to mix. Pour in the water. Lock on the lid and bring to pressure over high heat, 4 to 5 minutes. Remove from the heat without further cooking and set aside for 5 minutes.

2. With the steam vent pointed away from your face, gently release any remaining pressure. Transfer the cabbage to a serving bowl and dot with the butter all across the top. Sprinkle a generous amount of pepper and a double pinch of parsley or dill over the top. Place on the table and toss just as serving.

Brussels Sprouts with Kumquats and Prosciutto

In better produce markets, you might find Brussels sprouts on the stem during their season, late fall to early winter. It's a good idea to purchase a stem or two because the sprouts stay fresher that way and the decorative value is outstanding. When plucking the sprouts for the kitchen, I always leave two or three top ones on the stem so they can go to flower and provide visual interest in a tall vase as cooked ones provide edible interest on the plate.

Makes 4 servings

1 pound Brussels sprouts
2 tablespoons butter
½ cup water
¼ pound kumquats, cut lengthwise into thin slivers
6 not-too-thin slices prosciutto (about 2 ounces),
    torn into long strips

1. Trim the stem ends of the Brussels sprouts and pull off any wilted or yellowing leaves. Rinse in a colander and set aside.

2. Heat the butter in the pressure cooker over medium heat until beginning to melt. Add the still moist Brussels sprouts and the water and stir to coat. Lock on the lid and bring to pressure over high heat, 4 to 5 minutes. Reduce the heat to medium and cook for 2 minutes. Remove from the heat and let sit for 2 minutes to finish cooking.

3. With the steam vent pointed away from your face, gently release any remaining pressure. With a slotted spoon, transfer the Brussels sprouts to a serving bowl, leaving the liquid in the pot. Set the bowl aside in a warm place.

4. Add the kumquats to the pot and cook, stirring, over medium heat until wilted, about 2 minutes. Spoon the kumquats and liquid over the Brussels sprouts, top with the prosciutto strips, and serve right away.

◈ Cauliflower with Melted Cheese and Cracker Crumbs

Billowy, white, almost cloud-like cauliflower florets invite the eye. In spite of their reputation for malodorous vapors filling the air, when they are properly prepared, any unpleasant smell dissipates quickly as the dish is cooked. Since cauliflower lends itself so well to pressure cooking, I offer several recipes throughout the book, including this somewhat American-style casserole.

Makes 3 to 4 servings

1 large head cauliflower (about 2 pounds), trimmed and
    cut into 1-inch florets
¼ cup freshly squeezed lemon juice
¼ cup water
2 tablespoons butter
¼ teaspoon salt
Pinch of ground nutmeg
1 cup coarsely grated sharp white melting cheese, such as
    Manchego, Canadian white cheddar, or *kefalotyri*
½ cup toasted cracker crumbs (see right), for topping

1. Combine the florets, lemon juice, and water in a medium-size bowl. Toss to mix and set aside at room temperature for at least 15 minutes, or up to 30 minutes.

2. Melt the butter in the pressure cooker over medium heat. Drain the cauliflower and add it to the pot, along with the salt, nutmeg, and cheese. Stir to mix and lock on the lid. Bring to pressure over high heat, about 2 minutes. Reduce the heat to medium–high and cook for 2 minutes. Remove from the heat and let sit for 5 minutes to finish cooking.

3. With the steam vent pointed away from your face, gently release any remaining pressure. Transfer the cauliflower to a serving dish and sprinkle the cracker crumbs over the top. Serve right away, while the cheese is still runny.

Making and Toasting Crumbs

Toasted crumbs, whether bread or cracker, are of supreme importance to any dish that calls for them. That means they must be homemade and, unless otherwise specified, coarse enough to be recognizable as crumbs.

To make crumbs:

- Cracker crumbs: Spread saltine crackers on a counter and pulverize them with a rolling pin until broken up but not sandy. Or place them in a food processor and pulverize them with short pulses.
- Bread crumbs: Start with very stale bread, or dry out bread slices in a low-heat oven until no longer pliable. Chop the bread into coarse chunks about $\frac{1}{4}$ inch in size. At this point, you can set them aside in a brown bag in the cupboard for many weeks until ready to make crumbs. Or, if you'd like crumbs pronto, dry them a little more in a low oven until quite crunchy but not toasted, then pulverize them in a food processor or with a rolling pin.

Cracker crumbs or bread crumbs can be stored in a closed container in the cupboard almost indefinitely.

To toast crumbs: For $\frac{1}{2}$ cup crumbs, melt 2 tablespoons butter or margarine in a skillet over medium heat. Add the crumbs and stir until they begin to turn golden, about 6 minutes. Use right away or set aside for several hours but not overnight.

◈ **Creamed Radishes** *When bigger was better for radishes because they were considered a plate vegetable, similar to baby turnips, and not just a garnish, they were often cooked and served in a cream sauce. Making them that way is a bit old-fashioned, but the dish is still luscious and pretty. The radishes tint the cream a soft, peachy orange, and the little nubs of green tops peeking out of the sauce add visual delight.*

Makes 4 servings

2 bunches large, round, red radishes, with tops (about 20)

2 tablespoons butter

2 tablespoons all-purpose flour

1 cup water

⅓ cup heavy cream

⅛ teaspoon freshly ground white pepper

1. Cut the tops off the radishes, leaving 1 inch of green and reserving some of the very small leaves for garnish. Cut the radishes in half lengthwise.

2. Melt the butter in the pressure cooker over medium heat until beginning to foam. Add the flour and whisk to smooth. Add the water and whisk to smooth. Add the radishes, lock on the lid, and bring to pressure over high heat, about 2 minutes. Reduce the heat to medium-high and cook for 3 minutes. Remove from the heat and let sit for 2 minutes to finish cooking.

3. With the steam vent pointed away from your face, gently release any remaining pressure. With a slotted spoon transfer the radishes to a serving bowl. Stir the cream into the pot and boil until thickened, about 2 minutes.

4. Pour the sauce over the radishes. Add the pepper and gently stir to mix. Garnish with a few of the reserved radish leaves and serve.

◈ Rutabagas in Parsnip Puree with Sour Cream and Nutmeg

Rutabagas and parsnips, along with kohlrabies and salsify, for some reason or other have become relegated to the "odd roots" bin in produce markets. I always wonder why when I go to choose some for a stew or soup or root vegetable dish, like here. They're delicious, not hard for the American palate to understand, and eminently available. And, they're no more trouble to cook than carrots or beets or potatoes. I can assure you that the pressure cooker cooks them up easily. Most probably you'll go back for more.   Makes 4 servings

1 rutabaga (about ¾ pound), peeled, quartered, and sliced
    ¼ to ½ inch thick
2 parsnips, peeled, thin bottoms cut into ½-inch-thick rounds,
    thicker tops cut into ½-inch-thick quarter rounds
2 tablespoons butter
¼ teaspoon salt
¼ cup water
½ cup sour cream
Pinch of ground nutmeg, for garnish
1 teaspoon chopped flat-leaf parsley, for garnish

1. Place the rutabaga, parsnips, butter, salt, and water in the pressure cooker and stir to mix. Lock on the lid and bring to pressure over high heat, about 3 minutes. Reduce the heat to medium and cook for 2 minutes. Remove from the heat and let sit for 5 minutes to finish cooking.

2. With the steam vent pointed away from your face, gently release any remaining pressure. Stir in the sour cream, slightly mashing the parsnips as you do, and transfer the mixture to a serving bowl. Sprinkle the nutmeg and parsley over the top and serve.

Creamy Mashed Russet and Sweet Potatoes *Potatoes hold a spotlight in American cooking as in no other cuisine. True, the Irish relied on them for sustenance and the Belgians (or was it the French?) invented the best* frites *and the Lithuanians perfected the potato gratin to make a meal. But, on the hemisphere of their origin, the ways they're fixed with sundry adjuncts and augmentations could make a chapter all by itself. Mashed is one of the best of those*

dishes, and the pressure cooker steams the potatoes just right, so quickly the only question would be, how shall we have our mashed potatoes tonight?

Makes 6 to 8 servings

3 medium-size russet potatoes (1¼ pounds), peeled
   and cut into 1-inch chunks
1 large sweet potato (about 1 pound), peeled and cut into 1-inch chunks
¾ cup water, plus extra for mashing the potatoes if necessary
½ cup heavy cream
2 tablespoons butter, for dotting
Pinch of ground nutmeg, for garnish

1. Place the russet potatoes and sweet potato in the pressure cooker. Pour in the water, lock on the lid, and bring to pressure over high heat, about 5 minutes. Reduce the heat to medium and cook for 5 minutes. Remove from the heat and let sit for 5 minutes to finish cooking.

2. With the steam vent pointed away from your face, gently release any remaining pressure. Add the cream to the pot and mash the potatoes with a potato masher or sturdy wire whisk. Add up to ½ cup more water if necessary to keep the mixture from becoming too dry.

3. Spoon into a serving bowl. Dot the top with the butter and sprinkle on the nutmeg. Serve right away.

◈ Silken Yam Puree   *"Silken" is a description I more readily associate with Chinese or Japanese cooking. One taste and you'll see how it also most fittingly applies to pureed yams, inspired by South African–style chicken stew. Pressure cooking the yams allows them to soften in a small amount of water so they never become soggy or lose flavor to the cooking liquid.*

Makes 4 to 6 servings

2 large yams (1½ to 1¾ pounds), peeled and cut into 1-inch chunks

1 cup water

Salt to taste

Butter (optional), for dotting

1. Place the yams and water in the pressure cooker, lock on the lid, and bring to pressure over high heat, about 5 minutes. Reduce the heat to medium–high and cook for 12 minutes. Remove from the heat and let sit for 3 minutes to finish cooking.

2. With the steam vent pointed away from your face, gently release any remaining pressure, remove the lid, and let sit until cool enough to handle, about 5 minutes.

3. Puree the yams and liquid together in a food processor. Stir in salt. Spoon into a serving bowl, dot with butter, if using, and serve right away, while still warm.

Pass the Mashed Potatoes, Please

Mashed potatoes may seem a straightforward, uncomplicated topic. Until you get to the details. Should the potatoes be mealy, baking-type potatoes, or one of the firmer, waxy kinds? Myself, I usually opt for the former with the exception of Yukon golds, which seem to me to straddle the line between mealy and waxy varieties. Then, should they be whipped to smoothness, mashed with a potato masher so some chunks remain, or merely somewhat coarsely mashed to open them enough to receive seasonings but leave them in recognizable potato chunks? That, I think, depends on the embellishments and what role the potatoes are playing in the meal. Here are some possibilities to get your potato imagination going:

- Instead of sweet potato, combine potatoes with celery root, butternut squash, another variety of potato, or roasted garlic
- Instead of nutmeg, garnish them with tarragon, chives, dill, or paprika
- Instead of butter, top them with sour cream, cheddar cheese, bacon, gravy, or steamed broccoli
- Instead of serving the potatoes in a bowl, mound them on a plate, sculpt them into an interesting shape, and top them with steamed cabbage to make colcannon

◈ Carrots in Thyme Butter

Cinnamon, cayenne, cumin, cilantro, dill, chervil, thyme, cream, butter, olive oil, lemon, garlic. It's hard to enumerate all the flavors cooked carrots will embrace. Here's a basic recipe for the pressure cooker. Use it as a guideline for your own preferred seasonings.

Makes 4 servings

2 tablespoons butter
4 large carrots, peeled and cut into thick, 3-inch-long sticks (like French fries)
1½ teaspoons chopped fresh thyme, or ½ teaspoon dried
⅛ teaspoon salt
½ cup water

1. Heat the butter in the pressure cooker over medium heat until melted. Add the carrots, thyme, salt, and water. Lock on the lid and bring to pressure over high heat, about 1 minute. Immediately remove from the heat and let sit for 4 minutes.

2. With the steam vent pointed away from your face, gently release any remaining pressure. Serve right away.

◈ Braised Celery with Lemon and Capers

Years ago, I must have been attracted to this dish by its name, Celery Victor. That's awfully close to Celery Victoria. As a matter of routine, I keep two whole bunches of celery in the refrigerator just in case we need a good green for dinner.

Makes 4 servings

2 bunches celery, tops trimmed off and tough outer ribs removed,
    both reserved for another dish
1 cup Chicken Broth (page 18)
2 tablespoons butter
1 tablespoon freshly squeezed lemon juice

2 teaspoons capers, coarsely chopped

1 tablespoon chopped fresh flat-leaf parsley

1. Cut the celery lengthwise into quarters and rinse. Place in the pressure cooker, along with the broth and butter. Lock on the lid and bring to pressure over high heat, about 5 minutes. Reduce the heat to medium–high and cook for 5 minutes. Remove from the heat and set aside for 5 minutes to finish cooking.

2. With the steam vent pointed away from your face, gently release any remaining pressure. With a slotted spoon, transfer the celery to a serving platter.

3. Place the lemon juice, capers, and parsley in a small bowl. Add 1 tablespoon of the celery cooking liquid and whisk together. Pour over the celery and serve.

Fennel in Lemony Rice Flour White Sauce

Fennel proliferates with abandon, flowers with grace, and succors bees and butterflies throughout the summer. I encourage it in my garden for those reasons and also to harvest the small, tender bulbs when they take almost no cooking at all. Before they've grown fat and staunch, I also enjoy the inevitable some I've missed in the early stage, steamed and blanketed with a light, rice flour white sauce. The extra measure of lemon in the sauce is because I think fennel always asks for it.

Makes 4 to 6 servings

4 medium-size fennel bulbs, fronds trimmed off and chopped, bulbs sliced
    lengthwise 1 inch thick

1½ cups milk (1% is okay)

2 tablespoons rice flour (see Note page 194)

2 tablespoons butter

2 tablespoons freshly squeezed lemon juice

½ teaspoon salt

1. Arrange the fennel slices in an overlapping layer in the pressure cooker. Reserve the fronds for later. Pour in 1 cup of the milk, lock on the lid, and bring to pressure over high heat, about 4 minutes. Reduce the heat to medium-low and cook for 7 minutes. Remove from the heat and let sit for 4 minutes to finish cooking.

2. With the steam vent pointed away from your face, gently release any remaining pressure. Transfer the fennel to a serving platter, reserving the liquid in the pot. Set the fennel aside in a warm place.

3. In a small bowl, stir together the rice flour and remaining $\frac{1}{2}$ cup milk to make a paste. Whisk it into the liquid in the pressure cooker. Add the butter, lemon juice, and salt and whisk until smooth. Pour over the fennel, sprinkle the chopped fronds over the top, and serve.

Note: Rice flour is readily available in the Asian foods section of better supermarkets.

◇ Leeks in Spiced Honey Mustard Dressing

One day at my deli, Pig-by-the-Tail, my friend and coworker Penny Brogden presented what seemed to me an improbable composition she thought would work well for our fresh salad selections—a tangle of lightly steamed leeks tossed with a honey and mustard dressing inspired by a recipe she'd read in the San Francisco Chronicle *food section. It was perfect, and it remained in our repertoire, even showing up in* American Charcuterie: Recipes from Pig-by-the-Tail. *The pressure cooker version here is an adaptation. The leeks are good hot or cold.*

Makes 4 to 6 servings

1 tablespoon olive oil
2 tablespoons finely chopped shallot
$\frac{1}{4}$ teaspoon red pepper flakes

3 medium-size leeks (white and light green parts only), cut lengthwise
    into ½-inch-wide strips, well washed, and drained

½ teaspoon salt

¼ cup water

3 cups finely shredded iceberg lettuce

2 teaspoons honey

1 teaspoon Dijon mustard

2 teaspoons freshly squeezed lemon juice

2 teaspoons white wine vinegar

2 tablespoons chopped fresh flat-leaf parsley, for garnish

1. Combine the oil, shallot, and pepper flakes in the pressure cooker. Heat over medium heat until beginning to bubble. Add the leeks, salt, and water and toss to mix. Lock on the lid and bring to pressure over high heat, about 1 minute. Reduce the heat to medium and cook for 1 minute. Remove from the heat and let sit for 3 minutes to finish cooking.

2. With the steam vent pointed away from your face, gently release any remaining pressure. Spread the lettuce on a serving platter. Lift the leeks out of the pot with kitchen tongs and mound over the lettuce.

3. Whisk the honey, mustard, lemon juice, and vinegar into the juices in the pot. Set over medium–high heat until beginning to boil, then immediately pour over the leeks. Sprinkle the parsley over the top and serve. Or refrigerate overnight and serve cold.

Broccoli, the Italian Way

Broccoli done the Italian way is long simmered until it almost melts into itself, but not quite, because it retains some shape. With the pressure cooker's ability to sauté and then steam ever so quickly, the time for making Italian-style broccoli condenses from long to short, with undiminished depth of flavor.

Makes 4 servings

1¾ pounds broccoli, stems and florets

2 tablespoons olive oil

4 large cloves garlic, smashed

1 small dried cayenne or other red chile pepper, chopped, or
   ¼ teaspoon red pepper flakes

¼ teaspoon salt

½ cup water

1 tablespoon finely chopped lemon zest, for garnish

1 tablespoon freshly squeezed lemon juice, for garnish

1. Cut the tops off the broccoli and slice them into ½-inch-thick florets. Peel the stems with a vegetable peeler or paring knife and cut them into ¼-inch-thick rounds.

2. Heat the oil in the pressure cooker over medium-high heat until beginning to smoke. Add the garlic and chile pepper and cook, stirring occasionally, until the garlic is golden, 1 to 1½ minutes. Stir in the broccoli, salt, and water. Lock on the lid and bring to pressure over high heat, about 2 minutes. Immediately remove from the heat and let sit for 2 minutes to finish cooking.

3. With the steam vent pointed away from your face, gently release any remaining pressure. Transfer the broccoli to a serving platter, sprinkle the zest and lemon juice over the top, and serve.

◇ Spaghetti Squash, Many Ways *Hot or cold, spaghetti squash moves from luncheon dish to dinner side plate to picnic or buffet table with the greatest of ease and invites a different dressing for each of those occasions (see right).*

Makes 4 to 6 servings

1 small spaghetti squash (about 2¼ pounds), halved crosswise,
   then lengthwise, and seeded

1 cup water

2 tablespoons butter or olive oil

Salt and freshly ground black pepper to taste

½ cup freshly grated parmesan cheese, for serving

1. Place the squash quarters facedown in the pressure cooker, fitting them as much as possible in a single layer. Pour in the water, lock on the lid, and bring to pressure over high heat, about 5 minutes. Reduce the heat to medium–high and cook for 7 minutes. Remove from the heat and let sit for 3 minutes to finish cooking.

2. With the steam vent pointed away from your face, gently release any remaining pressure. When cool enough to handle, pull the strands out of the squash shells with a fork. Mound on a platter and toss with the butter and salt and pepper. Serve with the cheese on the side.

◇ ◇ ◇

Other Stylish Dress for Spaghetti Squash

- Instead of just butter, toss the squash strands with curry butter, olive oil with lemon and garlic, pine nuts, or crumbled bacon.
- Garnish with a fresh herb, such as parsley, chives, cilantro, tarragon, mint, rosemary, or thyme.
- Top with a light sauce, like pesto (see page 157), Very Quick Fresh Tomato Sauce (page 289), or Tomato Caper Sauce (page 210).
- Spread in a casserole, top with a melting cheese and bread crumbs, and bake until golden.
- Make a wonderful gooey dessert of spaghetti squash strands stuck together with maple syrup and draped over ice cream.

◈ Zucchini Simmered Italian Style

The mere word "zucchini" seems to ring out Italian, and it certainly is a representative without equal in the class of summer squash for that cuisine. The word also rings out "Watch out, neighbors, my zucchinis are out of control and about ready to invade your kitchen." If you're ever out of zucchinis, however, there are other squash waiting on the sidelines that simmer up just as well—like yellow crookneck; oblong, pale green–striped cucuzza; or pattypan (also called cymling).

Makes 2 to 3 servings

2 tablespoons olive oil
4 large cloves garlic, smashed
1 small dried cayenne or other red chile pepper, chopped, or
    ¼ teaspoon red pepper flakes
4 medium-size zucchinis (about 1 pound), cut ¼- to ½-inch-thick
    diagonal slices
¼ teaspoon salt
¼ cup water
1 tablespoon grated lemon zest, for garnish
1 tablespoon freshly squeezed lemon juice, for garnish
1 teaspoon chopped fresh flat-leaf parsley (optional), for garnish

1. Heat the oil in the pressure cooker over medium–high heat until beginning to smoke. Add the garlic and chile pepper and cook, stirring occasionally, until the garlic is golden, 1 to 1½ minutes. Stir in the zucchinis, salt, and water. Lock on the lid and bring to pressure over high heat, about 2 minutes. Immediately remove from the heat and let sit for 2 minutes to finish cooking.

2. With the steam vent pointed away from your face, gently release any remaining pressure. Transfer to a serving platter and sprinkle on the lemon zest, lemon juice, and parsley, if using. Serve right away or at room temperature.

◫ Red Bell Peppers with Garlic and Capers

When the aroma of sautéing red bell peppers wafted out the door of my deli, Pig-by-the-Tail, as it did on many afternoons, it was like a siren call. From up and down the block and both sides of the street, people would head for the door, noses twitching, taste buds tingling, asking, "What's cooking? Is it ready?" We always tried to make the answer yes, and they always came back for more. You can't do better with red bell peppers than to cook them this way, and the pressure cooker does justice to the dish, right down to the wafting aroma.

Makes 6 to 10 servings

2 tablespoons olive oil
3 pounds red bell peppers, seeded and cut into ½-inch-wide strips
12 large cloves garlic, coarsely chopped
2 teaspoons chopped fresh oregano, or 1 teaspoon dried
½ teaspoon salt
¼ cup capers
¼ cup water

1. Warm the olive oil in the pressure cooker over medium heat for about 1 minute. Add the peppers, garlic, oregano, and salt and stir to mix. Add the capers and water and stir again. Lock on the lid and bring to pressure over high heat, about 3 minutes. Reduce the heat to medium and cook for 5 minutes. Remove from the heat and let sit for 5 minutes to finish cooking.

2. With the steam vent pointed away from your face, gently release any remaining pressure. Transfer to a serving bowl and serve right away. Or store in the refrigerator, covered, for up to 1 week and reheat or serve cold.

◫ ◫ ◫

◈ Ratatouille

My defining lesson about ratatouille came from Madame Deschamps, a genuine French mère de cuisine. I worked in her kitchen a mere six months, during which time I learned more than I could ever calculate. One thing was the ratatouille. She set me in charge of a large pot of it one afternoon; it was to be served for dinner. Full of energy, I put my spoon into the pot and began stirring, somewhat vigorously, sad to report. Madame turned from what she was doing and, somewhat horrified, but kindly as she could, said, "No, no, Victoria. Doucement, laisse la frissoner. Ça c'est le secret de la bonne ratatouille." Frissoner is a French word that means shiver, and it describes a state of quiet, slow cooking at the bottom of the simmer stage. It was a revelation for which I have been grateful ever since. The seeming tons of ratatouille cooked at my deli were simmered slow and long so the vegetables could gently release their juices and thoroughly blend with one another. I'm happy to report that the pressure cooker does a fine job of simulating a slow-cooked ratatouille. Makes 4 to 6 servings

2 tablespoons olive oil
1 small eggplant, cut into ½-inch dice
1 medium-size green bell pepper, seeded and cut into ¼-inch-wide strips
1 small yellow or white onion, cut into ¼-inch dice
1 large zucchini, cut into ½-inch dice
2 medium-size tomatoes, coarsely chopped
4 large cloves garlic, coarsely chopped
1 tablespoon tomato paste
1 teaspoon chopped fresh oregano, or ½ teaspoon dried
1 teaspoon salt
½ teaspoon freshly ground black pepper

1. Warm the olive oil in the pressure cooker over medium heat for about 1 minute. Add the eggplant and stir to coat. Add the bell pepper, onion, zucchini, tomatoes, and garlic and stir to mix. Add the tomato paste, oregano, salt, and pepper and stir again.

2. Lock on the lid and bring to pressure over high heat, about 1 minute. Reduce the heat to medium–low and cook for 10 minutes. Remove from the heat and let sit for 10 minutes to finish cooking.

3. With the steam vent pointed away from your face, gently release any remaining pressure. Serve right away, at room temperature, or chilled. The ratatouille will keep in the refrigerator for up to 1 week.

◌ ◌ ◌

Getting to the Garlic

You can go about preparing garlic several ways. Sometimes the choice depends on how it fits into the dish; sometimes it depends on your taste of the moment. Options are:

- Whole cloves, peeled, for stewed or roasted garlic to be used as a vegetable itself
- Coarse chopping, for dishes where you want the garlic as a noticeable vegetable ingredient and that cook long enough for the garlic to soften
- Slivering, for quickly cooked dishes, especially vegetables and sauces, where *al dente* garlic is the point and slivers add a nice look
- Mincing, for dishes either quick cooked or long cooked where the garlic should disappear as a visual element, and also for using raw
- Pressing, for the same dishes as minced garlic, but when the nip of garlic juices is desired
- Smashing, for dishes similar to those for pressed garlic, but a method preferred by cooks who believe pressing taints the garlic, and for dishes similar to those for coarsely chopped garlic but where more tang is desirable

◇ Eggplant Stewed with Olive Oil, Garlic, and Oregano

Pressure stewing eggplant allows it to soften and cook through with very little oil. Use the stew as a warm side dish with grilled leg of lamb or roast chicken. Or serve it as a separate salad on a bed of butter lettuce leaves, garnished with black olives and accompanied with thin baguette toasts. Or fill pita pockets with the eggplant stew and sliced tomatoes and top with crumbled feta cheese. Asian eggplants, sliced one half inch thick, or tiny boutique eggplants, quartered, work as well as regular globe eggplants.

Makes 4 servings

2 medium-size eggplants (about 2 pounds), cut into 1-inch chunks
1 teaspoon salt
2 tablespoons olive oil
3 large cloves garlic, halved
2 teaspoons chopped fresh oregano, or 1 teaspoon dried
½ teaspoon freshly ground black pepper
3 tablespoons dry white wine
2 tablespoons water
3 tablespoons chopped fresh flat-leaf parsley
½ tablespoon freshly squeezed lemon juice
1 tablespoon grated lemon zest, for garnish

1. Toss together the eggplant and salt in a medium-size bowl and set aside for 10 minutes.

2. Heat the oil in the pressure cooker over medium-high heat until beginning to smoke. Stir in the eggplant, garlic, oregano, pepper, wine, and water. Lock on the lid and bring to pressure over high heat, 1 to 2 minutes. Immediately remove from the heat and let sit for 5 minutes to finish cooking.

3. With the steam vent pointed away from your face, gently release any remaining pressure. Stir in the parsley and lemon juice and sprinkle the zest over the top. Serve right away or cool and store in the refrigerator, covered, for up to 5 days and serve cold.

◇ Vegetable Curry of Sunchokes, Eggplant, and Tomatoes

In Indian cuisine, there are zillions of variations on the theme of curried vegetables; cauliflower (gobi) and potato are two prominent stars. So is broccoli. The combination of sunchokes (also known as Jerusalem artichokes), eggplant, and tomatoes particularly suits my taste.

Makes 4 servings

1 tablespoon peanut oil
2 teaspoons peeled and minced fresh ginger
2 small fresh red chile peppers, minced
1 small yellow or white onion, quartered and thinly sliced
1 pound sunchokes, peeled and cut into ½-inch dice
5 Thai eggplants (5 to 6 ounces total), quartered
1 medium-size tomato, peeled (see page 24), seeded, and coarsely chopped
¼ teaspoon ground turmeric
1 teaspoon ground cumin
1 teaspoon curry powder
1 teaspoon salt
1 cup pea sprouts or fresh sprigs cilantro, for topping

1. Heat the oil in the pressure cooker over medium-high heat until hot but not smoking. Add the ginger, chile peppers, and onion and cook, stirring occasionally, until the onion is wilted, about 2 minutes. Add the sunchokes, eggplants, and tomato and stir to mix. Stir in the turmeric, cumin, curry powder, and salt.

2. Lock on the lid and bring to pressure over high heat, 2 to 3 minutes. Reduce the heat to medium and cook for 5 minutes. Remove from the heat and let sit for 6 minutes to finish cooking.

3. With the steam vent pointed away from your face, gently release any remaining pressure. Serve right away, topped with the sprouts.

◇ ◇ ◇

◇ Asian Steamed Vegetable Pot with Silken Tofu

With the tofu, an Asian-style mix of steamed vegetables served with rice is a complete meal. Using daikon radish in rounds in the pot rather than finely grated as a side slaw was a surprise discovery from exploring Japanese Zen cooking. Enoki, sometimes called straw mushrooms, have become available vacuum wrapped in supermarkets and produce stores that carry a range of international vegetables. Fresh oyster mushrooms, equally delicate and exotic, would also do. If you don't have either one available, skip the mushrooms and make the dish without them. Makes 4 servings

3 tablespoons light soy sauce

3 tablespoons sake or Chinese rice wine

1 teaspoon peeled and grated fresh ginger

½ teaspoon sugar

3 tablespoons water

1 medium-size leek (white and light green parts only),
    cut into 3-inch long slivers, well washed, and drained

6 cups mustard greens, preferably Chinese mustard greens,
    coarsely chopped, well washed, and drained

6 ounces daikon radish, peeled and cut into ¼- to ½-inch-thick rounds

8 ounces firm silken tofu, cut into 1-inch cubes, for topping

3 ounces enoki (straw) mushrooms, stems trimmed, for topping

1. Combine the soy sauce, sake, ginger, sugar, and water in the pressure cooker over medium–high heat. When beginning to boil, stir in the leek and mustard greens. When the greens wilt, add the daikon. Lock on the lid and bring to pressure over high heat, 2 to 3 minutes. Immediately remove from the heat and let sit for 3 minutes to finish cooking.

2. With the steam vent pointed away from your face, gently release any remaining pressure. Transfer the vegetables to a serving platter, top with the tofu and enokis, and serve right away.

◈ Acorn Squash with Celery Sage Stuffing and Tangerine Juice

Of all the winter squashes, acorn is one of the easiest to handle for cutting open. Once opened, it reveals one of the largest wells for filling. It's also just the right size for serving two to four, depending on how it's filled. Its flavor is not remarkable on its own, so I like to give it a little personality perk with an herb filling and a splash of tangerine juice.

Makes 2 to 4 servings

1½ tablespoons minced celery

1½ tablespoons minced yellow or white onion

1 teaspoon finely chopped fresh sage, or ¼ teaspoon dried

¼ teaspoon salt

2 tablespoons butter, at room temperature

1 medium-size acorn squash, halved lengthwise and seeded

½ cup water

1 tablespoon freshly squeezed tangerine juice, for sprinkling

1. Combine the celery, onion, sage, salt, and butter in a small bowl.

2. Fill the center of each squash half with the celery mixture. Set the halves, filled side up, in the pressure cooker. (You will probably have to arrange them with one partly atop the other.) Pour the water around, not into, the squash and lock on the lid. Bring to pressure over high heat, about 5 minutes. Reduce the heat to medium–high and cook for 5 minutes. Remove from the heat and let sit for 5 minutes to finish cooking.

3. With the steam vent pointed away from your face, gently release any remaining pressure. For 4 servings, cut the squash in half and place on a serving platter. Sprinkle with the tangerine juice and serve right away.

◇ Stuffed Bell Peppers

Sometimes it's beef, sometimes it's lamb, and sometimes there's no meat at all. Rice or another grain is always the essential ingredient for stuffed vegetables, called dolmas, *all around the eastern Mediterranean. If you prefer, you can make the filling with rice and the seasonings only. Zucchinis or large tomatoes, along with or in place of the peppers, also make an authentic* dolma *dish.*

Makes 6 to 8 servings

8 medium-size bell peppers, any color, or pasilla peppers, or a mixture
4 cups Meat and Rice Filling for Stuffed Vegetables (recipe follows)
½ cup water
1 cup plain yogurt, whisked smooth, for serving

1. Cut the tops off the peppers, reserving them. Gently pull the seeds out of the pepper cavities. Stuff the cavities with the filling, about ½ cup per pepper, and set the tops back on the peppers.

2. Pour the water into the pressure cooker and set the trivet in it. Pack in the peppers as much in a single layer as possible. Lock on the lid and bring to pressure over high heat, 3 to 4 minutes. Cook over medium heat for 8 minutes. Remove from the heat and let sit for 3 minutes to finish cooking.

3. With the steam vent pointed away from your face, gently release any remaining pressure. When cool enough to handle, transfer the peppers to a serving platter or bowl. Serve right away with a bowl of yogurt on the side.

◇ ◇ ◇

Meat and Rice Filling for Stuffed Vegetables *Though it's more traditional to make the stuffing with raw rice and then cook the dolmas until the rice is tender, I find it sometimes expeditious to have the grains already cooked. That way the stuffed vegetables pressure cook ever so quickly. But raw rice also works; add 10 minutes to the cooking time and 7 minutes to the sitting time.*

Makes 4 cups

6 ounces ground beef or lamb

2½ cups cooked long grain white rice

1 small yellow or white onion, finely chopped

1 cup chopped fresh flat-leaf parsley

¼ cup chopped fresh mint

1 tablespoon finely chopped lemon zest

2 tablespoons tomato paste

1½ teaspoons salt

½ teaspoon freshly ground black pepper

Pinch of ground nutmeg

½ cup dry white wine or water

1 tablespoon freshly squeezed lemon juice

Combine all the ingredients in a medium-size bowl and mix until well blended. Use right away or store in the refrigerator, covered, for up to 3 days.

Beefsteak Tomatoes Stuffed with Bulgur on a Bed of Potato Slices

I grew up with dolmas. *Stuffed green peppers, zucchinis, and tomatoes were part of our family fare. Never would I have thought to put sliced potatoes on the bottom of a tomato* dolma *dish until my friend and sometimes co-author, Susanna Hoffman, introduced the notion to me, part of the way they cook stuffed tomatoes on the Greek island of Santorini, where she has done anthropology fieldwork for more than three decades. It's a summer dish, good only with ripe, juicy tomatoes.*

Makes 4 main dish servings, or 6 side dish servings

3 large or 6 medium-size tomatoes, ¼ inch of tops cut off and reserved, centers
    scooped out, and juices strained and reserved for the stuffing
1½ cups Bulgur Stuffing (recipe follows)
1 large russet potato, sliced into ¼-inch rounds
Salt and freshly ground black pepper to taste
1 tablespoon olive oil
¼ cup dry white wine
1½ cups plain yogurt, whisked smooth, for serving

1. Fill the tomatoes with the stuffing almost, but not quite, to the top and cover with their "caps." Set aside.

2. Arrange the potato slices in an overlapping layer in the pressure cooker and sprinkle lightly with salt and pepper. Pour in the oil and wine. Place the tomatoes on top. Lock on the lid and bring to pressure over high heat, 3 to 4 minutes. Reduce the heat to medium and cook for 15 minutes. Remove from the heat and let sit for 3 minutes to finish cooking.

3. With the steam vent pointed away from your face, gently release any remaining pressure. Transfer the tomatoes to a serving platter, taking care to keep them intact. Spoon the potatoes and juices around the tomatoes and serve right away, with a bowl of yogurt on the side.

Bulgur Stuffing   *When stuffed into tomatoes, the bulgur mixture is a little like tabbouleh in a box. But don't save it just for that: Fill chicken, acorn squash halves, grape leaves. You can also let the stuffing stand at room temperature for an hour or so and the grains will rehydrate and soften to make a fresh grain salad bed for grilled vegetables, quail, or baby chickens.*   Makes 1½ cups

½ cup coarse bulgur wheat
½ small green bell pepper, seeded and finely chopped
1 rib celery, trimmed and finely chopped
½ small yellow or white onion, finely chopped
1 tablespoon chopped fresh flat-leaf parsley
1 tablespoon chopped fresh dill

½ cup reserved tomato juices, or ⅓ cup water mixed with
1 tablespoon tomato paste
¼ teaspoon salt

Combine all the ingredients in a medium-size bowl and toss to mix. Use right away or set aside at room temperature for up to 30 minutes. Do not store any longer or the stuffing will get too soft for cooking.

◇ Cabbage Leaves with Beef, Onion, and Apple Stuffing and Tomato Caper Sauce *At first glance, this may look like a dish that includes a bit of everything in the pantry. Oddly, though, the elements come together in a unique way that pays obeisance to stuffed-cabbage lovers from northern Europe on down to the Mediterranean and comes to the plate with a very modern lilt.* Makes 12 large rolls

1 large Savoy or regular cabbage (1½ pounds)
1½ cups Beef, Onion, and Apple Stuffing (recipe follows)
Salt to taste
1½ cups Tomato Caper Sauce (recipe follows), for serving
1 cup sour cream (optional), for serving

1. Bring a pot of water to a boil. Core the cabbage with a paring knife and gently pull away 14 of the outer leaves. Place the leaves in the water, pressing them down to submerge them, and blanch for 3 minutes. Drain and let cool.

2. Making a small V cut, remove the remaining core from the bottom of each leaf. Place 2 tablespoons or so of the stuffing in the center of 12 of the leaves and roll up each leaf to make a neat packet. Use toothpicks to secure the rolls, if necessary.

3. Place a trivet in the pressure cooker and set the cabbage rolls on it in 1 or 2 layers. Pour in 2 cups water and sprinkle the rolls liberally with salt. Set the 2 extra leaves over the rolls, lock on the lid, and bring to pressure over high heat, 3 to 4 minutes. Reduce the heat to medium and cook for 7 minutes. Remove from the heat and let sit for 5 minutes to finish cooking.

4. With the steam vent pointed away from your face, gently release any remaining pressure. Carefully transfer the cabbage rolls to a serving platter. Dollop a bit of the sauce over the top. Serve with the remaining sauce and the sour cream, if using, in separate bowls on the side.

Beef, Onion, and Apple Stuffing

Makes 1½ cups

1 small yellow or white onion, finely chopped, blanched for
    1 minute in simmering water, and drained
1 small Pippin or other tart apple, peeled, cored,
    and finely chopped
1 pound ground round beef
2 tablespoons chopped fresh dill
¼ teaspoon ground allspice
1 teaspoon salt
½ teaspoon freshly ground black pepper

Combine all the ingredients in a small bowl and mix well. Use right away or refrigerate, covered, for up to 2 days.

Tomato Caper Sauce

Makes 1½ cups

2 tablespoons olive oil
2 medium-size tomatoes, peeled (see page 24),
    seeded, and coarsely chopped
2 large cloves garlic, coarsely chopped
2 tablespoons capers
1 teaspoon finely chopped lemon zest
½ teaspoon salt

Heat the oil in a medium-size saucepan over medium-high heat until beginning to smoke. Add the remaining ingredients, stir to mix, and bring to a boil. Remove from the heat without further cooking. Use right away or let cool and refrigerate for up to 3 days.

◇ Zucchini Stuffed with Spinach, Cream Cheese, and Pine Nuts

With zucchinis galore at the end of summer, what's a gardener cook to do besides send friends and neighbors running away from yet another zucchini offering? Here's one answer: Invite them for a stuffed zucchini dinner. A bowl of hot steamed rice (see page 215), another of salad greens, and a third of yogurt—and a glass of wine—would convince anyone that zucchini is worth it.

Makes 4 to 6 servings

4½ ounces good-quality cream cheese, at room temperature
1 tablespoon minced shallot
1 cup packed chopped spinach leaves, well washed and drained
2 tablespoons pine nuts
1 tablespoon plus 1 teaspoon chopped fresh dill
1 tablespoon heavy cream
Big pinch of cayenne
¾ teaspoon salt
1 very large zucchini (13 to 16 ounces)
8 cherry tomatoes, halved
1 tablespoon freshly squeezed lemon juice
1 tablespoon extra virgin olive oil
¼ teaspoon freshly ground black pepper

1. Mix together the cream cheese, shallot, spinach, pine nuts, 1 tablespoon dill, cream, cayenne, and ½ teaspoon of the salt in a medium-size bowl.

2. Cut the zucchini in half lengthwise and scoop out the pulp with an apple corer or paring knife, leaving a ½-inch wall intact. Place the pulp in the bottom of the pressure cooker, along with the tomatoes, remaining 1 teaspoon dill, lemon juice, olive oil, remaining ¼ teaspoon salt, and pepper. Stuff the zucchini halves with the cream cheese mixture and set the halves on top of the tomato mixture.

3. Lock on the lid and bring to pressure over high heat, about 2 minutes. Cook over medium heat for 3 minutes. Remove from the heat and let sit for 2 minutes to finish cooking.

4. With the steam vent pointed away from your face, gently release any remaining pressure. Remove the lid and let sit, uncovered, for 2 minutes more. Transfer the zucchini halves to a serving platter and cut each crosswise into 6 pieces. Spoon the juices and extra pulp from the bottom of the pot over the pieces and serve right away.

Note: The bed of zucchini pulp and tomatoes releases so much juice so rapidly, there's no reason to add extra liquid to the pot for cooking the stuffed zucchini dish.

◇ ◇ ◇

Grains:

Worldly Ways with Rice, Wheat, and Corn

Grains are a natural for pressure cooking. You can turn out a batch of basic rice so quickly and so easily that you'll never look at a box of instant rice again. Composed rice dishes, wheat pilafs in styles that range the world from Italy to India, Asia and the Pacific Rim to Turkey and Greece, and otherwise long-cooking brown rice, wild rice, and pearl barley, all fluff to perfection in a flash. The modern darling of rice cookery, risotto, is ready, *al dente* and creamy, in the time it takes you to set the table. A surprise bonus from the pressure cooker is the way special corn dishes become so manageable: Tamales to die for were one of my early-on successes; so was spoon bread, the American, pudding-y version of polenta (although polenta itself doesn't work to my taste). There are other bonuses. Long-forgotten grains like pearl barley and wheat berries, abandoned largely because the time they take to cook didn't fit into modern life, can be cooked in one third the time and tasted anew. Tender, pillowy Asian pasta dumplings can be part of your regular home fare rather than the occasional exotic treat. Following are some of the best from a vast repertoire of possibilities for pressure cooking grains.

Grains: Worldly Ways with Rice, Wheat, and Corn

◇ Basic Steamed Rice

Long grain from Texas, short grain from California, basmati from India, Thai jasmine, Italian Arborio, the precious "new" rice from Japan, healthful brown rice—all are treated well in the pressure cooker. The method is pretty much the same for all the kinds, except some take a little longer (brown rice, wild rice) and some need a brief soaking as well as rinsing to remain true to their origin (Japanese rice, Mexican rice). See page 220 for a brief summary of the differences.

Makes 3 cups, or 4 side dish servings

1 cup rice (see page 220 for special instructions)
1½ cups water

1. Rinse the rice and place it in the pressure cooker along with the water. Cover the pot and bring to pressure over high heat, about 5 minutes. Reduce the heat to medium high and cook for 3 minutes. Remove from the heat and let sit for 10 minutes to finish cooking.

2. With the steam vent pointed away from your face, gently release any remaining pressure. Remove the lid. Fluff the rice with a fork, replace the lid without locking it, and let the rice rest for at least 10 minutes (20 minutes is better) before serving.

How Long Can the Rice Sit?

For rice, there's no need to heed the "let sit then remove the lid" instruction at the end of cooking to an absolute T. As with regular steaming, rice can sit off the heat for some time before serving. That means, if the cooking is done and you need to run an errand, turn your attention to other matters, or take a break, it's okay for up to several hours. In fact, you can prepare the rice through Step 2 and let it rest up to overnight. Reheat in the microwave, over low heat on the stove top, or in a moderate oven before serving.

◇ Spanish or Mexican Red Rice

Spanish rice might just as well be called Mexican rice. They share Latin flavors—tomato, garlic, onion, green pepper. When it comes to detail, it's the green pepper that distinguishes them: bell pepper is the choice for Spanish rice; mild pasilla chile pepper, perhaps with an added touch of fresh jalapeño, takes the dish to the Mexican table (though I sometimes mix the cuisines by adding jalapeño to Spanish rice). More subtle differences are that Spanish rice is often further reddened with a touch of tomato paste; Mexican rice is often augmented with fresh peas. The following recipe includes options that leave it up to you which sunny clime to visit, for the rice dish, that is. Also, keep in mind that in Spain, olive oil is de rigueur, whereas in Mexico it is virtually never used; vegetable oil is the staple.

Makes 3 main course servings, or 6 side dish servings

2 tablespoons vegetable or olive oil

1 small yellow or white onion, peeled and chopped

1 clove garlic, peeled and choppped

1 medium-size green bell pepper or 1 medium-size pasilla chile pepper,
    seeded and chopped

1 jalapeño chile pepper (optional), seeded and chopped

1 cup long or medium grain rice, well rinsed

2 medium-size, very ripe tomatoes, seeded and finely chopped or
    pureed, with juices

1½ cups Vegetable Broth (page 20) or Chicken Broth (page 18)

½ teaspoon salt

½ tablespoon tomato paste (optional)

½ cup shelled fresh peas (optional)

¼ cup coarsely chopped fresh flat-leaf parsley, for garnish

1. Heat the oil in the pressure cooker. Add the onion, garlic, bell pepper or pasilla chile, and jalapeño, if using. Cook, stirring, over medium-high heat until wilted, about 3 minutes. Add the rice and

To Rinse or Not to Rinse

In general, rice is rinsed before cooking. This is not for sanitation reasons; rather it's to wash away some of the exterior starches so the rice cooks up clean and clear. I enjoy rinsing the rice and swishing it around before adding it to the pot. On the other hand, when I'm otherwise occupied, I often skip the step and cook the rice straightaway unless the dish or culinary style calls for soaking the rice before cooking.

stir to mix. Add the tomatoes and their juices, the broth, salt, and tomato paste, if using, and stir to mix.

2. Lock on the lid and bring to pressure over high heat. Reduce the heat to medium-high and cook for 5 minutes. Remove from the heat and let sit for 10 minutes to finish cooking.

3. With the steam vent pointed away from your face, gently release any remaining pressure. Stir in the peas, if using. Set the lid ajar and let rest for 5 minutes more.

4. Sprinkle the parsley over the top and serve.

Lemongrass Coconut Rice with Toasted Coconut Topping and Dressed Cilantro

In a dish such as this, you can taste the reason for searching out the basmati or jasmine strains of long grain rice. The good news is, both are homegrown these days. Texas is the big producer and has extended its output to designer grains, such as Texmati and Jasmati. Each of these fancifully named rices delivers the distinct nutty fragrance and nonsticky texture so favored in Indian and Thai cooking.

Makes 4 to 6 servings

1 cup basmati or jasmine rice

One 8-inch length lemongrass, cut into 1-inch pieces

1½ cups unsweetened coconut milk

½ cup water

¼ cup Toasted Coconut (recipe follows), for topping

1 cup Dressed Cilantro (recipe follows), for topping

1. Place the rice, lemongrass, coconut milk, and water in the pressure cooker, lock on the lid, and bring to pressure over high heat, 4 to 5 minutes. Reduce the heat to medium-high and cook for 3 minutes. Remove from the heat and let sit for 10 minutes to finish cooking.

2. With the steam vent pointed away from your face, gently release any remaining pressure. Fluff the rice with a fork. Set the lid ajar and let rest 5 to 10 minutes. Top with the toasted coconut and dressed cilantro and serve warm.

Toasted Coconut *The success of this topping depends on having unsweetened coconut flakes. They are available in health food stores and many produce markets.* Makes ¼ cup

¼ cup unsweetened coconut flakes

Spread the coconut flakes on a microwave plate and microwave on high for 2 minutes. Stir and microwave on high for 2 minutes more, until golden. Or toast the flakes in a very lightly greased skillet over medium heat for 4 to 5 minutes, stirring constantly. Use right away or store in an airtight jar for up to 1 month.

About the Proportion of Rice to Liquid in the Pressure Cooker

For pressure cooking, the proportion of rice to liquid is less than for stove-top steaming. So, for adapting a favorite rice recipe, decrease the water or broth to a ratio of 1 part rice to 1½ parts liquid and be sure to take into account juices that might be rendered from tomatoes or other moist vegetables that are included.

Dressed Cilantro *Dressed cilantro can be used as a topping or garnish for any dish that asks for a little moisture and crisp pungency.*

Makes 1 cup

1 cup sprigs fresh cilantro, tough stems removed
½ teaspoon cider vinegar
½ teaspoon peanut or extra virgin olive oil
⅛ teaspoon salt

Place all the ingredients in a small bowl and toss to mix. Use right away or within 2 hours, before the cilantro wilts.

◇ Brown Rice Risotto with Leeks, Fennel, Fontina Cheese, and Black Pepper

Inspired by Deborah Madison, doyenne of vegetarian cooking, and spurred on by Justin Schwartz, food maven and one of the astute editors of this book, who wanted more brown rice, please, I came up with a risotto-type brown rice dish that can serve as a meal-in-a-moment on a bone-chilling day when you've had to work late. Like any risotto, it should be served exactly when done, before it gets gluey.

Makes 4 servings

3 tablespoons butter
2 medium-size leeks (white and light green parts only),
    quartered lengthwise, then sliced crosswise ¼ inch thick,
    well washed, and drained
1 small fennel bulb, fronds trimmed off and chopped to make ¼ cup,
    bulb cut into ¼-inch dice
2 cups short grain brown rice
½ teaspoon salt
¼ cup dry white wine
2½ cups water
¾ cup grated fontina cheese
1½ teaspoons coarsely ground black pepper

1. Heat the butter in the pressure cooker over medium-high heat. Stir in the leeks and fennel bulb and cook until beginning to wilt, 1 minute. Add the rice and cook, stirring, until beginning to turn golden, 1 minute. Add the salt, wine, and water and stir to mix. Lock on the lid and bring to pressure over high heat, about 3 minutes. Reduce the heat to medium and cook for 20 minutes. Remove from the heat and let sit for 10 minutes to finish cooking.

2. With the steam vent pointed away from your face, gently release any remaining pressure. Remove the lid and stir in the cheese and chopped fennel fronds. Sprinkle with the pepper and serve right away.

Various Kinds of Rice

Short grain or pearl grain rice: used especially for rice puddings and Japanese dishes. For the latter, rinse the rice, soak it for 30 minutes, and rinse again before cooking.

Medium grain rice, including Arborio: for paella, many other Spanish rice dishes, and risottos. Also for many Mexican and Japanese dishes, presoaked as described above for short grain rice.

Long grain rice, including basmati, jasmine, and Carolina long grain rice (often grown in Texas or California rather than South Carolina these days): especially for Indian, Thai, Persian, Chinese, and Creole dishes.

Brown rice: long or short grain rice that has been husked to remove the bran but not milled and polished. The nutritional benefits of brown rice are that it is higher in calcium, iron, B vitamins, and protein than white rice. It is also less easy to digest and may even interfere with the absorption of calcium, zinc, and iron. That means that brown rice need not be embraced for its holistic value to the exclusion of other rices but should be enjoyed for its nutty flavor and appealing crunch.

If you are using brown rice for Basic Steamed Rice (page 215), reduce the heat to medium and increase the cooking time to 20 minutes.

◈ Brown Rice Stir-Fry

For me, brown rice is the best kind for a stir-fry. Its chewy texture and nutty flavor, combined with vegetables and a bit of ham, make a substantial dinner in a bowl, so quickly done in a pressure cooker.

Makes 4 servings

2 tablespoons peanut oil

2 cups short or long grain brown rice

2 small carrots, peeled and cut into ¼-inch dice

4 ounces thick-sliced ham, cut into small dice

¼ cup low-sodium soy sauce

2½ cups water

4 ounces snow peas, ends trimmed and cut diagonally into 1-inch pieces

1½ cups bean sprouts

4 small scallions, trimmed and thinly sliced, for garnish

1. Heat the oil in the pressure cooker over medium–high heat until beginning to smoke. Add the rice and cook, stirring, until beginning to turn golden around the edges, about 1 minute. Add the carrots and ham and stir to mix. Add the soy sauce and water and stir again. Lock on the lid and bring to pressure over high heat, 2 to 3 minutes. Reduce the heat to medium and cook for 20 minutes. Remove from the heat and let sit for 10 minutes to finish cooking.

2. With the steam vent pointed away from your face, gently release any remaining pressure. Stir in the snow peas and bean sprouts. Set the lid back on without locking it and let sit for 5 minutes.

3. Sprinkle the scallions over the top and serve.

◈ ◈ ◈

◇ Basic Classic Risotto

For me, it's not the no-stirring advantage of making risotto in a pressure cooker; I like the stirring, it's contemplative. Rather, the advantage is to have a good dinner quickly, and one that is widely appealing and widely variable according to the moment, the day, and the crowd. Also, risotto so neatly fits into the menu either as the primo piatto, *first course, or as the main course for simple family fare. Saffron turns the most basic classic risotto into risotto Milanese. The optional white truffle shavings transform any risotto into a truly elegant dish suitable for the best company.*

Makes 4 servings

2 tablespoons butter
1 tablespoon olive oil
¼ cup finely chopped shallots
1½ cups Arborio rice
4 cups Chicken Broth (page 18)
Pinch of saffron threads (optional)
⅓ cup freshly grated parmesan cheese
White truffle shavings or white truffle oil (optional), for garnish

1. Heat the butter and olive oil together in the pressure cooker over medium-high heat until the butter melts. Stir in the shallots and then the rice. Continue stirring until the rice begins to turn translucent, 1 to 2 minutes.

2. Stir in the broth and saffron, if using. Lock on the lid and bring to pressure over high heat, 3 to 4 minutes. Reduce the heat to medium and cook for 5 minutes. Remove from the heat and let sit for 8 minutes to finish cooking.

3. With the steam vent pointed away from your face, gently release any remaining pressure. Stir in the cheese and serve right away, topped with the white truffle shavings or a drizzle of white truffle oil, if using.

◇ Risotto with Shrimp, Fennel Seeds, and Saffron

Yellow saffron, orange-pink shrimp, and flecks of green parsley combine to make this an exceptionally colorful risotto. The yellow is essential to the appeal, so if you don't have saffron, turmeric will provide the same tint, though not the same fragrance.

Makes 4 servings

1 pound medium-size shrimp, deveined if necessary
5 cups Chicken Broth (page 18)
2 tablespoons butter
1 tablespoon olive oil
¼ cup finely chopped yellow or white onion
1½ cups Arborio rice
½ cup dry white wine
¼ teaspoon fennel seeds
Large pinch of saffron threads
½ teaspoon salt
⅓ cup freshly grated parmesan cheese
2 tablespoons chopped fresh flat-leaf parsley

1. Remove the shells from the shrimp, leaving the tails attached. Set the shrimp aside in the refrigerator and place the shells in a small saucepan with 1 cup of the broth. Bring to a boil and simmer briskly until the shells are pink, about 3 minutes. Remove and discard the shells and set the broth aside.

2. Heat the butter and oil in the pressure cooker over medium–high heat until the butter melts. Stir in the onion and then the rice. Continue stirring until the rice begins to turn translucent, 1 to 2 minutes. Stir in the wine, then add the remaining 4 cups broth, the fennel seeds, saffron, salt, and reserved shrimp broth.

3. Lock on the lid and bring to pressure over high heat, 3 to 4 minutes. Reduce the heat to medium and cook for 5 minutes. Remove from the heat and let sit for 8 minutes to finish cooking.

4. With the steam vent pointed away from your face, gently release any remaining pressure. Remove the lid and stir in the shrimp. Put the lid back on without locking it and let sit 4 minutes. Stir in the cheese and parsley and serve right away.

◇ ◇ ◇

Four Especially Delicious Risotto Variations

Judging from modern cookbooks, newspaper food section recipes, and restaurant menu offerings, risotto has been roundly embraced, not only in its traditional form but also for its cross-cultural possibilities, which allow the cook to innovate with unusual ingredients while staying true to the spirit. Following are four such.

Peas and Asparagus Risotto

This is for spring, when peas and asparagus are among the first vegetables to show verdant color after the darker-hued produce of winter. For 1 recipe Basic Classic Risotto (page 222), snap the ends off ¾ pound asparagus. Rinse the spears and cut them on the diagonal into ½-inch pieces, reserving the tips separately. Add the asparagus pieces and 1 cup shelled fresh peas in Step 1, along with the rice. Meanwhile, blanch the tips in a small pot of simmering salted water for 3 minutes. Drain and set aside. When done, garnish the risotto with the asparagus tips and some ribbons of prosciutto.

Gravlax Risotto

Seafood is a familiar embellishment for risottos, especially clams and shrimp. Gravlax, Swedish-style cured but not smoked salmon, is within that tradition but still a bit out of the ordinary. You can find gravlax at fine fish counters. A very lightly smoked salmon would be a good substitute. For 1 recipe Basic Classic Risotto (page 222), add 1 cup ½-inch pieces gravlax in Step 3, as you stir in the cheese.

Chicken Giblet and Sage Risotto

Using chicken giblets is a bit of stretch for American cooks, but it ought not to be. Follow the lead of Italian cooks and make them the meat of the day twirled into a hearty risotto or swirled into pasta. You'll be surprised at how tasty they are and delighted at how clever and thrifty you are. For 1 batch Basic Classic Risotto (page 222), finely chop 1 chicken heart, 1 chicken liver, and 1 set of chicken gizzards. Thinly shred 4 to 6 sage leaves. Add the giblets and sage in Step 1, along with the shallots, and stir before including the rice. Grind some black pepper over the top of the risotto just before serving.

Molded Risotto with Saffron, Carrot, and Sorrel Cream

Risotto lends itself nicely to being pressed into a mold. With rivulets of sorrel cream across the top, molded risotto makes a lovely decoration for the center of the table or, in a smaller version, for individual plates. For 1 recipe Basic Classic Risotto (page 222), peel and finely dice 1 carrot. Add it in Step 1 along with the shallots. In Step 2, increase the saffron to 2 pinches. When the risotto is done, stir in the cheese, as in Step 3. Right away, spoon the risotto into one or several molds, depending how you are serving the dish, pressing down firmly to make sure the nooks and crannies of the mold(s) are filled and the risotto is compacted. When ready to serve, invert the mold(s) and gently pry out the risotto with a knife. Spoon over some heavy cream that has been heated at the last minute with a little finely shredded sorrel.

Risotto with Porcinis, Escarole, and Red Wine

It's unlikely you will find porcini mushrooms fresh outside Italy, but they are widely available dried and, reconstituted, are as flavorful as the fresh ones, in fact more so according to the renowned Italian cookbook author Marcella Hazan. Fresh cremini mushrooms or fresh shiitakes will also do in place of the porcinis. The faintly bitter flavor of the escarole complements the fragrance and earthy taste of the porcinis, and both stand up in balance to garlic's pungence.

Makes 4 servings

½ ounce dried porcini mushrooms (about ½ cup)

2 tablespoons butter

1 tablespoon olive oil

2 large cloves garlic, minced or pressed

1½ cups Arborio rice

1 cup dry red wine

4 cups Beef Broth (page 15)

2 cups packed shredded escarole leaves

½ teaspoon salt

½ cup freshly grated parmesan cheese

2 tablespoons chopped fresh flat-leaf parsley, for garnish

1. Place the mushrooms in a medium-size bowl and pour 1 cup boiling water over them. Set aside to rehydrate for 20 minutes. When ready to use, strain through a fine-mesh sieve into a bowl, pressing down to squeeze dry the mushrooms. Set the mushrooms and their liquid aside separately.

2. Heat the butter and oil in the pressure cooker over medium-high heat until the butter melts. Stir in the garlic, then the rice. Continue stirring until the rice begins to turn translucent, 1 to 2 minutes. Stir in the wine, broth, escarole, salt, mushrooms, and ½ cup of the reserved soaking liquid.

3. Lock on the lid and bring to pressure over high heat, 3 to 4 minutes. Reduce the heat to medium and cook for 5 minutes. Remove from the heat and let sit for 8 minutes to finish cooking.

4. With the steam vent pointed away from your face, gently release any remaining pressure. Stir in the cheese, sprinkle the parsley over the top, and serve right away.

◇ ◇ ◇

Pilafs:
A Mediterranean Grain Specialty

Pilafs appear all around the eastern and southern Mediterranean, including North Africa, and east all the way to Armenia, as well as India. Those lands also feature many rice dishes. The distinction between pilaf and flavored rice is somewhat blurry. For instance, why aren't Asian stir-fried rice dishes pilafs? Why is Spanish rice not a pilaf? Probably because pilaf is not a word of their language. To complicate matters, in its home region, bulgur is as common a pilaf grain as rice, and in India certain lentil dishes are called pilafs. In this section, I offer a representative selection of dishes that are called pilafs, from rice to bulgur. Similar dishes made with lentils are in the legume chapter.

Armenian Pilaf

I have no idea how the vermicelli noodles wound up in the basic pilaf of all the cooks on the Armenian side of my family. But they did, and we never made pilaf without them. Other than the simple flourishes of freshly ground black pepper and a pat or two of butter at the end, there were no other this's or that's. To this day, it serves at my table as a mandatory side dish for almost any lamb preparation.

Makes 4 to 6 side dish servings

1½ tablespoons butter, plus extra for dotting
½ cup broken-up vermicelli
1 cup long grain white rice
2 cups water
Freshly ground black pepper to taste

1. Heat the butter in the pressure cooker over medium-high heat until melted. Add the vermicelli and stir until beginning to turn golden, about 1½ minutes. Add the rice and continue stirring until well coated and translucent, about 2 minutes.

2. Add the water, lock on the lid, and bring to pressure over high heat, about 3 minutes. Reduce the heat to medium-high and cook for 5 minutes. Remove from the heat and let sit for 10 minutes to finish cooking.

3. With the steam vent pointed away from your face, gently release any remaining pressure. Fluff the rice with a fork, sprinkle lots of black pepper over the top, and dot with butter. Without stirring, set the lid ajar and let rest, undisturbed, for 5 minutes. Fluff again and serve.

◇ Vegetable Pilaf
With a generous handful of North African spice-bazaar aromatics and a mélange of vegetables you might find in a tagine, vegetable pilaf could be considered something of a rice couscous. With a trio of frills to accompany, consider it for dinner.

Makes 4 servings

1 tablespoon vegetable oil
1 tablespoon butter
2 cloves garlic, minced
½ small yellow or white onion, thinly sliced
One ½-inch-piece fresh ginger, peeled and minced
1 serrano chile pepper, minced
1½ cups small cauliflower florets
1 cup green beans, ends trimmed and cut into 1-inch pieces
1 medium-size carrot, peeled and cut into thin diagonal slices
3 teaspoons North African Spice Blend (recipe follows)
½ teaspoon salt
1 cup long grain white rice
1½ cups water
A trio of condiments (optional; see right)

1. Heat the oil and butter in a pressure cooker over medium heat until the butter melts. Add the garlic, onion, ginger, and chile pepper and stir to mix. Stir in the cauliflower, green beans, and carrot and raise the heat to medium-high.

2. Stir in the spice mix, salt, and rice. Add the water, lock on the lid, and bring to pressure over high heat, about 3 minutes. Reduce the heat to medium-high and cook for 5 minutes. Remove from the heat and let sit for 15 minutes to finish cooking.

3. With the steam vent pointed away from your face, gently release any remaining pressure. Fluff with a fork and serve right away, accompanied by the condiments, if using.

North African Spice Blend *Kept in a tightly covered jar as you would any other ground spice, this blend will remain fresh and aromatic for up to six months.*   Makes ¼ cup

> 1 teaspoon ground cumin
> ½ teaspoon ground turmeric
> ¼ teaspoon cardamom seeds
> 1 teaspoon chili powder
> ⅛ teaspoon ground cloves
> ⅛ teaspoon Aleppo pepper (see page 232) or hot paprika

Mix together all the ingredients. Use right away or store in an airtight container for up to 3 months.

Elevating Condiments

Small bowls of colorful garnishes set alongside the main dish can turn ordinary fare into something special. Throughout this book, you will find many such condiments I rely on to dress a meal. A complete list, from the totally effortless to the more complicated, is given on pages 10 through 12.

For the vegetable pilaf, to keep things easy, my selections are slivered almonds, blanched or not, lightly toasted (see page 41); fresh pineapple, somewhat finely chopped; or cilantro sprigs.

◇ Bulgur Pilaf

Old as the hills, good as gold, bulgur wheat is a grain not much used in American cooking. Perhaps it needs a new spin on its name because its taste and texture are as appealing as any rice and equally nutritious. And it's not at all complicated to use. In the cuisines where it is favored—Greece, Turkey, Armenia—it is as often the grain of pilaf as rice. Earthy and nutty, bulgur makes a basic dish that can be garnished and embellished in pan-Mediterranean ways. Following is a basic home-style bulgur pilaf, which may be served as a customary part of the main meal.

Makes 4 to 6 side dish servings

2 tablespoons olive oil
1 small yellow or white onion, finely chopped
1 cup coarse bulgur wheat (see below)
1½ cups Chicken Broth (page 18), Beef Broth (page 15), Vegetable Broth
    (page 20), or water
Salt and freshly ground black pepper to taste

1. Heat the oil in the pressure cooker over medium-high heat. Add the onion and bulgur and cook, stirring, until the onion is translucent and the bulgur begins to smell nutty, about 3 minutes.

Bulgur Wheat: A Fine to Coarse Grain

Not any old bulgur wheat will do for a particular recipe. Bulgur has its refinements. Pilafs require the coarse-ground version of the grain so the granules absorb the liquid and seasonings and remain fluffy without becoming soggy. For tabbouleh, the famous grain salad of Middle Eastern cuisines, a medium-size grain is preferred because it soaks to suppleness without requiring any cooking. For *kufta*, one of the undoubted queen dumplings of the world, fine-ground bulgur is the only way to achieve the desired lightness of texture in conjunction with the full flavor required for royal praise.

2. Stir in the broth, lock on the lid, and bring to pressure over high heat, about 5 minutes. Reduce the heat to medium–high and cook for 3 minutes. Remove from the heat and let sit for 10 minutes to finish cooking.

3. With the steam vent pointed away from your face, gently release any remaining pressure. Fluff the bulgur with a fork and season with salt and pepper. Set the lid ajar and let rest for 5 minutes more, then serve.

◎ Bulgur Pilaf with Sprouts, Aleppo Pepper, and Thickened Yogurt

Somewhere between the eastern Mediterranean and my imagination, this recipe sprouted up. It's not so much a recipe as a concoction. Pressure-cooked bulgur makes it a no-fuss dish for a light vegetarian meal.

Makes 4 servings

Thickened Yogurt

As they have it in Greece and the eastern Mediterranean, yogurt is creamy, sweet/tart, and thick enough to stand a spoon in. To simulate that, first choose a good-quality yogurt. Place it in a cheesecloth-lined strainer set over a bowl deep enough for the strainer to rest above the bottom of the bowl. Set aside at room temperature for at least 2 hours or refrigerate overnight. Whisk with a fork or wire whip to smooth before serving.

1 batch Bulgur Pilaf (page 230), warm
1 cup fresh sprouts, such as alfalfa, onion, soybean, mung bean, pea, or sunflower
Aleppo pepper (see page 232) or freshly ground black pepper to taste
1 cup Thickened Yogurt (left), for serving

Spoon the warm bulgur into a serving bowl. Spread the sprouts across the top and sprinkle with Aleppo pepper. Serve with a dish of Thickened Yogurt.

◎ ◎ ◎

Aleppo as Allegory

Aleppo pepper, named after the city in Syria that is its most prominent source, is my favorite ground red pepper, bar none, including the best of the Hungarian paprikas, the finest of the Cayman Island cayennes, and the finest pure chile pepper from the high plains of the Southwest. Aleppo pepper retains the taste and aroma of its vegetable origin (fresh red capsicum) while offering a red pepper punch that is not too hot, just enough. For me, it also evokes a heritage since it is typical of Armenian cooking around the area in Turkey near Syria that my paternal relatives called home before emigrating to the United States. Though a bit hard to scout out, you can find it in Middle Eastern groceries, especially those that cater to a Turkish, Syrian, or Lebanese clientele. Or you can mail order it from Kalustyan's, 123 Lexington Avenue, New York, NY 10016, or www.kalustyans.com on the Internet.

Pilaf of Wild Rice with Pecans and Dried Apricots

Though not a rice grain but the seed of an aquatic grass (Zizania aquatica), wild rice nonetheless acts like a rice culinarily. Not only is it esteemed for its texture and flavor, it is also admired as few other botanicals for its rarity and place in American agricultural history. It was once available only in a small section of the Great Lake marshes; the desire for it gave rise to a whole new cultivation, and it is now grown in California and Oregon as well as Minnesota. That means wild rice is widely available and not so expensive; the drawback is that cultivated wild rice is often not worth any expense at all because it doesn't open its grains and remains needle-y no matter how long you cook it. For that reason, I recommend choosing true wild rice. Christmas Point (www.christmaspoint.com) is a particularly good brand at an excellent price. Plain and simple or mixed with some of its seasonal companions, it makes a worthy offering on a fall or winter holiday table.

Makes about 4 cups, or 6 side dish servings

1½ tablespoons butter

½ cup pecans, coarsely chopped

½ medium-size yellow or white onion, finely chopped but not minced

1 tablespoon chopped fresh mint, or 1 teaspoon dried

1 cup good-quality wild rice

¼ cup coarsely chopped dried apricots

1½ tablespoons chopped lemon zest

2 cups water

Wild Rice with Peas and Chèvre: A Pilaf of Another Color

The instructions for cooking wild rice hold true with or without the extra elements. You can omit them and cook the grains plain. While the rice cooks, bring a medium-size pot of water to a boil. Add 1½ pounds fresh English peas (about 1½ cups shelled) and blanch for 1 minute. Right away, drain in a colander and run under cool water to stop the cooking. Set aside to drip-dry while the rice finishes cooking. When the rice is done, add the peas, along with ⅓ cup crumbled chèvre; 2 tablespoons walnut, hazelnut, or extra virgin olive oil; and salt and pepper to taste. Toss ever so gently so as not to smash everything together, and serve right away, while still warm.

1. Heat the butter in the pressure cooker over medium-high heat until melted. Add the pecans, onion, and mint and cook, stirring, until the onion begins to wilt, about 2 minutes. Stir in the wild rice, then the apricots, lemon zest, and water.

2. Lock on the lid and bring to pressure over high heat, 2 to 3 minutes. Reduce the heat to medium-low heat and cook for 15 minutes. Remove from the heat and let sit for 10 minutes to finish cooking.

3. With the steam vent pointed away from your face, gently release any remaining pressure. Drain any remaining liquid and serve right away.

Note: If you are using cultivated rice and the grains have not opened, add a bit more water and boil with the lid ajar for 5 to 10 minutes more.

◇ ◇ ◇

⬙ Pan-Asian Steamed Dumplings

A few shreds of lemongrass, a bit of Szechwan pepper, a daring dollop of grated fresh ginger or an undeniable measure of lemon zest, and pork, mushrooms, shrimp, chicken livers take on a new meaning for the Western palate. Bundled in Asian-style pasta wrappers, the fillings turn into delicate packets of taste, tender and lusciously rendered in the pressure cooker. More, you can stuff the wrappers with Italian-style fillings for a quick, almost ready-made pasta treat. For the wrappers, use wonton (square) wrappers, gyoza (round) wrappers, or egg roll wrappers cut into quarters. They're pretty much the same dough; just the shape differs. All are available in most supermarkets these days in the refrigerated Asian foods section, where you'll also find tofu and fresh Asian noodles

.

Makes 16 dumplings, or 4 to 6 side dish servings

16 dumpling wrappers
1¼ cups filling (recipes follow)
Dipping sauces of your choice (recipes follow)

1. Lay out the wrappers on a counter. Place 1 tablespoon filling in the center of each. With your fingers or a pastry brush, moisten the edges of each wrapper. Fold in half to make a triangle or half-moon shape, depending on the wrapper you are using, and pinch together the edges to seal. As you go, place the dumplings on a lightly oiled trivet that will fit inside the pressure cooker, setting them side by side in 1 layer but not overlapping.

2. Place a heatproof plate in the pressure cooker and pour in ¾ cup water. Set the trivet on top of the plate, so that the trivet rests just above the liquid. Lock on the lid and bring to pressure over high heat, about 2 minutes. Reduce the heat to medium–high and cook for 3 minutes. Remove from the heat and set aside for 5 minutes to finish cooking.

3. With the steam vent pointed away from your face, gently release any remaining pressure. Let rest with the lid ajar for 10 minutes before serving.

4. To serve, arrange the dumplings on a serving platter and accompany with dipping sauces on the side.

Note: You can cover the dumpling packets with a damp cloth or paper towel to keep them from drying out until ready to cook. They will hold this way for up to a couple of hours, but then they should be cooked and not refrigerated or held longer.

Shrimp and Lemongrass Filling

Makes about 1¼ cups, enough for about 16 dumplings

½ pound shrimp meat, minced (about 1 cup)

2 tablespoons minced lemongrass (tender white part only)

¼ cup finely chopped fresh cilantro

¼ cup coarsely grated carrot

1 teaspoon minced scallion

2 teaspoons freshly squeezed lime juice

½ teaspoon salt

Combine all the ingredients in a medium-size bowl and mix well. Use right away or refrigerate, covered, for up to 2 hours.

Ginger Pork Filling

Makes about 1½ cups, enough for about 16 dumplings

4 ounces ground pork

2 tablespoons peeled and coarsely grated fresh ginger

1 cup finely shredded green cabbage

2 tablespoons minced scallion

2 tablespoons low-sodium soy sauce

1 tablespoon dry sherry

Combine all the ingredients in a medium-size bowl and mix well. Use right away or refrigerate, covered, for up to 2 days.

Mushroom Spinach Filling

Makes about 1½ cups, enough for about 16 dumplings

⅔ cup finely chopped spinach leaves, well-washed, and drained

1 teaspoon coarsely grated fresh ginger, preferably young ginger

2 tablespoons finely chopped scallion

1 cup coarsely chopped fresh shiitake mushroom caps

¼ teaspoon sesame oil

½ teaspoon low-sodium soy sauce

¼ teaspoon freshly ground black pepper

Combine all the ingredients in a medium-size bowl and mix well. Use right away or refrigerate, covered, for up to 2 days.

Chicken Liver and Asian Greens Filling

Makes about 1½ cups, enough for about 16 dumplings

Livers from 3 chickens, rinsed, patted dry, and minced (about ¾ cup)

¾ cup minced Asian greens, such as bok choy, chrysanthemum leaves,
    or tender watercress leaves

1 tablespoon finely chopped lemon zest

1 tablespoon minced shallot

1 teaspoon smashed Szechuan peppercorns (optional, see Note page 85)

1 teaspoon salt

2 teaspoons dry sherry

Combine all the ingredients in a medium-size bowl and mix well. Use right away or refrigerate, covered, for up to 2 hours.

◇ ◇ ◇

Thai- or Vietnamese-Style Dipping Sauce *Neither one nor the other, classically speaking, this is a combination of* nam prik *(Thai) without the dried shrimp and* nuoc cham *(Vietnamese), and with less sweetening than normally desired in either of those cuisines. Like an Asian salsa, this is a table sauce, to be used for adding a sprightly note to this and that throughout the meal. The fish sauce is essential for authentic taste; you can find it in most supermarkets in the international foods section. If you can't find it, substitute an equal amount of light soy sauce mixed with ¼ teaspoon mashed anchovy fillet.*

Makes ¾ cup

1 small fresh or 2 small dried red chile peppers, finely chopped
2 tablespoons freshly squeezed lime juice
2 tablespoons rice vinegar
2 tablespoons fish sauce (*nam pla*)
1 small clove garlic, finely chopped
Pinch of sugar

Combine all the ingredients in a small bowl. Set aside until ready to serve. This will keep at room temperature for up to 3 hours.

Following are two quick and easy-to-make flavor accents for Pan-Asian Steamed Dumplings (page 234). They will take the dumplings in a Chinese direction and are especially good used together, in separate dishes. Place coarsely shredded daikon radish, coarsely shredded carrot, and mint or basil leaves on a small plate next to the dishes.

Hot Mustard Paste

Makes about ¼ cup

2 tablespoons powdered mustard, preferably Colman's
3 tablespoons water

Place the mustard in a small bowl. Using a fork or small whisk, slowly stir in the water. Use right away or within 30 minutes.

Sweet-and-Sour Dipping Sauce

Makes ¾ cup

½ cup ketchup
¼ cup firmly packed dark brown sugar
2 tablespoons granulated sugar
1 teaspoon ground ginger
2 tablespoons freshly squeezed lemon juice
1 tablespoon water

1. Place all the ingredients in a heavy saucepan. Bring to a boil over medium heat, stirring constantly.

2. Reduce the heat to low and simmer very gently until slightly sticky, about 5 minutes. Cool and use right away or store in the refrigerator, covered, for up to 1 week.

◇ ◇ ◇

Raviolis in Asian Pasta Wrappers

A s many ways as there are to fill Asian dumplings, there are also as many for stuffing raviolis. Following are two fillings, with sauce and other filling suggestions, that work well with an Asian pasta wrap in the spirit of the Mediterranean, and a tempting list of how to go from there.

Butternut Squash–Filled Raviolis with Toasted Bread Crumb Topping

Makes about 16 raviolis, or 4 to 6 side dish servings

1 cup cooked butternut squash (see steps 1 and 2 on page 33)

¼ teaspoon ground coriander

Small pinch of ground cloves

1 tablespoon heavy cream

¼ teaspoon salt

About 16 dumpling wrappers

¼ cup (½ stick) butter, melted and kept warm, for topping

¼ cup toasted bread crumbs (see page 187), for topping

1. Combine the squash, coriander, cloves, cream, and salt in a food processor and puree.

2. Fill and cook the wrappers as described in Steps 1 through 3 on page 234.

3. To serve, arrange the raviolis on individual plates or a serving platter. Pour the melted butter over the top and sprinkle with the bread crumbs.

Marco Polo Cooks in Modern Times

Many of the recipes in this book can be used to fill and sauce Asian pasta wraps and create a quick hors d'oeuvre or light meal.

For the filling, try:

Creamed Corn Filling (page 249)

Black Bean and Plantain Tamale Filling (page 250)

Shredded Chicken in Tomatillo Sauce Filling (page 249)

Spicy Beef Filling (page 250)

Shredded Beef, from Hash to Picadillo (page 64)

Sweet Italian Sausage (page 108)

Savory Azukis (page 344)

Chard with Garlic and Black Olives (page 179)

Spaghetti Squash, Many Ways (page 196)

Spinach, Cream Cheese, and Pine Nut Stuffing (page 211)

For saucing the packets, try:

Parsley Sauce (page 150)

Black Olive Butter Sauce (page 151)

Arugula Pesto (page 157)

Soft Garlic Anchovy Oil (page 176)

Tomato Caper Sauce (page 210)

Very Quick Fresh Tomato Sauce (page 289)

Arayah's Marinara Sauce (page 290)

Vegetarian "Ragu" (page 294)

Tomato Concassé Sauce (page 324)

◈ Chard and Chèvre–Filled Raviolis

Makes about 16 raviolis, or 4 to 6 side dish servings

4 cups packed coarsely chopped chard, well washed and drained
¼ cup soft chèvre, at room temperature
1 large shallot, cut up
¼ teaspoon salt
About 16 dumpling wrappers
½ cup Very Quick Fresh Tomato Sauce (page 289), for serving
¼ cup freshly grated parmesan cheese, for serving

1. Combine the chard, chèvre, shallot, and salt in a food processor and puree as fine as possible.

2. Fill and cook the wrappers as described in Steps 1 through 3 on page 234.

3. To serve, arrange the raviolis on individual plates or a serving platter. Nap with the tomato sauce and serve the parmesan cheese on the side.

◈ Wheat Berries

Since discovering wheat berries a few years ago while working on recipes for Greek cooking, I've adopted them and taken to praising them as a personal mission. They are so good, I can't imagine why they've been cast into the shadows of grain cooking. But that can change. With the help of a pressure cooker, versatile and good-for-you wheat berries can be ready in less than an hour instead of three, and you can let your imagination run free serving them up with various toppings, including them in rice pilafs, adding them to breads, placing them cooked and unadorned in a snack bowl to munch as the day goes on.

Makes 6 side dish servings

1 cup wheat berries
4 cups water

1. Place the berries and water in the pressure cooker, lock on the lid, and bring to pressure over high heat, about 8 minutes. Reduce the heat to medium and cook for 20 minutes. Remove from the heat and let sit for 15 minutes to finish cooking.

2. With the steam vent pointed away from your face, gently release any remaining pressure, drain, and briefly rinse. Serve warm with a pat of butter or garnish with any of the toppings described in the pilaf recipes (pages 227 to 233).

Note: Wheat berries are available in natural food stores and produce markets that carry bulk grains.

◈ ◈ ◈

Two Wheat Berry Pilafs with Mushrooms as the Meat

Twice a year, in the wet seasons, mushrooms appear like an earthbound cloudburst across the forest floor and nearby meadows. Those are just the right times for a robust, legume-studded wheat berry pilaf with mushrooms providing the "meat." In spring, the mushrooms might be chanterelles coupled with fresh fava beans. In fall, they might be shiitakes with fresh soybeans punctuating the wheat berries. In either season, the mushrooms together with the legumes provide a substantial dish that leaves nothing to be desired.

For pilafs, the berries should be cooked through but with a little crunch left. The age and type of wheat determines the actual cooking time, and so it varies a bit, as with dried beans. If the berries are underdone and the liquid in the pot hasn't been well absorbed, boil a little longer, uncovered, before adding the remaining ingredients.

◈ Wheat Berries with Shiitake Mushrooms and Fresh Soybeans

Fresh soybeans, called edamame, *have become available in the produce or freezer sections of many supermarkets and specialty Asian markets. They are a snack treasure on their own and also a special ingredient to use in a wheat berry pilaf. If you can't find them, use baby lima beans instead.*

Makes 4 servings

1½ tablespoons soy or peanut oil

½ small yellow or white onion, thinly sliced

2 ounces fresh shiitake mushrooms, stemmed and sliced ¼ inch thick

1 cup wheat berries

2 cups Chicken Broth (page 18)

½ cup fresh soybeans

¾ cup soybean, mung bean, or sunflower sprouts, for topping

1. Heat the oil in the pressure cooker over medium heat until beginning to smoke. Add the onion and cook, stirring occasionally, over medium heat until wilted, 1 minute. Stir in the shiitakes and continue to cook, stirring occasionally, for 2 minutes more.

2. Raise the heat to medium-high, stir in the wheat berries, and cook, stirring occasionally, until the berries begin to turn golden, 1 minute. Add the broth, lock on the lid, and bring to pressure over high heat, 2 to 3 minutes. Reduce the heat to medium and cook for 20 minutes. Remove from the heat and let sit for 15 minutes to finish cooking.

3. With the steam vent pointed away from your face, gently release any remaining pressure. Remove the lid and boil a little longer if the wheat berries are not done. Stir in the soybeans. Top with the sprouts and serve right away.

◈ Wheat Berry Pilaf with Chanterelles and Fresh Fava Beans *Fresh peas could replace the fava beans and dried porcinis could be the mushrooms.*

Makes 4 servings

1 tablespoon butter

4 ounces chanterelle mushrooms, stemmed and sliced ½ inch thick

1 cup wheat berries

2 cups Chicken Broth (page 18)

1 pound fresh fava beans, shelled

1 teaspoon coarsely chopped fresh tarragon, or pinch of dried

1. Melt the butter in the pressure cooker over medium-high heat. Add the chanterelles and cook, stirring occasionally, until beginning to wilt, about 1 minute. Add the wheat berries and broth, lock on the lid, and bring to pressure over high heat, about 4 minutes.

Reduce the heat to medium and cook for 20 minutes. Remove from the heat and let sit for 15 minutes to finish cooking.

2. While the wheat berries sit, bring a small pot of water to a boil. Drop in the fava beans and, as soon as the water returns to a boil, drain. Rinse the beans with cool water and peel away the skins with your fingers.

3. With the steam vent pointed away from your face, gently release any remaining pressure from the pressure cooker pot. Remove the lid and boil a little longer if the berries are not cooked. Stir in the fava beans and tarragon. Serve right away.

Farro

For years, wheat berries have languished in the back pages of the occasional cookbook that mentions them. Suddenly, farro, a wheat berry, arrives on the scene and takes the culinary mavens by storm. A few tablespoons of butter stirred in just before serving is all that's needed if you're serving the farro as a side dish with roasted or grilled meats. If serving with a stew, such as Game Hens Bistro Style in Vinegar Tomato Sauce with Farro (page 141), or another dish that has an accompanying sauce, the butter is not necessary. Makes 4 to 6 side dish servings

1½ cups farro
3 cups water
1 teaspoon salt
3 tablespoons butter (optional)

1. Combine the farro, water, and salt in the pressure cooker. Lock on the lid and bring to pressure over high heat, about 5 minutes. Reduce the heat to medium and cook for 3 minutes. Remove from the heat and let sit for 10 minutes to finish cooking.

2. With the steam vent pointed away from your face, gently release any remaining pressure. Stir in the butter, if using, and serve.

◯ Farro Risotto with Roasted Tomatoes, Marjoram, and Beef Broth

Farro, like Arborio rice, another pearly, hard grain, is happily cooked risotto style. Farro's wheat flavor takes well to other known and recently devised rice risotto seasonings, especially the hearty renditions of Emilia-Romagna and points east. Roasted tomatoes do take some precious minutes to prepare, but they add a smoky flavor that elevates the dish above the more sanguine canned Italian plum tomatoes. Makes 4 to 6 servings

3 tablespoons butter

2 small shallots, finely chopped

3 teaspoons chopped fresh marjoram, or 1½ teaspoons dried

2 Roasted Tomatoes (left), coarsely chopped

1½ cups farro

3 cups Beef Broth (page 15)

1 teaspoon salt

½ cup freshly grated parmesan, romano, or aged asiago cheese

Roasted Tomatoes

Place the tomatoes you are roasting on a baking sheet in a preheated 500°F oven or on the grill rack over a hot barbecue fire. Either way, cook for 10 to 15 minutes, turning once, until charred all around. Remove and let cool enough to handle, then peel and seed them with your fingers. Some cooks like to roast or char tomatoes over a gas burner on the stove top, but I find that too messy a proposition.

1. Heat the butter and shallots together in the pressure cooker over medium-high heat, stirring occasionally, until the shallots begin to wilt, about 1 minute. Stir in the marjoram and tomatoes, then the farro. Add the broth and salt, lock on the lid, and bring to pressure over high heat, about 5 minutes. Reduce the heat to medium-low and cook for 5 minutes. Remove from the heat and let sit for 10 minutes to finish cooking.

2. With the steam vent pointed away from your face, gently release any remaining pressure. Remove the lid. If too soupy, boil uncovered for a minute or two. Stir in the cheese and serve right away.

◯   ◯   ◯

Tamales with Four Fillings
and Mint Lime Butter

n court with squash blossoms, grape leaves, tortillas, pitas, and lavash bread, corn husks encasing tender tamale dough stand as one of the princesses of wraps. When it comes to the pressure cooker, they are downright queen, turning out delectably in any size from small bite to main plate. The corn husks, particularly good when fresh, can be stockpiled in the freezer to await a New Year's celebration. Or dried corn husks, now available in most supermarkets, are easily made supple for wrapping with a brief soak in water.

◇ Basic Tamales *The recipe can easily be doubled to make a sumptuous party platter. In that case you will need to cook the tamales in two batches.*

Makes 8 to 10 tamales, or 4 to 8 servings, depending on how you use them

¾ cup (1½ sticks) butter

2 cups water

2 cups masa harina (see Note page 249)

1½ teaspoons baking powder

¾ teaspoon salt

18 to 25 fresh or dried corn husks (depending on size), soaked in water for
    30 minutes if dried and drained

2 cups tamale filling, all one kind or a selection (pages 249 to 251)

½ cup Mint Lime Butter (page 252), warm, for serving

1. Combine the butter and water in a small saucepan over medium heat and warm until the butter melts. Set aside.

2. Place the masa harina, baking powder, and salt in a large bowl and stir with a fork to mix well. Whisk in the butter mixture, beating well as you go, until the dough is the consistency of a wet cake batter.

3. Select 8 to 10 husks large enough to roll into a tube 1 to 1½ inches in diameter and lay them out on a counter. (Or, select smaller husks and overlap 2 or 3 for each wrapper.) Place ¼ cup of the dough in the center of each husk and press into a rectangle about 4½ × 2½ inches and ¼ inch thick. Spread 2 tablespoons of the filling you are using down the center of the dough. Roll up the husks into a tube to enclose the filling. Fold the pointed top ends of the husks under, toward the seam side of the tube. Leave the bottom of the tube unfolded. At this point, you can cook the tamales right away or cover them with a damp towel and set them aside at room temperature for 2 to 3 hours.

4. To cook the tamales, pour 2 cups water into the pressure cooker and set a trivet in the cooker (you may have to elevate it on a heat-proof plate in order to keep it up out of the water). Set the tamales,

Corn: An Amazing Grain

One delight of exploring the twists and turns of pressure cooking was the discovery that many of my favorite corn recipes work not only well but beautifully. Tamales I will never do another way. Spoon bread is so much easier than the more labored mix, mix again, and into the oven method. A disappointment was polenta; I found it was so clunky and gluey as not to be worth a second thought. However, a modified version, using eggs to lighten the load, makes a wonderful alternative and has the bonus of being sweetly adaptable for a dessert pudding. The key for all the successes, I found, is to treat the cooking as essentially steaming. For tamales, this took no conceptual modifying. They are a dish traditionally steamed; the pressure cooker is just faster. For the corn pudding (see page 323), it was more of a surprise to find how cooking it in a pressure cooker *à la bain marie* could truly simulate the slow oven-steamed water bath method with the same excellent results. In the following section, you'll find lots of tips, variations, sauces, and accoutrements to keep you in corn cooking from July to January.

seam side down, in 2 layers on top of the trivet. Cover with a layer of corn husks. Lock on the lid and bring to pressure over high heat, about 4 minutes. Reduce the heat to medium-high and cook for 12 minutes. Remove from the heat and set aside for 8 minutes to finish cooking.

5. With the steam vent pointed away from your face, gently release any remaining pressure. Serve the tamales warm in the husks, to be unwrapped as eaten, with the warm Mint Lime Butter on the side.

Note: You can find masa harina in the Mexican foods section of most supermarkets. Better still is to look for it in bulk in a market that caters to a Latino clientele or one that carries a variety of grains in bulk.

Creamed Corn Filling

Makes 2 cups

1½ cups fresh corn kernels, plus liquid collected from shaving the cobs
⅓ cup finely chopped yellow or white onion
1 jalapeño chile pepper, finely chopped
1 cup grated semisoft cheese, such as Monterey Jack, farmer's cheese,
　　or *queso asadero*
2 tablespoons sour cream

Combine all the ingredients in a medium-size bowl. Use right away or store in the refrigerator, covered, up to overnight (not longer).

Shredded Chicken in Tomatillo Sauce Filling

Makes 1½ cups

1 cup shredded cooked chicken
1 cup Tomatillo Sauce (page 251)
Salt to taste

Combine the chicken and Tomatillo Sauce in a medium-size bowl. Season with salt and use right away or store in the refrigerator for up to 3 days.

Black Bean and Plantain Tamale Filling

Makes 2½ cups

1 tablespoon olive or vegetable oil
½ small yellow or white onion, chopped
2 cloves garlic, chopped
⅛ teaspoon anise seeds
1 bay leaf, minced
1½ cups cooked black beans, with cooking liquid (page 279)
1 medium-size, ripe plantain, peeled
½ teaspoon salt

Heat the oil in a small skillet over medium heat. Add the onion, garlic, anise seeds, and bay leaf. Cook, stirring occasionally, until the onion is wilted, about 3 minutes. Transfer the contents of the skillet to a food processor. Add the beans, plantain, and salt and puree as fine as possible. Use right away or store in the refrigerator, covered, for up to 2 days (not longer).

Spicy Beef Filling

Makes about 1½ cups

½ tablespoon olive or vegetable oil
½ cup finely chopped yellow or white onion
½ pound lean ground beef
¼ teaspoon dried marjoram
1½ teaspoons chili powder
¾ teaspoon salt
¼ teaspoon freshly ground black pepper
¼ cup dry white wine
1 tablespoon freshly squeezed lime juice

1. Heat the oil in a medium-size skillet over medium heat. Add the onion and cook, stirring occasionally, until it begins to wilt, about 2 minutes. Stir in the beef, marjoram, chili powder, salt, and pepper. Cook, stirring occasionally, until the beef is nicely browned, about 5 minutes.

2. Add the wine and lime juice and continue cooking until the liquid is mostly evaporated, about 1 minute more. Cool and use right away or store in the refrigerator, covered, for up to 5 days.

Tomatillo Sauce

Tomatillo sauce, otherwise known as salsa verde, is so useful and so easy to make and so much better homemade than canned or jarred that I have adopted it as one of my always-in-the-fridge items. If you can't find fresh tomatillos, canned will do—even Mexican cooks often resort to them in winter when tomatillos are out of season.

Makes 1½ cups

5 or 6 tomatillos

½ medium-size yellow or white onion, coarsely chopped

3 to 5 small green chile peppers, coarsely chopped

1½ cups packed fresh cilantro sprigs

Salt to taste

1. Peel away the papery husks from the tomatillos and rinse them. Place in a saucepan with the onion and barely enough water to cover. Bring to a boil and simmer briskly for 5 minutes. Remove from the heat and let sit until cool enough to handle.

2. Drain, reserving the liquid. Transfer the tomatillos and onion to a food processor, add the chile peppers, cilantro, and ¼ cup of the tomatillo cooking liquid, and puree. Season with salt and use right away or store in the refrigerator, covered, for up to 10 days.

Mint Lime Butter

Makes ½ cup

½ cup (1 stick) butter
1 teaspoon minced serrano chile pepper (optional)
2 tablespoons freshly squeezed lime juice
1 tablespoon shredded fresh mint, or 1 teaspoon dried

1. Place the butter and chile pepper, if using, in a small saucepan or microwave bowl. Heat over medium heat on the stove top or on high in the microwave until beginning to melt, about 1 minute.

2. Remove from the heat, whisk in the lime juice, and then swirl in the mint. Return to the heat for 1 minute more. Serve right away or set aside at room temperature and gently reheat just before serving.

◈ Pearl Barley

Pearl barley doesn't too often make the headlines, except as the companion player in beef barley soup. That's an excellent role, but it can also put in a worthy solo performance. A pressure cooker can bring this tasty grain quickly to the table, and there's an economic plus: From raw grain in the pot to serving bowl on the table, its expansion properties are impressive, making it a good bet as a filler carb on a plate of vegetables, poached chicken, or roast beef when there's a crowd to feed.

Makes 6 side dish servings

2 tablespoons butter
½ cup pearl barley, well rinsed
1 teaspoon salt
2 cups water

1. Melt the butter in the pressure cooker over medium-high heat. Add the barley and salt and stir until well mixed. Add the water,

Featuring Pearl Barley

To highlight pearl barley as a side dish, top it with:

- Cranberry Sauce with Ginger and Tangerine (page 299) and Crispy Shallot Rings (page 54)
- Creamy Horseradish Sauce (page 65) and flat-leaf chopped parsley
- Thickened Yogurt (page 231) and shredded fresh mint
- Wilted greens and Salted Lemon Rounds (page 40)
- Fresh sprouts, such as pea or sunflower sprouts, and a drizzle of walnut oil
- Slivers of sun-dried tomato and slivers of ham

lock on the lid, and bring to pressure over high heat, 3 to 4 minutes. Reduce the heat to medium-high and cook for 20 minutes. Remove from the heat and let sit for 10 minutes to finish cooking.

2. With the steam vent pointed away from your face, gently release any remaining pressure. Set the lid ajar and let sit for 10 minutes more (see Note). Serve warm. Store in the refrigerator, covered, for up to 5 days, then reheat before using.

Note: If the barley seems too wet, cook it a little longer over medium-high heat, without the lid, until it's no longer soupy but still moist.

Kasha

Kasha is the homey term used in Russian and eastern European Jewish cooking for buckwheat groats. Though it seems like a cereal grain, such as bulgur or rice, it is more closely related to sorrel and rhubarb, members of the same family, except buckwheat is grown for its seeds rather than its leaves or stalks. Odd as it is to contemplate, the same plant, actually a native of Asia, in Japanese cooking is more commonly turned into soba, the noodle of such poetically named dishes as moon viewing noodles and summer noodles. Either as noodle or whole grain, kasha retains a pronounced flavor that stands on its own or melds smoothly with other elements.

Makes 6 to 8 side dish servings

2 tablespoons butter, plus extra for topping
1 cup kasha (whole buckwheat groats)
2 cups Chicken Broth (page 18), Beef Broth (page 15), or water
Salt to taste

1. Melt the butter in a pressure cooker over medium-high heat. Add the kasha and cook, stirring, until toasty, about 2 minutes. Stir in the broth and lock on the lid. Bring to pressure over high heat. Reduce the heat to medium and cook for 3 minutes. Remove from the heat and let sit for 10 minutes to finish cooking.

2. With the steam vent pointed away from your face, gently release any remaining pressure. Add the salt and fluff with a fork. Top with several pats of butter and, without stirring, set aside with the lid ajar for 5 to 10 minutes. Serve while still warm.

Kasha Variations

To further plump a bowl of steaming kasha, top it with one or all of these: sunflower or pea sprouts, Crispy Shallot Rings (page 54), or thinly sliced dates.

To turn kasha into a breakfast porridge, cook 1 cup kasha with 3 cups milk (in place of the broth) according to the directions above. Serve with sugar and cream on the side, as you would oatmeal or other hot cereals.

To make kasha fritters, mix 2 cups cooked kasha with 1 large egg, 2 tablespoons all-purpose flour, and 2 tablespoons finely chopped yellow or white onion. Form into individual patties and fry in 2 tablespoons vegetable oil over medium-high heat until golden on both sides, about 5 minutes alto-gether. Drain on paper towels and serve warm. For dinner, accompany with sour cream on the side. For breakfast, accompany with jam, especially strawberry or rhubarb. For brunch, serve with both sour cream and jam and also smoked salmon on the side. Makes eight 2-inch patties.

Lively Legumes

The Leguminosae family of plants includes some of the most important and familiar food crops known to man: beans and peas. Botantists divide the family into two genera—*phaseolus*, or beans, and *lathyrus*, or peas. When it comes to the common names of the different cultivars of each genera, the distinctions are somewhat arbitrary. By now all have crisscrossed the oceans and seas to become established crops and garden edibles regardless of their original continental or ethnic boundaries. And that's a good thing, because dried beans and peas are among the most nutritious and, when freshly cooked, not canned, delicious of foods. The pressure cooker is a dream machine for turning out pot after pot of them on the spot.

A genuine benefit of pressure cooking legumes is that there is no need for pre-soaking. All the recipes in this chapter, with the exception of Boston beans, have been designed and tested to avoid that time-taking step.

A note: In all my years of cooking both professionally and casually, I have been mystified by the inherent nature of dried beans. When they're done, they're done. And, when they're not done and you stop the cooking, they cannot be coaxed in any way into softness. *Al dente* beans remain *al dente* beans forever. For tender beans, it's best to err on the side of a little too much and then let them rest to room temperature so they refirm a bit and won't disintegrate at the next stage of the recipe.

Lively Legumes

◇ Boil'd Peanuts

I always wondered what to do with raw peanuts. Roast them, yes, but that's already done for you and so nicely with many choices about exactly how: in or out of the shell, salted, not salted, pureed into chunky peanut butter. Then I was introduced to boil'd peanuts by Keith Fullington, a backyard neighbor, who grew up in Macon, Georgia. Now I think there's not a better way to have a bowl of peanuts in the shell. Like the Japanese nibble, edamame (soybeans in the pod), they're salty on the outside, legumy good on the inside, and, with a pressure cooker, easy to have.

Makes ½ pound

½ pound raw peanuts in the shell
5 cups water
1½ tablespoons salt

1. Place all the ingredients in the pressure cooker and stir to dissolve the salt a bit. Lock on the lid and bring to pressure over high heat, 5 to 6 minutes. Reduce the heat to medium-low and cook for 50 minutes, adjusting the heat from time to time to prevent boiling over. Remove from the heat and let sit for 15 minutes to finish cooking.

2. With the steam vent pointed away from your face, gently release any remaining pressure. Drain in a colander. Let sit until cool enough to handle and enjoy warm.

Note: Peanuts cooked this way are essentially a fresh, albeit well-done, vegetable. They will keep at room temperature overnight, but after that store them in the refrigerator, covered, for up to 1 week, or they will mold.

◇ ◇ ◇

◈ Basic Chickpeas

Somehow chickpeas (also known as garbanzo beans) have come to mean canned morsels to puree into a ho-hum dip or toss into salad almost as an afterthought. I strongly recommend, instead, cooking them in a pressure cooker. I can almost guarantee a taste revelation that will lead to more chickpeas. With one batch of the basic cooked chickpeas below, you can make a fabulous vegetable side dish or vegetarian entrée, a crunchy snack, the ever popular hummus, or the equally popular three-bean salad (see page 270).

Makes 5 cups

2 cups dried chickpeas
6 cups water

1. Place the chickpeas and water in the pressure cooker and lock on the lid. Bring to pressure over high heat, about 7 minutes. Reduce the heat to medium–high and cook for 10 minutes. Remove from the heat and let sit for 15 minutes to finish cooking.

2. With the steam vent pointed away from your face, gently release any remaining pressure. Use right away or cool and refrigerate, covered, for up to 1 week.

Roasted Chickpeas

Makes 2 cups

5 cups Basic Chickpeas (above), drained
Olive oil, for greasing the pans
Salt to taste

1. Preheat the oven to 300°F. Spread the chickpeas on 2 baking sheets generously greased with olive oil. Roll the chickpeas around to coat all over. Roast, shaking once or twice, until a bit crunchy and golden, about 1¼ hours.

2. Remove, lightly sprinkle with salt, and serve in a snack bowl.

Hummus *Tahini paste (also known as sesame paste) is available in some supermarkets along-side the matzo crackers and kosher salt in the Jewish or Middle Eastern foods section. It's also available in natural food stores. Be sure to stir it well before using.*

Makes 2 cups

1 cup Basic Chickpeas (page 258)
5 cloves garlic, pressed or minced
⅓ cup freshly squeezed lemon juice
3 tablespoons tahini paste
½ cup extra virgin olive oil
½ teaspoon salt

Place all the ingredients in a food processor and puree as fine as possible. Use right away or store in the refrigerator, covered, for up to 1 week.

Dried Beans and Peas: Pretty as a Picture in the Field or Garden

The Leguminosae family also includes many decorative plants that are better known by their common names. They range from trees, such as the broad-canopied, spring-flowering acacias, with iridescent yellow blossoms that light up the landscape in spring when the sun still rests low on the horizon for most of the day, to decorative sweet peas, which elicit a similar bright joy with their many-hued, multiple flowers on vines that sprawl around and about the ground and reach over fences in their spring exuberance.

Then there are the other edibles of the family that have evolved both underground and above seemingly for the specific purpose of seasoning and spicing. A few are:

- Licorice: Grown for its sweet root and similar in flavor to anise, licorice has been used since Grecian times for medicinal purposes and, more familiarly, licorice candy.
- Tamarind: A legume harvested for its pod more than for its seed, it adds a sweet/tart taste similar to sun-dried apricots. Tamarind is much adored in many cuisines, especially Turkish, North African, South African, and Indian.
- Fenugreek: Its seeds are a major component of many curry spice blends; its ground leaves are used in eastern Mediterranean cooking to add a pungent, musty seasoning; and its leaves, freshly steamed, are enjoyed as a side dish in Indian cooking.

Omi's Chickpeas with Lime and Onion Ring Topping

I met Omi Aurora and her husband, Indir, when they came several times from India to visit with their son, his wife, and the two grandchildren who were schoolmates of my son. Eventually, Omi and Indir decided to retire close by to be near family. That's how it came to be that in their parlor, I was the lucky recipient of the best cup of tea I've ever sipped and of this recipe Omi so generously shared. The garam masala spices are not difficult to find and blend together. Or you can purchase the mix in ethnic markets that cater to an Indian clientele.   Makes 6 to 8 servings

2 tablespoons vegetable oil

3 cups Basic Chickpeas (page 258), plus 1 cup of the cooking liquid

½ teaspoon Garam Masala (recipe follows)

¼ teaspoon red pepper flakes

1 tablespoon peeled and coarsely grated fresh ginger

½ teaspoon anardana (optional; see right)

1 teaspoon salt

1 tablespoon freshly squeezed lime juice

Thinly sliced onion rings, for garnish

Sprigs fresh cilantro, for garnish

Lime wedges, for garnish

1. Heat the oil in the pressure cooker over medium-high heat. Stir in the chickpeas and their cooking liquid, the Garam Masala, pepper flakes, ginger, anardana (if using), and salt. Lock on the lid and bring to pressure over high heat, about 1 minute. Reduce the heat to medium-high and cook for 5 minutes. Remove from the heat and let sit for 5 minutes to finish cooking.

2. With the steam vent pointed away from your face, gently release any remaining pressure. Stir in the lime juice and adjust the salt. Top with the onion rings and cilantro sprigs and serve the lime wedges on the side.

A Mystery Spice

Anardana is a spice of Indian cooking, and it's a true exotic. I haven't found it in any other cuisine, even in the most esoteric concoctions of my Armenian relatives in Sacramento, California, who had bushels of pomegranates right off the trees in their gardens. Essentially anardana is pulverized dried pomegranate seeds. As with all special spices, it gives a certain *sine qua non* to the dish. You can substitute a teaspoon of juice from a fresh pomegranate or a tiny pinch of tamarind rind with a tiny pinch of sugar, which together suggest the special sour/sweet taste of anardana.

Garam Masala *Not just for spicing Indian foods, garam masala travels east to Singapore and west to the Pacific coast of the United States, where innovative chefs, inspired by its immigrant users, employ it for all manner of vegetable and meat and grain dishes.*   Makes ¼ cup

1 tablespoon freshly ground black pepper
1 tablespoon coriander seeds, smashed
1 tablespoon cardamom seeds, smashed
1 teaspoon ground cumin
¼ teaspoon ground cloves
¼ teaspoon ground cinnamon

Grind all the ingredients together in a spice grinder mill. Store in a tightly closed jar for up to 1 month.

◊ ◊ ◊

Lentils: A Dried Pea of Many Hues

A yellow lentil looks like a green split pea, only yellow. A green lentil looks a bit like a brown lentil, only rounder and flatter, and neither are split. All are dried peas. All are ancient legume goodness for both the land, whereon they're grown not only for food but also to replenish the soil with their nitrogen-fixing power, and for the table, where upon they're set in many a style around the world.

How to Avoid Foaming Up

Unlike other legumes or grains, lentils and split peas will invariably foam up and boil over even with a close watch on the pot. The sound creates a terrible fright and the overflow creates a terrible mess. So, I always cook lentils and split peas with a teaspoon or so of oil—somehow it prevents that unwelcome surprise.

◈ Basic Brown or Green Lentils

Brown lentils are the kind that come in packages in the pasta and grains section in the grocery store. Green lentils are the kind that come in boxes in upscale or gourmet markets. Both can be found in bins in markets that carry bulk grains and legumes. The taste difference between the two is subtle: I find the green lentils nuttier, the brown lentils a bit less flavorful. There are also texture differences: The green lentils are firmer and tend to remain individual, so they're the better choice for salad. Brown lentils are starchier and tend to mash more easily into a puree. An important difference to note, however, is that for salad the lentils, brown or green, cook for a mere one minute in the pressure cooker, whereas lentils destined for soup need five minutes to soften.

Makes about 2½ cups

1 cup dried brown or green lentils
2 cups water
1 teaspoon vegetable oil

What About the Red Lentils?

Red lentils are a delight to behold, wondrous in their red-orange color that is not often matched in the world of vegetables, except maybe for some of the heirloom tomato or beet varieties. I use them as a salad with barely blanched green peas, fresh parsley, and a soupçon of olive oil. I also use them to perk up a main plate dish that cries out for a bit of color. In any case, I never cook them in the pressure cooker because in my experience, red lentils are ready to drain and cool almost the very minute they come to a boil on the stove top.

1. Rinse the lentils and place them in the pressure cooker with the water and oil. Lock on the lid and bring to pressure over high heat, about 5 minutes.

If using for salad, reduce the heat to medium and cook for 1 minute.

If using for soup, reduce the heat to medium and cook for 5 minutes. Remove from the heat and let sit for 5 minutes to finish cooking.

2. With the steam vent pointed away from your face, gently release any remaining pressure. Drain and rinse briefly under cool water. Use right away or store in the refrigerator, covered, for up to 3 days.

◇ Lentil Salad with Feta Cheese and Walnut Oil *Fresh-cooked*

lentils, preferably the French green kind because they're nuttier; feta cheese, preferably imported; and pure walnut oil. Not such out-of-the-way ingredients these days; you can find them in most (or many) urban groceries. But the combination is extraordinary. From mainstay of my deli counter to soccer team potlucks, neighborhood holiday buffets, and backyard summer picnics, this salad is a take-out dish that never gets tired. Makes about 3 cups, or 6 to 8 side dish servings

2 to 2½ cups Basic Brown or Green Lentils (page 262)

3 scallions, trimmed and thinly sliced

2 tablespoons chopped fresh flat-leaf parsley

¼ cup freshly squeezed lemon juice

Salt and freshly ground black pepper to taste

⅓ cup walnut oil or extra virgin olive oil,
    plus extra for drizzling

Inside leaves from 1 head romaine lettuce

½ cup crumbled feta cheese

Place the lentils, scallions, parsley, lemon juice, salt and pepper, and oil in a large bowl and toss to mix. Cover the bottom of a serving platter with the lettuce leaves. Spoon the lentils on top of the lettuce and sprinkle the cheese over the lentils. Drizzle a little extra walnut oil over all and serve.

◈ Basic Yellow Lentils or Split Peas

Most cookbook writers addressing the pressure cooker speak only about brown or green lentils for soup; some even say lentils are not candidates for the pressure cooker at all because they turn mushy. However, for a yellow lentil Greek porridge or Indian dal, mush is the point, and the pressure cooker can produce it in a veritable flash. Vary the spices and you can fly from the Mediterranean Sea to the Indian Ocean in the flick of a wrist and solve many a menu quandary in the process.

Makes about 3 cups, or 6 to 8 side dish servings

1 cup dried yellow lentils, rinsed

3 cups water

1 teaspoon vegetable oil

Salt to taste

Butter (optional), for serving

Freshly ground black pepper to taste (optional), for serving

1. Combine the lentils, water, and oil in the pressure cooker. Lock on the lid and bring to pressure over high heat, about 5 minutes. Reduce the heat to medium–low and cook for 3 minutes. Remove from the heat and let sit for 10 minutes to finish cooking.

2. With the steam vent pointed away from your face, gently release any remaining pressure. Season with salt. Serve warm with a pat of butter and a few grinds of black pepper, if desired. Or see the following recipes.

◌ Yellow Lentil or Split Pea Porridge in the Mediterranean Style

I will be forever thankful to my sometime cookbook co-author and longtime dear friend, Susanna Hoffman, for opening my eyes to the yellow lentils in the side-by-side lentil bins where we often shop together for recipe ingredients. Yellow lentils have a special earthy taste and gentle glow, unique among the dried pea family, that she came to know well during her sojourns on Santorini. You can put together the lentils and other ingredients in a microwave dish in advance of serving and set it aside at room temperature for up to three hours. Just before you're ready to place it on the table, heat it in the microwave on high for one to two minutes, until it's as warm as you like.

Makes 6 servings

3 cups Basic Yellow Lentils or Split Peas (page 264), warm
½ teaspoon finely shredded fresh sage, or ¼ teaspoon dried
1 tablespoon chopped fresh chives
1 tablespoon capers
1 tablespoon freshly squeezed lemon juice
1 tablespoon extra virgin olive oil

Place the lentils in a serving dish. Sprinkle on the sage, chives, and capers. Pour the lemon juice and olive oil over the top and toss to mix (the lentils will mash into a porridge). Serve warm.

◎ Yellow Lentil Fritters

If you make a batch of yellow lentils just for these fritters, they need to be cooled completely and refrigerated overnight so they're like leftovers, even if they're not. Otherwise, you won't get nicely crisp fritters.

Makes six 2½-inch fritters

1 cup Basic Yellow Lentils or Split Peas (page 264)
1 small egg, lightly beaten
¼ to ⅓ cup all-purpose flour, plus extra for dusting
1 teaspoon chopped fresh oregano, or ½ teaspoon dried
1 tablespoon minced scallion (green part only)
Salt and freshly ground black pepper to taste
Olive oil, for frying
Thin lemon wedges, for garnish

1. Place the lentils in a medium-size bowl. Whisk in the egg, then the flour, and mix. Blend in the oregano, scallion, and salt and pepper. Set aside.

2. Pour olive oil into a heavy skillet to a depth of ¼ inch. Set over medium-high heat until beginning to smoke. Make six ½-inch-thick patties, ¼ to ⅓ cup each. Dust the outside of each patty with a little flour. Add as many as will fit in the pan without crowding and fry, turning once, until golden on both sides, about 3 minutes altogether. Transfer to a paper towel and continue with another round until all are fried. Serve warm, garnished with the lemon wedges.

◎ Yellow Lentil or Split Pea Dal with Cilantro Mint Chutney

To those not familiar with Indian cuisine, dal is a somewhat confusing term because it refers both to all of the dried legumes—peas, beans, and lentils—and also to the culinary preparations of them. To further complicate matters, so extensive and refined are the dal dishes that there's a distinction made between the yellow split peas used in European cooking and the yellow lentils of the Indian kitchen. Practically speaking, however, yellow split peas work fine for dals. Here, turmeric exponentially increases the yellow of the dal, and the chutney adds a zesty green to the composition.   Makes 4 side dish servings

¼ teaspoon ground turmeric
3 cups Basic Yellow Lentils or Split Peas (page 264), warm
⅔ cup Cilantro Mint Chutney (recipe follows), for serving

Stir the turmeric into the lentils and, if necessary, heat them on the stove top or in a microwave oven. Spoon ¼ cup of the chutney over the top. Serve with the remaining chutney on the side.

Cilantro Mint Chutney *Certainly not Major Grey's famous chutney so full of chunky mango bits, this cilantro, mint, and fresh chile pepper mixture is nonetheless a traditional Indian uncooked chutney. It will keep overnight in the refrigerator, covered, but loses its punch after that.*

Makes about ⅔ cup

1 cup chopped fresh cilantro
½ cup chopped fresh mint leaves
1 fresh jalapeño chile pepper, coarsely chopped
¼ teaspoon ground coriander
¼ teaspoon salt
¼ teaspoon sugar
1½ tablespoons freshly squeezed lemon juice
1 tablespoon water

Combine all the ingredients in a food processor and finely chop without pureeing. Use right away or store in the refrigerator up to overnight.

◈ Basic Black-Eyed Peas

Black-eyed peas, also called cowpeas, grace the garden in summer with their lilac-tinged creamy white flowers and provide lacy fill to flower arrangements. In fall and on through winter, the seeds fill many a nourishing pot from Asia to Africa to the American South, where they're considered a token of good luck for the new year.

Makes about 4 cups

1 cup dried black-eyed peas
4 cups water
½ teaspoon salt

1. Place the peas, water, and salt in the pressure cooker, lock on the lid, and bring to pressure over high heat, about 5 minutes. Reduce the heat to medium-high and cook for 5 minutes. Remove from the heat and let sit for 5 minutes to finish cooking.

2. With the steam vent pointed away from your face, gently release any remaining pressure and drain into a colander. Set aside to drip-dry for a few minutes, then use right away or store in the refrigerator, covered, for up to 5 days.

◈ Black-Eyed Peas with Sun-Dried Tomatoes, Shallot, Thyme, and Shredded Ham

Long after I grew up, went away to college, and established my own home, my mother often traveled from her house to mine with a pot of black-eyed peas on January 1 to make sure I would fare well in the coming year. In a bold-faced revisionist version, I tender the black-eyed peas in the same spirit. (She actually likes mine, and sometimes we serve the two side by side.) If you have a large family for such celebrations, double the recipe.

Makes about 4½ cups, or 6 side dish servings

4 cups Basic Black-Eyed Peas (page 268), warm

4 oil-packed sun-dried tomato halves, drained

1 small fresh tomato, finely diced

2 tablespoons chopped shallot

1 teaspoon chopped fresh thyme, or $\frac{1}{2}$ teaspoon dried

1 tablespoon balsamic vinegar

1 tablespoon olive oil

1 cup shredded thinly sliced ham, for topping

$\frac{1}{4}$ cup chopped fresh flat-leaf parsley, for topping

Toss together all the ingredients except the ham and parsley. If necessary, reheat on the stove top or in the microwave. Top with the ham and parsley and serve with warm good spirit.

◇ Basic Red Kidney Beans

Red kidneys are the bean of at least three renowned dishes of American cooking: red beans and rice, chili, and three-bean salad. Recipes for each of those follow, but first the basics.

Makes 3 cups

1$\frac{1}{2}$ cups dried red kidney beans

6 cups water

1$\frac{1}{2}$ teaspoons salt

1. Place the beans and water in the pressure cooker. Lock on the lid and bring to pressure over high heat, about 6 minutes. Reduce the heat to medium and cook for 20 minutes. Remove from the heat and let sit for 10 minutes to finish cooking.

2. With the steam vent pointed away from your face, gently release any remaining pressure, taking good care because there will probably be some. Carefully remove the lid and stir in the salt. Use right away or cool completely and refrigerate, covered, in the cooking liquid for up to 5 days.

◇ Red Beans, Green Beans, and Chickpeas in a Classic Three-Bean Salad

In a fresh take on what has perhaps become too staid and routine an offering for picnics and buffet fare, three-bean salad is given new life with just-now cooked, not canned, ingredients.

Makes 6 cups, or 8 to 10 side dish servings

2 cups Basic Red Kidney Beans (page 269)

2 cups fresh green beans, ends trimmed and cut into ½-inch pieces, blanched in simmering water until soft (6 to 8 minutes), and drained

2 cups Basic Chickpeas (page 258)

1 small yellow, white, or red onion, halved and thinly sliced

2 teaspoons chopped fresh oregano, or 1 teaspoon dried

¼ cup chopped fresh flat-leaf parsley

¼ cup red wine vinegar

1 tablespoon freshly squeezed lemon juice

Tiny pinch of cayenne (optional)

½ cup extra virgin olive oil

Salt and freshly ground pepper to taste

Place all the ingredients in a large bowl and toss to mix. Set aside to marinate for at least 2 hours or store in the refrigerator, covered, for up to 2 days. Serve at room temperature.

◇ ◇ ◇

◎ Not-So-Classic Red Beans and Rice with Fresh Thyme and Andouille Sausage

There's almost no way to go wrong with a combination of beans, whatever color, and rice, whichever style. Even so, the red beans and rice of Louisiana are renowned in that field. The blue ribbon is given not only for the undoubtable nutrition the dish proffers but also for its rich flavor and good looks. In my modern take on the classic, red beans and rice are seasoned with fresh, not dried, thyme, garnished with a few thin rounds of sausage or ham over the top, not mixed in, and sprinkled with fresh parsley. Otherwise, it's the same hearty, filling, satisfying dish of tradition. Makes 4 to 6 servings

3 cups Basic Red Kidney Beans (page 269),
    plus ¼ cup of the cooking liquid, warm
1 teaspoon chopped fresh thyme
2 tablespoons butter, at room temperature
1 tablespoon red wine vinegar
Salt and freshly ground black pepper to taste
3 cups cooked long grain white rice, warm
1 small andouille sausage, cut into 12 thin rounds, or 4 slices
    smoked ham, cut into thin shreds, for garnish
¼ cup chopped fresh flat-leaf parsley, for garnish
Tabasco or other hot pepper sauce, for serving

1. Combine the kidney beans and their liquid, the thyme, butter, vinegar, and salt and pepper in a large bowl and toss to mix.

2. Place the rice on a serving platter. Mound the beans over the rice. Arrange the sausage rounds over the top and garnish with the parsley. Serve warm with the hot sauce on the side.

Basic White Beans

White beans vary widely in size, cooking time, taste, and use, to the extent that it's not possible to pinpoint one neat instruction or basic recipe. Below is a guide that tells the measurements and basic cooking times for the sorts often used, with the proviso that you may have to boil them a bit, uncovered, if they are not quite tender. On the following pages are recipes for some of the best ways to make each kind a bean to remember.

For 1 cup unsoaked dry beans (all take about 5 minutes to come to pressure):

- *Great Northern (large white) beans:* Cook for 25 minutes in $2\frac{1}{2}$ cups water and let sit for 5 minutes. Makes about $2\frac{1}{2}$ cups.

- *Navy (pea or small white) beans:* Cook for 25 minutes in 2 cups water and let sit for 5 minutes. Makes 2 cups.

- *Lima (butter) beans, large or small:* Cook for 15 minutes in 2 cups water and let sit for 10 minutes. Makes 2 cups for large limas, about $2\frac{1}{2}$ cups for baby limas.

- *Cannellini (Italian white kidney) beans:* Cook for 25 minutes in 2 cups water and let sit for 10 minutes. Makes about 2 cups.

Flageolets

Traditionally, flageolets, the French light green dried haricots (beans), are used for white beans Bretonne. Upscale supermarkets and fancy food stores carry them, usually in boxes but sometimes in bulk bins. As on the stove top, flageolets take longer to pressure cook than Great Northerns: Add 1 cup more water to the basic recipe for Great Northern white beans, increase the cooking time to 40 minutes, and allow the flageolets to sit for 10 minutes before using. If they are not yet tender, boil them with the lid ajar for 5 to 10 minutes more, adding a little water, if necessary.

◈ White Beans Bretonne

I discovered Elizabeth David's white beans Bretonne style at the beginning of my cooking career, when I was the chef at Chez Panisse restaurant in its formative days. I used the Italian white kidney beans called cannellini and served them with lamb, as David describes and as they do in Brittany. Now, as then, it's an all-satisfying combination and an all-satisfying way to have white beans. For the just-right lamb dish, see Lamb Shanks Braised with Garlic, Rosemary, and White Wine (page 92).

Makes 3 cups, or 6 to 8 side dish servings

2 tablespoons butter
1 small yellow or white onion, chopped
2 medium-size tomatoes, peeled (see page 24),
    seeded, and coarsely chopped
1 small bay leaf
1 teaspoon chopped fresh thyme, or ½ teaspoon dried
½ cup dry white wine
¼ teaspoon salt
2 cups cooked Great Northern, cannellini, or flageolet beans (see page 272),
    plus ½ cup of the cooking liquid
Juices from a lamb dish (optional)
1 tablespoon chopped fresh flat-leaf parsley, for garnish

1. Melt the butter in a heavy sauté pan over medium heat. Add the onion and cook, stirring occasionally, until wilted but not browned, about 5 minutes. Stir in the tomatoes, bay leaf, thyme, and wine. Continue cooking, stirring occasionally, until the mixture has become saucy, about 5 minutes.

2. Add the salt, and beans and their cooking liquid. Continue cooking until everything is heated through, about 5 minutes. Stir in the lamb juices, if using, sprinkle with the parsley, and serve.

Lima Bean Salad with Watercress, Yogurt Garlic Dressing, and Cracked Black Pepper

Lima beans are named for the city in Peru where they first grew. They are also called butter beans, maybe for their soft, mealy texture similar to a well-cooked potato that cries out for butter and needs not much more to be delicious. They are the bean of succotash and many other Southern dishes. They also give themselves over to a modern, somewhat fusion interpretation in a warm salad bedded on watercress and moistened with an unusual yogurt dressing. Either large or baby limas will do. They cook in about the same time; the baby limas yield slightly more than the large ones.

Makes 2 cups, or 4 to 6 side dish servings

3 cups watercress, leaves and tender sprigs only
2 cups cooked lima beans (see page 272)
½ cup Yogurt Garlic Dressing (recipe follows)
2 teaspoons black peppercorns

1. Rinse and spin dry the watercress. Arrange the leaves on a serving platter. Spread the limas over the watercress and spoon the dressing over the beans.

2. Place the peppercorns on a wood counter, cover with a towel, and pound them until coarsely cracked. Sprinkle over the dressing and serve.

Note: If you have a spice grinder or pepper mill that is adjustable to a rough grind, either works equally well to crack the peppercorns without the noise of pounding.

◌ ◌ ◌

Yogurt Garlic Dressing   *Plain blanched or boiled vegetables, otherwise unadorned chicken breast or fish fillet, and sturdy salad greens, such as escarole, radicchio, or Belgian endive, all come alive with this dressing. Romaine lettuce leaves mixed with croutons and tossed with it gives new meaning to a Caesar-type salad.*   Makes 1 cup

²⁄₃ cup plain yogurt
¹⁄₃ cup extra virgin olive oil
4 cloves garlic, pressed, then minced with ¾ teaspoon salt
3 tablespoons freshly squeezed lemon juice

In a medium-size bowl, whisk the yogurt until smooth. Slowly whisk in the oil until completely incorporated. Stir in the garlic and salt mixture and the lemon juice. Use right away or refrigerate, covered, for up to 1 week.

◈ Basic Cranberry Beans   *Cranberry beans, mottled creamy beige, cordovan brown, and mulberry red on the outside, cook up faintly pink. But that subdued color merely hints at the intense legume flavor.*   Makes 2½ cups

1 cup dried cranberry beans
2 cups water
½ teaspoon salt

1. Combine the beans and water in the pressure cooker. Lock on the lid and bring to pressure over high heat, about 4 minutes. Reduce the heat to medium-low and cook for 30 minutes. Remove from the heat and let sit for 15 minutes.

2. With the steam vent pointed away from your face, gently release any remaining pressure. Remove the lid and stir in the salt. Use right away or cool to room temperature and refrigerate in the cooking liquid, covered, for up to 4 days.

◇ Cranberry Bean Salad with Arugula, Dried Cranberries, and Hazelnut Oil

A salad of cranberry beans with dried cranberries takes the fall/winter beans and berries beyond Thanksgiving and the winter holidays to the next season, perhaps a picnic or summer buffet table. Since the salad is equally good warm or chilled the next day, I let the occasion dictate which way I serve it.

Makes 4 to 6 servings

¼ cup dried cranberries
2 cups arugula leaves
2½ cups Basic Cranberry Beans (page 275), drained but still warm
2 tablespoons minced shallot
2 tablespoons hazelnut oil
½ teaspoon salt

1. Place the dried cranberries in a small saucepan and add water barely to cover. Bring to a boil, drain right away, and press with a spoon to get rid of excess moisture.

2. Spread 1½ cups of the arugula on a serving platter. Combine the warm beans, shallot, oil, salt, cranberries, and remaining ½ cup arugula in a medium-size bowl. Gently toss to mix and mound on top of the arugula on the platter. Serve right away.

◇ Pasta e Fagioli

Pasta together with beans in the same bowl may seem an odd pairing, but that's pasta e fagioli, one of the most satisfying peasant dishes ever devised. Cranberry beans are traditional, or use Great Northern or white cannellini beans.

Makes 4 servings

1 pound pork spareribs
5 cups water
3 cups Beef Broth (page 15)

2 large cloves garlic, minced or pressed

2 tablespoons tomato paste

1 small dried red chile pepper

1 bay leaf

1 cup dried cranberry beans

¼ cup elbow macaroni

1 teaspoon salt

Extra virgin olive oil, for garnish

½ cup freshly grated parmesan cheese, for serving

1. Combine the spareribs and 4 cups of the water in the pressure cooker. Bring to a boil and skim the foam off the top. Add the broth, garlic, tomato paste, chile pepper, bay leaf, and cranberry beans and stir to mix. Lock on the lid and bring to pressure over high heat, about 5 minutes. Reduce the heat to medium-low and cook for 40 minutes. Remove from the heat and let sit for 15 minutes to finish cooking.

2. With the steam vent pointed away from your face, gently release any remaining pressure. Remove the lid and take out and discard the pork ribs, chile pepper, and bay leaf. Lift out about 2 cups of the beans with a slotted spoon and puree them in a food processor.

3. Bring the beans and the liquid left in the pot, along with the remaining 1 cup water, to a boil. Add the macaroni and cook until *al dente*, 5 to 6 minutes. Stir in the salt and the bean puree. Ladle into individual bowls and garnish with a swirl of olive oil. Serve right away, with the parmesan cheese on the side.

Pressure-Cooked Boston Beans

Boston beans hardly need an introduction; they are a heralded bean staple of American cooking. Still, there's conversation about how exactly they should be prepared. There's no question about mustard being a necessary ingredient, but the addition or not of tomato paste has become a matter of scholarly interest. From established and reliable cookbook authors to modern ones, there's no agreement. I'd say the taste scale tilts toward no tomato paste. On the other hand, with a little touch of it, the earthy brown takes on a deeper red glow, so I leave it up to you. Garnish lover that I am, I am never tempted to embellish a pot of Boston beans. Any extra topping might distract from that lovely color.

Makes 3 cups, or 4 to 6 side dish servings

1 teaspoon vegetable oil
2 ounces blanched salt pork (see Note page 70), coarsely chopped
³⁄₄ cup chopped yellow or white onion
1½ tablespoons prepared mustard
1 teaspoon tomato paste (optional)
2 tablespoons dark brown sugar
2 tablespoons molasses
1 cup dried small white beans
2 cups water
½ teaspoon salt
¼ teaspoon freshly ground black pepper

1. Place the oil and salt pork in the pressure cooker. Stir over medium heat until the salt pork begins to curl, about 1 minute. Add the remaining ingredients and stir to mix. Lock on the lid and

Herbal Prowess

Epazote is an herb native to the Americas. It grows wild like a weed from Mexico and California to as far east as Florida. Though it has been used for centuries in Native American cooking, its musty flavor and, to some, overpowering aroma never caught on beyond Mexico and somewhat in the Caribbean. Its botanical name, *Chenopodium ambrosiodes*, gives a certain lilt to its more mundane aliases—goosefoot, pigweed, wormweed (because it is supposed to purge hookworm), and bean herb (because it is thought to be anti-flatulent). In Mexican cooking, especially for the black beans and other soups of Oaxaca, I suspect it is mainly used for its singular flavor reminiscent of dry lands and sagebrush.

bring to pressure over high heat, about 3 minutes. Reduce the heat to medium and cook for 25 minutes. Remove from the heat and let sit for 5 minutes to finish cooking.

2. With the steam vent pointed away from your face, gently release any remaining pressure. Let sit another 5 minutes, then serve.

◈ Basic Black Beans

In Oaxaca, Mexico, frijoles almost surely means black beans. There they are the pot bean of choice, the stuff of tamale fillings, the base of refrito-style bean paste to accompany grilled beef, and the "soup" for masa dumplings. Rendered as black bean chili, their deep, rich taste and unique ebony color have become popular in American cooking to the extent of being a staple of the new healthy menus. Adding the herb epazote is a finesse of Mexican cooking; marjoram will approximate its flavor.

Makes 3 cups

Black Beans for Dinner, or Breakfast

If you're one who adores a fresh egg and also a pot of beans, putting the two together makes an unbeatable comfy meal, especially if the beans are black ones and the eggs are very fresh. To serve yourself and maybe another too: Dish some warm black beans into 1 or 2 large soup bowls, 1 bowl per serving. Fry or poach 1 or 2 eggs per serving, depending on the hunger factor. Set the eggs on top of the warm beans, serve with tomato salsa if you have some, and enjoy.

1½ cups dried black beans
3 cups water
2 large sprigs fresh epazote, or 1 teaspoon dried (optional)
Salt to taste

1. Combine the beans, water, and epazote, if using, in the pressure cooker. Lock on the lid and bring to pressure over high heat, about 6 minutes. Reduce the heat to medium-high and cook for 25 minutes. Remove from the heat and let sit for 10 minutes to finish cooking.

2. With the steam vent pointed away from your face, gently release any remaining pressure. Stir in the salt and use right away or cool completely and refrigerate in the liquid, covered, for up to 1 week. May be frozen for up to 6 weeks.

◈ ◈ ◈

◎ Black Bean Chili with Chipotle Cream

I regularly use my large, 8-quart cooker to make a huge batch of black bean chili so there's some to freeze. The chipotle cream soothes as it adds extra spice.

Makes 6 generous servings

Warming Tortillas

For warming tortillas, there are several ways to go:

- Spread them out on a rack in a 400°F oven for about 3 minutes.
- Stack them and wrap in a damp dish towel and place in a 300°F oven for 20 minutes, or up to 30 minutes. This is a good method if you are serving a crowd because the tortillas will hold in the oven when it's turned off for up to another 20 minutes.
- Spread them in an overlapping layer in a toaster oven and toast on a light setting until softened but not crisp.
- Toast them on a barbecue grill or over a gas burner flame until beginning to char in spots, 15 to 20 seconds.
- Heat 1 or 2 tortillas at a time in a microwave for 30 seconds.

1 tablespoon peanut oil

2 medium-size yellow or white onions, finely chopped

2 large cloves garlic, finely chopped

2 teaspoons ground cumin

2 tablespoons chile powder

2 teaspoons hot paprika

1 tablespoon chopped fresh oregano, or 1 teaspoon dried

1 canned chipotle chile in adobo sauce, minced

1½ cups chopped canned tomatoes, with juices

2 cups dried black beans

4 cups water

1½ teaspoons salt

½ cup Chipotle Cream (recipe follows), for topping

Several sprigs fresh cilantro, for garnish

12 warm corn tortillas (see left), for topping

1. Heat the oil in the pressure cooker over medium-high heat until beginning to smoke. Add the onions and garlic and cook, stirring occasionally, over medium heat until wilting, about 2 minutes. Add the cumin, chile powder, paprika, oregano, chipotle chile, tomatoes and their juices, black beans, and water. Stir to mix, lock on the lid, and bring to pressure over high heat, 6 to 7 minutes. Reduce the heat to medium-low and cook for 30 minutes. Remove from the heat and let sit for 15 minutes to finish cooking.

2. With the steam vent pointed away from your face, gently release any remaining pressure. Remove the lid, stir in the salt, and let rest for 15 to 30 minutes.

3. Ladle into individual bowls, swirl some Chipotle Cream over the top, and garnish with cilantro sprigs. Serve with the warm tortillas.

Chipotle Cream *The heavy cream mixed with sour cream simulates the thick and slightly tart Mexican crema. You can also use Crème Fraîche (page 282). Chipotle chiles canned in adobo sauce are essential because they are softened and pickled in the brine-like sauce. They're different from dried chipotles, which simply won't do.*

Makes about ½ cup

½ cup heavy cream
1 tablespoon sour cream
1 canned chipotle chile in adobo sauce, minced

Combine the ingredients in a small bowl and whisk to smooth. Use right away or store in the refrigerator, covered, for up to 2 days.

◈ Black Bean Cakes with Crème Fraîche and Tomato Salsa

Makes 6 servings

2 cups Basic Black Beans (page 279), plus ¼ cup of the cooking liquid
½ small yellow or white onion, minced
2 serrano chile peppers, minced
½ teaspoon ground cumin
¼ cup all-purpose flour, plus extra for forming the cakes
Vegetable oil, for frying
½ cup Crème Fraîche (page 282), for serving
6 sprigs fresh cilantro, for serving
1 cup Tomato Salsa (page 282), for serving

1. Place the beans and their cooking liquid in a medium-size bowl and mash them with a fork or potato masher. Add the onion, chile peppers, cumin, and flour and stir to mix. Form into cakes about 3 inches wide and ¼ inch thick, coating your hands with extra flour to prevent sticking.

2. Heat 2 tablespoons oil in a large, heavy skillet over medium-high heat until beginning to smoke. Add as many cakes as will fit without crowding and fry until golden, about 1 minute on each side. Continue with another round until all the cakes are fried, transferring them to a serving platter as you go.

3. Serve right away with a dollop of the Crème Fraîche and a sprig of cilantro on each cake and with a bowl of the salsa and another of the remaining Crème Fraîche on the side.

Crème Fraîche

Makes about 1½ cups

1½ cups heavy cream
2 teaspoons buttermilk

1. Stir the cream and buttermilk together in a glass or heavy plastic container. Cover and set aside at room temperature overnight, or up to 36 hours if the weather is cool, until thick as sour cream.

2. Whisk to smooth and store in the refrigerator until ready to use. Will keep in the refrigerator, covered, for 2 weeks.

Tomato Salsa

Makes 2 cups

6 small chile peppers, such as jalapeño, serrano, or yellow wax
¼ medium-size green bell pepper, seeded
1 clove garlic, peeled
½ medium-size yellow or white onion
3 medium-size tomatoes
1 cup fresh cilantro leaves and tender stems
½ to 1 cup water
1 tablespoon tomato paste (optional)
Salt to taste

1. Coarsely chop the chile peppers, bell pepper, garlic, onion, tomatoes, and cilantro with a chef's knife or in a food processor. If using a food processor, process in batches and take care not to cut the vegetables too fine.

2. Transfer to a medium-size bowl. Stir in ½ to 1 cup water, depending on how juicy the tomatoes are. Add the tomato paste unless the tomatoes are extremely, densely rich on their own, and the salt. Cover and refrigerate for at least 3 hours (overnight is best). Will keep in the refrigerator for 1 week.

◇ Basic Pinto Beans

Pintos are a pot bean par excellence. You can cook them up and serve them as is in their tasty juices, turn them into hot New Mexico–style beans (see page 284), puree them into refritos (see page 285), use them to fill burritos, or refrigerate and save them for the day after tomorrow.

Makes about 3 cups

1½ cups dried pinto beans
6 cups water
Salt to taste

1. Place the pintos and water in the pressure cooker. Lock on the lid and bring to pressure over high heat, 6 to 8 minutes. Reduce the heat to medium and cook for 20 minutes. Remove from the heat and let sit for 10 minutes to finish cooking.

2. With the steam vent pointed away from your face, gently release any remaining pressure. Season with salt and use right away or cool and refrigerate in the pot liquid, covered, for up to 5 days.

◇ ◇ ◇

◈ Bill's New Mexico Pinto Beans

First of all, let me explain that Bill was my step-grandmother on the maternal side. She was much maligned by many in the family because she more or less rustled my grandfather away in a most unseemly manner (not that he didn't always have his own agenda). I liked her a lot, what little I knew of her, because when I knew her I was a child, outside the circle of adult concatenations. She made pot pinto beans so hot with home-grown green chiles that you would cry or die or laugh and maybe die anyway as you ate them. That's where I learned to love chiles, in the New Mexico dirt and sagebrush countryside outside Silver City, in a kitchen in an adobe house, surrounded with heat, horses (my grandfather raised and raced them, along with the cars he did the same thing with), and lots of New Mexico tumbleweed hospitality. This recipe is an approximation from the best I can remember of that eye-opening, palate-expanding taste.

Makes 4 cups, or 4 to 8 side dish servings

2 cups cooking liquid from Basic Pinto Beans (page 283)
6 jalapeño chile peppers, cut into long slivers
3 cups Basic Pinto Beans (page 283)
Salt to taste
Warm corn tortillas (see page 280), for serving

1. Combine the liquid and chiles in a large pot and bring to a boil over medium heat. Cook until the chiles are soft, about 10 minutes.

2. Add the beans to the pot and continue cooking at a gentle simmer until heated through, 5 minutes. Season with salt, ladle into bowls, and serve with a stack of warm corn tortillas.

◈ ◈ ◈

◇ Classic Refritos and Then Some

The "refrying" of the beans for refritos is not exactly a subtle proposition. It's done over high heat, in a sturdy, preferably cast-iron, skillet, and rapidly. The advantage is that both the pressure cooking of the beans and the final second refrying are quick, as long as you're on your toes. As you're stirring the beans in the skillet and judging the exact moment to stop, remember that the mixture will thicken a lot as it sits before serving.

Makes 3 cups, or 6 to 8 side dish servings

3 cups Basic Pinto Beans (page 283), with cooking liquid
2 tablespoons vegetable or olive oil
½ medium-size yellow or white onion, finely chopped
1 clove garlic, finely chopped
Salt to taste
1 cup grated Monterey Jack, white cheddar, or other tasty melting cheese,
　　for topping

1. Mash the pintos in a food processor, along with enough of the cooking liquid to make a coarse, loose, very wet mixture.

2. Heat the oil in a cast-iron or other heavy skillet over medium-high heat until beginning to smoke. Add the onion and garlic and cook, stirring occasionally, until beginning to wilt, about 2 minutes. Add one third of the mashed pintos and stir them about with a wooden spoon until most of the liquid is evaporated.

3. Add the pintos in 2 more batches, stirring after each addition, until the mixture is like a wet puree or loose cake batter, 2 to 3 minutes each time.

4. Season with the salt. Sprinkle the cheese over the top and serve warm, allowing the cheese to melt slightly as the refritos move from kitchen to table.

Traveling with Refritos

There's no need to remain traditional and limit refritos to "the fill" alongside rice on a Mexican-style meal plate or the dip for tortilla chips at the cocktail hour. They have other places to go.

Refritos Go to Denver: Somewhere on the high Rocky Mountain plain where Denver, Colorado, sits, someone now might be serving pinto bean sandwiches. At least, that's what I hear from Susanna Hoffman's reminiscence of her childhood Denver fare. These bean sandwiches are made up of two pieces of bread, buttered on one side each, and slathered with refritos. That's plenty good enough, but if we were to go chic in modern style, a small dollop of thinly sliced onion steeped in 1 cup red wine vinegar with 1 tablespoon sugar for 30 minutes would be nice on the side.

Refritos Go to Boston: On the East Coast, similar bean sandwiches are enjoyed with Pressure-Cooked Boston Beans (page 277), a kind of sweet refritos. If you stretch your imagination, you can spread refritos on Boston brown bread.

Refritos Go to Italy: For an Italian interpretation, make individual bruschetta toasts, spread them with a tiny but generous mound of refritos, and top them with minced roasted red bell pepper.

Five

Notable Tomato Sauces

taly reigns supreme in the world of tomato sauces even though no one in Italy had seen a tomato, much less used tomatoes for cooking, until the sixteenth century when seeds from the age of exploration were planted in the Old World, grew, fruited, and finally became accepted as food in the seventeenth century. In fact, it was only when many Italian people left their homeland and emigrated to the New World in the mid-nineteenth century that the young Americans came to understand their native, ruby fruit as not only a foodstuff but also one of the earth's treasures. The Italian immigrants had brought along, in whatever meager baggage they carried, seeds for their gardens in the New World, including tomato seeds. It's a genuine "what goes around comes around" story, and their sauces of tomatoes, from smooth to chunky, quick cooked to long simmered, complex or with no extras at all, remain the convention in American cooking after all these years. Except, of course, for barbecue sauce, which is unabashedly American.

Five Notable Tomato Sauces

Very Quick Fresh Tomato Sauce

Peeling the tomatoes or not is a matter of style for this sauce. With peeled tomatoes, there's an extra smoothness. With unpeeled tomatoes, it's quicker than quick to make. Either way, the delicious-even-though-fast factor is heightened with summer ripe tomatoes, but good canned tomatoes, not preseasoned, can produce a tasty facsimile. Using tarragon as the herb rather than the more expected basil gives the sauce a French twist; in fact, I learned it from la Mère Deschamps when I was "la belle bouchère" in her kitchen at Casa Madrona in Sausalito, California.

Makes about 4 cups, or 6 to 8 servings

2 tablespoons olive oil
2 cloves garlic, minced or pressed
2½ pounds ripe tomatoes, peeled (see page 24) or not,
    seeded, and chopped, with juices
2 teaspoons chopped fresh tarragon, or 1 teaspoon dried
1 tablespoon balsamic vinegar
½ teaspoon sugar
½ teaspoon salt
Freshly ground black pepper to taste

1. Heat the oil and garlic together in the pressure cooker over medium-high heat until warm. Add the remaining ingredients, including the tomato juices. Lock on the lid and bring to pressure over high heat, 1 to 2 minutes. Reduce the heat to medium-high and cook for 10 minutes. Remove from the heat and let sit for 10 minutes to finish cooking.

2. With the steam vent pointed away from your face, gently release any remaining pressure. If the sauce is too soupy because the tomatoes were very juicy, boil it over medium-high heat for 5 minutes or so, until it's as thick as you like. Use right away or cool and store in the refrigerator, covered, for up to 1 week or freeze for up to 6 months.

Molto Exquisite Variations for Very Quick Tomato Sauce

The number of tomato sauces in Italian cuisine is almost without measure. Much depends on geography. In Corsica, prunes and cinnamon are included in the sauce and it is used between layers of lasagne noodles. In Emilia-Romagna, anchovy and tuna might expand the tomatoes. In Rome, the tomatoes might serve as a vehicle for a healthy amount of garlic and fresh basil leaves, nothing more, while in Venice, the tomatoes might be enriched with a generous amount of heavy cream and used to nap potato gnocchi. Other quick tomato sauce variations from the immense repertoire include:

• Sun-dried tomatoes, especially in southern Italy, in place of some of the fresh tomatoes

• Herbs such as basil, oregano, marjoram, parsley, or, more rarely, rosemary

• Spices, especially red pepper flakes, sometimes paprika, nutmeg, allspice, or cinnamon

• Black or green olives

• Anchovies, minced and added during cooking

• Pancetta together with red chile pepper, to make *amatriciana* sauce, originally Roman but now popular all over Italy

• Sardines, together with fennel, raisins, and pine nuts, for *pasta con sarde*, a signature Sicilian dish

• Capers, with olives and anchovies to make puttanesca sauce, or with parsley and lemon zest to make an uncooked tomato sauce

Arayah's Marinara Sauce

After her first trip to Italy, my sister, Arayah Jenanyan, came home with an exhilaration she described as having found her true origin. She also came home with marinara sauce on the mind. She had left her lush vegetable garden with many tomato plants to languish in the sun as she frolicked under another sun. On her return, the tomatoes were sprawling all over the garden and sweet as only vine ripened can be. With so much harvest to make use of, it was marinara sauce for family and friends the rest of that summer and marinara sauce from the freezer for many months thereafter. She served it plain and pure over spaghetti as she gleefully, if somewhat didactically, explained to her guests, wondering where was the seafood, "No, marinara sauce means plain, smooth tomato sauce. Then you add fish or clams if you want." The operative word is smooth, for marinara, even though quick to cook, is pureed. She enjoys that part of making marinara and always takes the time to press the sauce through a fine china cap sieve; nothing else will turn out quite the same silken texture. She doesn't add any extras, preferring the elegant simplicity of the life and marinara sauce she discovered in Italy. Here's her recipe.

Makes 4 to 5 cups, or 6 to 8 servings

2 tablespoons olive oil
1 head garlic, cloves separated, peeled, and coarsely chopped
4 medium-size yellow or white onions, coarsely chopped
4 to 5 pounds tomatoes, preferably summer ripe, coarsely chopped,
    with juices
1 teaspoon salt
1 teaspoon freshly ground black pepper
½ teaspoon red pepper flakes (optional)
1 large bay leaf
Handful of chopped fresh herbs, such as thyme, parsley, oregano, and basil

1. Heat the oil in the pressure cooker over medium heat until beginning to smoke. Add the garlic and onions and cook, stirring occasionally, until soft but not caramelized, about 10 minutes.

2. Add the remaining ingredients, including the tomato juices, lock on the lid, and bring to pressure over high heat, about 6 minutes. Reduce the heat to medium-low and cook for 15 minutes. Remove from the heat and let sit for 10 minutes to finish cooking.

3. With the steam vent pointed away from your face, gently release any remaining pressure. When cool enough to handle, push the sauce through a china cap sieve or puree it in a food processor or through a food mill.

4. Reheat and use right away. Or cool and store in the refrigerator, covered, for up to 5 days or freeze for up to 3 months.

Seafood to Make the Marinara "of the Sea"

Marinara is reputed to be a quick, uncomplicated sauce devised by fishermen to blanket the pasta and envelop a bit of the catch for their meal after a day at sea. The pureeing of the sauce after an arduous day on a boat has always seemed a bit of a fish tale to me, but a good one as stories go. On the other hand, some seafood included makes sense. To turn the marinara into a sauce with a whiff of the sea, you can add after it's pureed, as you reheat it at a gentle simmer:

- Clams, small Manila, littleneck, or cherrystone, until they open, 6 to 12 minutes, depending on the amount and the size of the clams
- Mussels, very fresh and not too large, until they open and are firm, 6 to 8 minutes
- Squid, cleaned (see page 168), including tentacles, until they turn barely pink, 3 minutes
- White fish fillets, such as, snapper, turbot, sea bass, or halibut, until just cooked through, 5 to 8 minutes

---

◇ Bolognese Sauce

Simmering up a Bolognese sauce, called ragu alla bolognese *in Italian, on the stove top requires nearly three and a half hours, with attentive stirring to keep it from burning on the bottom. The pressure cooker cuts the time in half and there's no stirring necessary. However, one step can't be quickened—the slow cooking of the vegetables that ensures a rich yet mellow sauce with no raw taste. Stirring in the milk at the end binds the meat and vegetables with the liquid and savory rendered fats so that the sauce is deeply flavored throughout. While you're at it, you might as well make a big batch; it freezes beautifully to serve on-the-run meals.*

Makes 10 cups, or 8 to 12 servings

¼ cup olive oil
1 large yellow or white onion, finely chopped
1 large carrot, peeled and finely chopped
2 ribs celery, finely chopped

4 large cloves garlic, finely chopped

2 small dried red chile peppers

1 pound ground beef chuck

1 pound ground pork

Two 28-ounce cans Italian plum tomatoes, coarsely chopped, with juices

1 bay leaf

$\frac{1}{8}$ teaspoon ground nutmeg

1 teaspoon salt

$\frac{1}{2}$ teaspoon freshly ground black pepper

$\frac{2}{3}$ cup dry red or white wine or water

$\frac{1}{2}$ cup milk

Bolognese, a Matter of Style

Bolognese sauce means meat and tomato sauce, but what meat and how much tomato is open to interpretation. Since tomatoes came to Italy long after the Bolognese began making their ragu, some think the amount of tomato should be minimal to maintain authenticity. Others, without the means to have much meat, adapted the sauce to be mostly tomato. In Sicily, the meat might be pork only with some Italian sausage. Elsewhere, the sauce is considered authentic only if it contains some prosciutto, and so on. From standard to idiosyncratic, variations might include bacon or pancetta (sautéed along with the vegetables), prosciutto, beef only, pork and sausage only, veal in place of half the pork, or chicken livers.

1. Heat the oil in the pressure cooker over high heat until beginning to smoke. Add the onion, carrot, celery, and garlic. Reduce the heat to low and cook, stirring frequently, until golden but not burned, about 15 minutes. Add the remaining ingredients, except the milk. Raise the heat to high and stir to mix, breaking up the chunks of meat.

2. Lock on the lid and bring to pressure over high heat, 5 to 6 minutes. Reduce the heat to medium and cook for 1 hour. Remove from the heat and let sit for 20 minutes to finish cooking.

3. With the steam vent pointed away from your face, gently release any remaining pressure. Remove the lid and stir in the milk. If time allows, set the lid ajar and let sit another 30 minutes. Use right away or cool and store in the refrigerator, covered, for up to 1 week or freeze for up to 3 months.

◇ ◇ ◇

◇ Vegetarian "Ragu"

Though ragu *in Italian means a sauce with meat, I think of this vegetarian sauce as a ragu because it is equally hearty and meal-worthy. Like ragu, it can top pasta, polenta, or risotto, or layer lasagne or eggplant parmesan. It's long cooked, but not quite so long as a Bolognese, because the vegetables meld and blend together more quickly than meat does. To make the sauce seem meatier, you can add diced eggplant or mushrooms to the other vegetables.*

Makes 6 cups, or 8 servings

Ragu or Ragout?

Though the words are etymologically related and even sound the same unless you have the perfect accent, they have different roles culinarily. The Italian ragu is a sauce, albeit rich enough to make a meal in itself sometimes. The French ragout can be made of meat, fish, or poultry, with or without vegetables, or of vegetables only, and there's no doubt it's a meal, a stew meal.

2 tablespoons olive oil

1 medium-size yellow or white onion, finely chopped

2 large cloves garlic, minced

1 carrot, peeled and finely chopped

1 small green, red, or yellow bell pepper, seeded and finely chopped

4 medium-size zucchinis, coarsely chopped

3 pounds ripe tomatoes, coarsely chopped

1 bay leaf

½ teaspoon dried marjoram

1 teaspoon chopped fresh basil

Salt to taste

1. Heat the oil in the pressure cooker over medium–high heat until beginning to smoke. Add the onion, garlic, carrot, bell pepper, and zucchinis and cook, stirring occasionally, over medium heat until softened, 10 minutes.

2. Stir in the tomatoes, bay leaf, marjoram, basil, and salt. Lock on the lid and bring to pressure over high heat, about 4 minutes. Reduce the heat to medium and cook for 40 minutes. Remove from the heat and let sit for 10 minutes to finish cooking.

3. With the steam vent pointed away from your face, gently release any remaining pressure. Let sit for another 15 minutes. Use right away or cool and store in the refrigerator, covered, for up to 5 days or freeze for up to 3 months.

Versatile Tomato Sauces

Any of the tomato sauces for pasta can also be used for:

• Saucing vegetables such as baked eggplant or baked potatoes

• Building layers in a lasagne

• Embellishing chicken, fish, or simple meat dishes

• Topping polenta to make a meal

• Finishing a plain risotto

Ye Olde Family Barbecue Sauce

A backyard barbecue scene: One part of the patio was turned into a stage for an impromptu performance by the young set while the other part was taken up for the barbecuing of chicken on the grill, not to touch because the chef, my uncle Harmon Black, had his own special timing for turning out the pieces perfectly amber, a little bit crispy on the outside, done but still moist all the way through. Besides the feeling of solidity that comes from the extended family being together, the pleasure for me was the perfect barbecued chicken. It became part of sunny summer Sundays in our house, thanks to my father, who was also a barbecuer par excellence. The story has an interesting twist because the recipe that came to seem homegrown was originally a collaboration between Wesson oil and Heinz ketchup; isn't that an early edition of combining brands to double market value? I boldly offer the recipe as I remember it, bottled sauces and all, adapted for the pressure cooker. The chili powder is my addition.

Makes 6 cups

2 tablespoons vegetable oil

2 medium-size yellow or white onions, finely chopped

4 cups ketchup

3 cups water

3 tablespoons prepared mustard, preferably Dijon

1 tablespoon Worcestershire sauce

1 tablespoon freshly squeezed lemon juice

2 teaspoons chili powder

Pinch of cayenne

Safe Handling Tip

If using the barbecue sauce for chicken, you'll have a tastier dish if you marinate the chicken in the sauce for a while, up to overnight. Take care to have the sauce cool before adding the chicken, and be sure to marinate it in the refrigerator.

1. Heat the oil in the pressure cooker over medium-high heat until beginning to smoke. Add the onions and cook, stirring occasionally, over medium heat until wilted, about 5 minutes. Stir in the remaining ingredients, mixing well. Lock on the lid and bring to pressure over high heat, about 6 minutes. Reduce the heat to medium-low and cook for 25 minutes. Remove from the heat and let sit for 15 minutes to finish cooking.

2. With the steam vent pointed away from your face, gently release any remaining pressure. Remove the lid and let sit another 15 minutes. Use right away or cool and store in the refrigerator, covered, for up to 2 weeks or freeze for up to 3 months.

Preserves:
Spiced and Pickled Fruits and Vegetables

hutneys, relishes, marmalades, and fruit preserves are by and large not good candidates for pressure cooking. The juice they release during cooking has no way to evaporate, so they turn out soupy and you need to spend an equal amount of time, or even more time, boiling them with the lid off so they thicken. There are a few, however, that I use the pressure cooker for because it hastens the softening of the components and the open-pot boiling to finish is brief, or else there's no extra reducing required at all, as with the cranberry sauce and applesauce. Following are recipes for those condiments I always make in the pressure cooker with outstanding results.

Preserves: Spiced and Pickled Fruits and Vegetables

◇ Essence of Apple Sauce

The trick to making applesauce in the pressure cooker is to remove the pot from the heat as soon as the pressure gauge is up so it doesn't boil into the steam vent and make a mess. I use very little sugar for applesauce, but if you prefer a sweeter sauce, add more sugar to taste. If you prefer a smooth applesauce, you can pass the mixture through a food mill when it's cool (in which case you wouldn't bother to peel the apples).

Makes 5½ to 6 cups

4 pounds firm sweet/tart apples, such as Granny Smith, Gala, or Winesap,
    peeled, cored, and cut into ½-inch dice
½ cup sugar, or more to taste
¼ cup freshly squeezed lemon or lime juice
Pinch of ground cinnamon

1. Place all the ingredients in the pressure cooker and stir to mix.

2. Lock on the lid and bring to pressure over high heat, 5 to 6 minutes. Immediately remove from the heat without further cooking. Let sit for 5 minutes to finish cooking.

3. With the steam vent pointed away from your face, gently release any remaining pressure. Use right away or cool and refrigerate, covered, for up to 3 weeks.

◇ Cranberry Sauce with Ginger and Tangerine

While it doesn't make sense to do many fruit sauces in the pressure cooker, cranberries work because they contain so much pectin that they thicken quickly without long open-pot reducing. The advantage of pressure cooking them is that you can make a lot at a time, much more than in the microwave, and you don't have to stir and watch that they don't burn on the bottom as you do with regular stove-top cooking. Just lock on the lid, bring to pressure, and remove from the heat.

Makes about 8 cups

8 cups fresh cranberries, rinsed and picked over
One 3-inch piece fresh ginger, peeled and cut into ½-inch-thick slices
½ cup freshly squeezed tangerine juice
2 cups sugar

1. Combine all the ingredients in the pressure cooker. Lock on the lid and bring to pressure over high heat, about 6 minutes. Immediately remove from the heat and let sit for 5 minutes to finish cooking.

2. With the steam vent pointed away from your face, gently release any remaining pressure. Stir vigorously to break up the cranberries. Remove the ginger and set aside to cool. Use right away while at room temperature or refrigerate and serve chilled. Will keep in the refrigerator, covered, for up to 3 months.

Cranberry Connections

Cranberries are one of the most versatile fruits for combining with other flavors. If you've stocked the freezer to have a supply even after the short fall harvest season, you can create cranberry sauce variations with:

• Kumquats, orange zest, or lemon zest
• Walnuts or slivered almonds
• Fresh red currants, dried currants, or raisins
• Cloves, allspice, powdered mustard, cracked black pepper, or small dried chile peppers
• Bay leaves or thyme
• Shallots
• Port wine

American as Cranberry Sauce

Cranberries are native to the East Coast of North America, where wet and sandy marsh bogs provide a natural habitat. Long before colonists began settling in New England, Native Americans of that area mixed cranberries with dried meat and fat for pemmican, a kind of fruity jerky, or with honey for a kind of sauce. Much later, the new arrivals made use of cranberries for vinegar, candles, soap, and a potion to prevent scurvy. They also instituted the cultivation of cranberries around Cape Cod in the early eighteenth century. In the twentieth century, cranberry farming was extended to the Oregon coast, where a similar landscape also furnishes the right environment for growing them. Today, a huge cranberry industry supplies tons of the nutritious, tart, ruby rounds for Thanksgiving condiments, winter holiday galettes, and dried cranberries for snacking.

◎ Onion-Raisin Marmalade

One of the sweet varieties of onion, like Vidalia, Maui, or Walla Walla, or Candy or First Edition if you grow your own, makes the most lip-smacking marmalade. I always employ a food processor fitted with the cutting blade to slice the onions. The thickness is just right, and since it's for a marmalade, the slices don't have to be uniform; you won't be able to tell after they cook down.

Makes 4 cups

4 medium-size sweet onions, halved and sliced ¼ to ½ inch thick
¾ cup golden raisins
1 cup honey
1 tablespoon cider vinegar

1. Place the onions in the pressure cooker and add water to cover. Bring barely to a boil and drain right away (see sidebar page 302).

2. Return the onions to the pot and add the raisins, honey, and vinegar. Mix well—this takes a bit of turning or the honey won't be evenly distributed throughout the onions. Lock on the lid and bring to pressure over high heat, about 5 minutes. Reduce the heat to low and cook for 10 minutes. Remove from the heat and let sit for 15 minutes to finish cooking.

3. With the steam vent pointed away from your face, gently release any remaining pressure. Remove the lid and boil, uncovered, for 5 minutes to thicken the juices. Cool for 5 minutes, then use warm or store in the refrigerator, covered, for up to 4 weeks.

◈ Red Bell Pepper Marmalade

Relish it with roast beef, venison, game, chicken, or turkey. Garnish a plate of fine white cheddar cheese and crackers with it. Spread cream cheese on a toasted bagel and slather the top with it. Fill cute little jars with it for holiday gift giving. However it's used, Red Bell Pepper Marmalade is attractive and awakens curiosity, a true conversation starter.

Makes 2 cups

Marmalade Magic

The step of presoaking is one regularly used for making marmalade to soften and mellow the ingredient, whether orange, grapefruit, onion, or red pepper. This can be done by covering the fruit or vegetables with water and letting them sit overnight. A quick bring-to-boil-and-drain treatment, as with the two vegetable marmalades in this chapter, also works.

4 large red bell peppers (about 2 pounds), quartered, seeded, and thinly sliced
1 small yellow or white onion, quartered and thinly sliced
2 cups sugar
2 tablespoons balsamic vinegar

1. Place the peppers and onion in the pressure cooker and add water to cover. Bring barely to a boil and drain right away (see left).

2. Return the peppers and onion to the pot and stir in the sugar and vinegar. Lock on the lid and bring to pressure over high heat, about 2 minutes. Reduce the heat to medium and cook for 5 minutes. Remove from the heat and let sit for 5 minutes to finish cooking.

3. With the steam vent pointed away from your face, gently release any remaining pressure and remove the lid. Simmer briskly over medium-high heat until thickened, about 6 minutes. Cool and chill, covered, overnight before using.

◈ Kumquat and Red Chile Pepper Relish

Kumquats, reminiscent of Seville oranges with their bittersweet tang, are ideal for a sparky, marmalade-like relish. The chile pepper adds a modest amount of heat, and the turmeric heightens the already bright orange color. If a fresh red chile pepper is not available, substitute a dried one, such as cayenne or japonés. Use the relish with poultry, pork, lamb, or beef dishes or have it on a toasted English muffin.

Makes 1½ cups

1 pound kumquats, quartered lengthwise and seeded
1 fresh red chile pepper, coarsely chopped
½ cup sugar
1 bay leaf, broken in half
¼ teaspoon grated fresh turmeric (see page 138), or small pinch of ground turmeric
2 tablespoons freshly squeezed lemon juice, preferably Meyer lemon

1. Combine all the ingredients in the pressure cooker. Stir to mix and dissolve the sugar a bit. Lock on the lid and bring to pressure over high heat, 2 to 3 minutes. Reduce the heat to medium-low and cook for 4 minutes. Remove from the heat and let sit for 4 minutes to finish cooking.

2. With the steam vent pointed away from your face, gently release any remaining pressure. Remove the lid, stir, then boil briskly, uncovered, over medium-high heat until thickened and sticky, 2 to 3 minutes. Cool to room temperature, remove the bay leaf, and use right away or store in the refrigerator, covered, for up to 3 weeks.

◈ ◈ ◈

◈ Mango and Dried Plum Chutney
Mango is one of the best fruits in the world. It grows from India to Africa, the Caribbean, South America, and on to Hawaii and the Pacific Rim. In one or another of those places, it's used green and hard for salad, somewhat ripe for chutney, soft and fragrant for drinks and sorbets. I have adored mango since my childhood days in Hawaii, where we had a tall, wide, and prolific mango tree forming a canopy across the back of our small garden. Mangoes were there for the taking most of the year. Here, in a fusion chutney, that early and simple taste love is married in a relish with the sophistication of Indian cuisine, to some dried plums. It goes with almost everything: greens, grains, meats, poultry, and ice cream.

Makes 2 cups

2 almost ripe, still firm but not green mangoes, peeled and
   cut off the pit into coarse ½-inch pieces
2 small green chile peppers, such as serrano, minced
1 large clove garlic, pressed
2 teaspoons peeled and coarsely grated fresh ginger, preferably young ginger
6 unsweetened dried plums, coarsely chopped
¾ cup firmly packed dark brown sugar
¾ cup raw cane sugar
1 cup white wine vinegar
2 teaspoons powdered mustard, preferably Colman's

1. Combine all the ingredients in the pressure cooker and stir to mix. Lock on the lid and bring to pressure over high heat, about 5 minutes. Remove from the heat and let sit for 7 minutes to finish cooking.

2. With the steam vent pointed away from your face, gently release any remaining pressure. Remove the lid and boil briskly over medium-high heat until thick, about 10 minutes. Cool completely and refrigerate, covered, overnight before using. Will keep in the refrigerator for up to 6 weeks.

◇ Green Tomato Chutney

Of the numerous ways to prepare green tomatoes—fry them, pickle them, relish them, turn them into pie—this is one of my favorites. In gardens and markets, the ingredients come together seasonally as if by design: tomatoes, green because they're at the end; peppers, red because they've ripened to the hilt; onions from the spring planting, ready to bring in before it gets too cold. Sometimes, I even have a few bunches of almost-dried-on-the-vine late grapes, halfway to raisin, that fill in for the currants. Together, they make a chutney bouquet, in good time for winter holiday tables.

Makes 5 cups

2 pounds green tomatoes, cut into ¼- to ½-inch dice
1 medium-size white onion, quartered lengthwise
    and sliced ¼ inch thick
1 small Anaheim chile pepper, preferably red, cut into thin rounds
¼ cup currants
4 small cayenne or other red chile peppers, minced
2 tablespoons peeled and coarsely grated fresh ginger
¾ cup firmly packed dark brown sugar
¾ cup distilled white vinegar

1. Place all the ingredients in the pressure cooker and stir to mix. Lock on the lid and bring to pressure over high heat, about 6 minutes. Reduce the heat to medium-high and cook for 10 minutes. Remove from the heat and let sit for 10 minutes to finish cooking.

2. With the steam vent pointed away from your face, gently release any remaining pressure. Cool and refrigerate overnight before using. Will keep in the refrigerator, covered, for up to 2 months.

◇ ◇ ◇

◈ Hot and Sweet Grape Mostarda

Mostarda is a specialty of Italian cooking, handed down from the Romans and perhaps before that from the Greeks. Basically, it's a condiment of fruits boiled with honey or sugar and spiked with a healthy amount of mustard. In my signature mostarda based on grapes, their seeds and those of mustard add texture to the fruit, and black peppercorns add extra zip. Use it alongside any meat or poultry dish, especially naturally bland turkey.

Makes about 1½ cups

1¾ pounds red or purple grapes, preferably with seeds, stemmed, rinsed, and halved
1 tablespoon cracked black peppercorns
1 tablespoon yellow mustard seeds
1 tablespoon powdered mustard, preferably Colman's
2 tablespoons freshly squeezed lemon juice
⅓ cup sugar
1 tablespoon water

1. Combine all the ingredients in the pressure cooker. Stir to mix and dissolve the sugar a bit. Lock on the lid and bring to pressure over high heat, about 2 minutes. Reduce the heat to low and cook for 5 minutes. Remove from the heat and let sit for 3 minutes to finish cooking.

2. With the steam vent pointed away from your face, gently release any remaining pressure. Carefully remove the lid and simmer, uncovered, over medium-high heat until thick and deep colored, about 4 minutes. This tastes best if cooled and refrigerated, covered, overnight before using. Will keep in the refrigerator, covered, for up to 6 weeks.

◈　◈　◈

◈ Pears in Blood Orange and White Wine Syrup
with Toasted Pistachio Topping

Pears are a little tricky to select because they must be picked when not completely underripe or they will never taste sweet. On the other hand, too ripe and they won't make it to market without bruises and turning to mush all the way through. Comice or Bartlett or Anjou are pretty sure bets for holding up during travel to market and, by nature, are not too grainy. For poaching, I judge by feel and fragrance and choose those somewhere between almost hard as a rock and fragrant at the stem end. In any case, this dish is pear poetry.

Makes 4 servings

1½ cups dry white wine

¼ cup freshly squeezed blood orange juice

¾ cup sugar

Seeds from 3 cardamom pods, or ¼ teaspoon ground cardamom

4 ripe but still firm pears

⅓ cup shelled pistachios, toasted (see page 41) and finely chopped, for topping

1. Combine the wine, orange juice, sugar, and cardamom in the pressure cooker and stir to dissolve the sugar a bit. Set a trivet in the pressure cooker.

2. Peel the pears, then halve them lengthwise and core them. Fit the halves, cut side down, in an overlapping layer on the trivet. Lock on the lid and bring to pressure over high heat, 3 to 4 minutes. Reduce the heat to medium and cook for 2 minutes. Remove from the heat and let sit for 2 minutes to finish cooking.

3. With the steam vent pointed away from your face, gently release any remaining pressure. Remove the lid and let sit for 5 minutes to cool down.

4. Carefully transfer the pears to a wide dish or bowl, setting them facedown. Set aside to cool.

5. Boil the liquid in the pot until it is reduced by one third and big bubbles form across the surface, 5 to 6 minutes. Remove from the heat and let cool for 5 minutes. Pour this syrup over the pears and set aside to cool to room temperature, or refrigerate, covered, for up to 5 days.

6. To serve, arrange 2 pear halves in each of 4 individual serving bowls, one half facing up, one half facing down. Spoon some of the syrup into each bowl and sprinkle the pistachios over the top.

◇ ◇ ◇

Stone Fruits

Here today and gone tomorrow. From the first cherries and apricots on to peaches and plums, the drupes, also called stone fruits, epitomize the admonition: *carpe diem*. Fortunately, they are one of the best kinds of fruits to put by. Spiced, pickled, poached in sweet water, softened into a conserve, they beckon the cook to think ahead through the advancing season and preserve some for later.

◇ Apricot Conserve with Slivered Almonds
The almonds add a nice crunch and take the apricot conserve in the direction of a Greek spoon sweet. You can omit them and the recipe turns out a pure apricot conserve.

Makes about 2 cups

1½ pounds ripe apricots, halved and pitted
1 tablespoon freshly squeezed lemon juice
½ cup sugar
½ teaspoon orange extract
⅓ cup slivered almonds (optional), toasted (see page 41)

1. Combine the apricots, lemon juice, sugar, extract, and almonds, if using, in the pressure cooker. Stir to mix, lock on the lid, and bring to pressure over high heat, 2 to 3 minutes. Immediately remove from the heat and let sit for 5 minutes to finish cooking.

2. With the steam vent pointed away from your face, gently release any remaining pressure. Remove the lid and boil, uncovered, over medium-high heat, stirring frequently, until the apricots have completely collapsed and the liquid is almost gone, about 7 minutes. Remove from the heat, cool, and refrigerate overnight before using. Will keep in the refrigerator, covered, for 6 weeks.

◈ Spiced Peaches, an Old-Fashioned Favorite
Spiced peaches often appeared on holiday tables to accompany the turkey, goose, or roast beef when sweet/tart condiments and conserves were a regular addition to the feast. I still enjoy such adornments and appreciate the pressure cooker as a quick do-it-now-for-later facilitator. Some say to tie the spices in a bag or else strain them out before pouring the brine over the fruit. But I don't bother with either of those steps because if the spices remain, they continue to flavor the peaches and syrup and can easily be brushed away when ready to serve. Small peaches that can be spiced whole are the easiest to deal with. Large peaches should be cut in half and, for that, freestone, rather than cling, peaches make the neatest halves.

Makes 1½ quarts

2 cups cider vinegar

2 cups firmly packed dark brown sugar

1 teaspoon whole cloves

1 teaspoon allspice berries

One 3-inch piece cinnamon stick

2 pounds small peaches (8 to 9 small or 4 to 5 large), gently washed to rub off the fuzz (see headnote)

1. Combine the vinegar, brown sugar, cloves, allspice berries, and cinnamon stick in the pressure cooker. Stir to mix and dissolve the sugar. Add the peaches, lock on the lid, and bring to pressure over high heat, 4 to 5 minutes. Immediately remove from the heat and let sit for 4 minutes to finish cooking.

2. With the steam vent pointed away from your face, gently release any remaining pressure and remove the lid. Lift out the peaches with kitchen tongs, taking care not to smash them, and transfer to a wide dish. Set aside to cool.

3. Boil the liquid in the pot on high heat for 3 minutes to reduce and thicken a bit. Set aside to cool.

4. Slip the skins off the peaches with your fingers and transfer the peaches to a glass jar or other storage container. Pour the liquid into the jar, without straining, and set aside until cooled to room temperature. Cover and refrigerate for at least 2 weeks before using. Will keep in the refrigerator, covered, for up to 4 months.

◇ ◇ ◇

◈ Plums Pickled in Port Wine and Balsamic Vinegar

Red and heady as they are, pickled plums make a lovely hostess gift for holiday occasions. One or two showcased in a small glass jar, floating in their sweet/tart brine, makes a beguiling jewel of an offering. Making them in a pressure cooker is a swift procedure: Bring to pressure, remove from the heat, cool, and it's done, except for the waiting while they rest in the refrigerator and mellow for a few weeks. The plums should be largish, firm, red ones so they hold up in the brief cooking and come out brilliantly colored.

Makes 1 to 1½ quarts

> 1 cup port wine
> ½ cup balsamic vinegar
> ⅔ cup sugar
> 3 whole cloves
> 1 teaspoon Szechwan pepper (see Note page 88)
> 10 medium-size tart red plums (1¾ pounds)

1. Combine the port, vinegar, sugar, cloves, and pepper in the pressure cooker. Stir to mix and dissolve the sugar a bit. Add the plums, lock on the lid, and bring to pressure over high heat, 3 to 4 minutes. Immediately remove from the heat and let sit for 5 minutes to finish cooking.

2. With the steam vent pointed away from your face, gently release any remaining pressure. Remove the lid and with a slotted spoon transfer the plums to a colander set over a bowl, taking care not to smash the fruit. Set aside the plums and the liquid remaining in the pressure cooker and let cool to room temperature.

3. Carefully transfer the plums to glass jars, filling them loosely. Pour the liquid over them, cover, and store in the refrigerator for at least 2 weeks before using. Will keep in the refrigerator, covered, until Groundhog Day (about 6 weeks).

◇ Cherries in Ouzo Syrup

When you've had your fill of cherries for their short season but dream of more later, suspending them in an anisey syrup of ouzo and sugar is a way to keep them, stored in the refrigerator, halfway to next year's cherry season. Use them as a topping for pancakes or ice cream, as a side sauce for Chocolate Ancho Chile Steamed Pudding Cake (page 339), or spooned directly out of the jar when you'd like a taste of cherry in November. Pernod or anisette will do as a substitute for the harder-to-find, and more expensive, ouzo.

Makes 3½ to 4 cups

2 pounds cherries, pitted
½ cup ouzo
1 cup sugar
2 tablespoons freshly squeezed lemon juice

1. Combine the ingredients in the pressure cooker and stir to dissolve the sugar a bit. Lock on the lid and bring to pressure over high heat, about 4 minutes. Immediately remove from the heat and let sit for 10 minutes to finish cooking.

2. With the steam vent pointed away from your face, gently release any remaining pressure. Remove the lid. If too moist, boil until the liquid is thickened and syrupy but still pourable, 2 to 3 minutes. Refrigerate overnight, covered, before using. Will keep in the refrigerator for up to 6 months.

A Savory Set of

Custards and Steamed
Puddings

◇ ◇ ◇

Custards and steamed puddings comfortably surround all manner of tidbits, chocolate to chicken, vegetables to nuts, candied fruit to chile peppers. The dishes in this chapter represent a range of multiethnic savory custards and steamed puddings, including a few surprises like a chèvre popover pudding and a bread pudding with lettuce and cheese. The guidelines are the same as for similar oven-cooked delights, with some special notes for individual custards in the pressure cooker:

- The cups are covered with aluminum foil and pinched around the edges to keep out moisture from the condensing steam during the sitting time.

- The recipes call for six-ounce ramekins. The ordinary custard cups available in grocery and hardware stores are just right, but you can go more upscale and use six-ounce small soufflé dishes or ramekins. The point is, the pressure cooker doesn't hold larger size ramekins side by side, so unless you want to cook the larger ones in several rounds, two at a time, it's more practical to use the smaller ones, and they're a good amount for single servings.

- When a recipe call for four individual ramekins, for instance, Asparagus Flan (page 317), you can set three cups on the bottom and place the fourth in the middle on top of those. When it yields five to six servings, you can set three on the bottom and two or three balanced on top of them. However, that's not such a stable structure, and rather than risk spilling the top cups while balancing them on the bottom cups, I set a second trivet on top of the bottom layer and set the remaining two or three ramekins on top of the second trivet. As long as the top trivet has holes for steam to escape and circulate, they'll all cook evenly.

A Cautionary Note for Cooking Custards and Puddings in the Pressure Cooker

The handled trivet that modern pressure cookers usually come equipped with is useful for some purposes. However, I never rely on the handle for removing custards and puddings. When trying to lift out the trivet, or anything else heavy for that matter, it will rock back and forth and the ramekins and the trivet are way too hot to touch even after the steam has subsided, so you really can't stabilize the situation with two bare hands. Rather, I use two heavy kitchen towels, terry cloth towels, not hot pads or decorative towels of any other sort, one in each hand. That way, *after the steam has subsided,* you can grasp the dishes one at a time to remove them.

Creating a Water Bath in the Pressure Cooker

P robably it's not problematic to think of setting a dish of custard or a lovingly constructed pâté in a water bath, called a *bain marie*, to cook in the oven. Clearly, the setup allows a soothing shroud of steam to cook the food gently, not forcefully. It's also a familiar technique to set a roast or whole bird on a rack in a baking dish so it's elevated out of the juices and fat rendered as it cooks. For the same purpose, Chinese steamed dishes are arranged on bamboo baskets that fit into a wok but rest above the bottom, so the food stays out of the liquid as the dish steams.

Pressure steaming custards and puddings combines a bit of all those traditional ways, but the setup is simpler. The pressure cooker method requires only a trivet to keep the dish off the bottom of the pot and an inch or so (one to two cups) of water to create the steam pressure. There's no need to add water to rise halfway up the side of the dish, as in a *bain marie*, nor is it necessary to keep the dish completely out of the water, as in Chinese-style steaming.

A Savory Set of Custards and Steamed Puddings

Asparagus Flan Flings

Comely and tasty as they are alone, asparagus flans invite decorative company. Good side dishes to garnish the plate would be:

• Mushrooms barely wilted with minced garlic and tarragon and tossed with lemon and olive oil

• Sautéed bell peppers

• A salsa of coarsely chopped tomato, parsley, and balsamic vinegar

• A slaw of shredded turnip and radish splashed with white wine vinegar

• Thinly sliced red onion rings wilted with red wine vinegar and a pinch each of salt and sugar

Or, once chilled and unmolded, you can slice the custards and use the slices to embellish other dishes, such as:

• A plate of smoked salmon garnished with dill and sprinkled with lemon juice

• An arugula and black olive salad dressed with lemon or red wine vinegar and walnut oil

• Consommé à la Madrilène (page 16) or Japanese-Inspired Beef Consommé with Tofu and Scallion Slivers (page 18)

◇ Asparagus Flan

Savory flan is an easy way to go for an elegant luncheon or first course dinner dish. These, in particular, unmold intact once they set to room temperature.

Makes four 6-ounce flans

2 tablespoons butter, plus extra for greasing the ramekins
1 tablespoon minced shallot
4 asparagus spears, cut into thin diagonal slices
1 cup half-and-half
4 large eggs, beaten
½ teaspoon salt
¼ teaspoon ground white pepper
Pinch of ground nutmeg

1. Lightly grease four 6-ounce ramekins with butter. Pour 1 cup water into the pressure cooker and set the trivet in it.

2. Melt the 2 tablespoons butter in a large, heavy frying pan over medium heat. Add the shallot and asparagus and cook, stirring occasionally, until beginning to wilt, 1 minute. Add the half-and-half and continue cooking until steaming but not boiling, about 3 minutes.

3. Remove from the heat and when no longer steaming whisk in the eggs, salt, pepper, and nutmeg. Ladle the mixture into the ramekins. Cover each with foil, pinching around the edges to seal. Set 3 of the ramekins on the trivet and the fourth in the middle on top of them. Lock on the lid and bring to pressure over high heat, about 4 minutes. Reduce the heat to medium-low and cook for 11 minutes. Remove from the heat and let sit for 4 minutes to finish cooking.

4. With the steam vent pointed away from your face, gently release any remaining pressure. Carefully remove the lid and let sit another 5 minutes. Using 2 thick terry cloth kitchen towels, one in each hand, lift out the ramekins and set aside to cool to room temperature.

5. Remove the foil. Run a knife around the edge of each ramekin and unmold onto individual serving plates. Serve right away. Or, chill the custards in the ramekins and unmold just before serving.

Two Tips for Cooking Individual Custard or Pudding Cups

1. Make sure the top of the pressure cooker clears the stack of ramekins by at least 2 inches. Otherwise, cook them in 2 rounds.

2. I have found it doesn't matter if the dishes come in contact with the sides of the pot. This is good, because given the size limitations of pressure cookers, they have to if you're going to steam more than 2 at a time.

Chawan Mushi, Japanese Savory Steamed Custard

Chawan mushi is a moist custard, considered a soup in Japanese cooking, and not meant to be unmolded. Chicken and shrimp are traditionally included, but I find them too heavy for the custard's soft texture and gentle taste, so I use shredded Napa cabbage and mild oyster mushrooms instead. The traditional garnish is mitsuba *(trefoil), which is almost impossible to find outside of Japanese markets. Its taste is reminiscent of celery leaf, so I substitute that, and festoon the custard with an extravagant dollop of caviar (see bottom right).* Makes five 6-ounce ramekins

1 tablespoon peanut oil
3 large Napa cabbage leaves, green parts thinly shredded,
     white parts finely chopped
3 fresh oyster mushrooms, trimmed and thinly sliced
2 scallions, trimmed and thinly sliced
1 teaspoon salt
1½ cups Chicken Broth (page 18)
1½ teaspoons low-sodium soy sauce
½ teaspoon sugar
4 large eggs, beaten
5 small celery leaves from the tender, inner ribs, for garnish
5 teaspoons *tobiko* (flying fish) roe (optional), for garnish

1. Pour 1 cup water into the pressure cooker and set a trivet in it. Use five 6-ounce ramekins, not greased (it's not necessary because the custards don't get unmolded).

2. Heat the oil together with the cabbage, oyster mushrooms, scallions, and salt in a skillet over medium-high heat until beginning to wilt, 2 to 3 minutes. Stir in the broth, soy sauce, and sugar. Remove from the heat, add the eggs, and whisk to mix.

3. Divide the mixture among the ramekins. Cover each with foil, pinching around the edges to seal. Set 3 of them on the trivet. Place a second trivet on top and set the remaining 2 ramekins on it. Lock on the lid and bring to pressure over high heat, about 4 minutes. Reduce the heat to medium and cook for 8 minutes. Remove from the heat and let sit for 6 minutes to finish cooking.

4. With the steam vent pointed away from your face, gently release any remaining pressure. Carefully remove the lid and let sit another 5 minutes. Using 2 thick terry cloth kitchen towels, lift out the ramekins. Remove the foil. Tuck a celery leaf in the top of each custard and place a dollop of the caviar alongside, if desired. Serve right away.

◇ ◇ ◇

Caviar Not in the Extreme

Caviar, the salted eggs of various fish, makes a perfect top note for many dishes. In spite of its reputation as one of the most out-of-reach luxury foods, it need not be so. Outside the kingly realm of beluga and sevruga sturgeon caviars, the roe of flying fish (called *tobiko*), crunchy and orange red; salmon, large, moist, and bright red-orange; and Great Lakes whitefish, small, crispy, and golden, all provide delicious caviars affordable enough to consider using for special occasions.

◇ Savory Coconut Custard with Chicken, Ginger, Snow Peas, and Pineapple Salsa   *Coconut custards may be served like Chawan Mushi (page 318), still warm and jiggling in their ramekins. A more striking presentation is to let them cool to room temperature so they can be unmolded onto a small plate and garnished with a spoonful of pineapple salsa alongside. Crabmeat, the real thing, instead of chicken makes an excellent variation on the theme.*

Makes five 6-ounce ramekins

2 teaspoons peanut oil, plus extra for greasing the ramekins
1 tablespoon finely chopped fresh ginger
1 large boneless and skinless chicken breast half ($^{1}/_{2}$ to $^{3}/_{4}$ pound),
    cut into $^{1}/_{4}$-inch dice
1 teaspoon salt
10 snow peas, tops trimmed and cut diagonally into $^{1}/_{4}$-inch pieces
1$^{2}/_{3}$ cups unsweetened coconut milk
4 large eggs
1 small fresh red chile pepper, seeded and coarsely chopped
2 tablespoons freshly squeezed lime juice
5 sprigs fresh cilantro, for garnish
1$^{1}/_{2}$ cups Pineapple Salsa (optional; recipe follows), for garnish

1. Lightly grease five 6-ounce ramekins with peanut oil. Pour 1 cup water into the pressure cooker and set a trivet in it.

2. Heat the 2 teaspoons peanut oil in a medium-size sauté pan over medium-high heat until beginning to smoke. Add the ginger and chicken, sprinkle with $^{1}/_{4}$ teaspoon of the salt, and cook, stirring occasionally, until beginning to turn white, about 2 minutes. Stir in the snow peas and continue to cook, stirring occasionally, until wilted, about 1 minute more. Remove from the heat and set aside.

3. Pour the coconut milk into a large bowl and whisk to smooth. Add the eggs and whisk to blend. Stir in the chicken mixture, chile pepper, lime juice, and remaining $^{3}/_{4}$ teaspoon salt.

4. Ladle the mixture into the prepared ramekins. Cover each with foil, pinching around the edges to seal. Set 3 of them on the trivet in the pressure cooker. Place a second trivet over them and set the remaining 2 ramekins on it. Lock on the lid and bring to pressure over high heat, about 4 minutes. Reduce the heat to medium-low and cook for 15 minutes. Remove from the heat and let sit for 10 minutes to finish cooking.

5. With the steam vent pointed away from your face, gently release any remaining pressure. Remove the lid and let sit for another 10 minutes.

6. Remove the foil. Garnish each custard with a cilantro sprig and serve warm. Or cool completely, then unmold the custards onto small serving plates. Garnish each with a cilantro sprig and a generous spoonful of the pineapple salsa alongside.

Pineapple Salsa *Red chile pepper makes the best color contrast with the yellow pineapple and green cilantro, but green chile pepper will do for the taste. What's important is to have the chile pepper fresh, not dried.*

Makes 1½ cups

¼ medium-size pineapple, including core, cut
    into ¼-inch dice (about 1½ cups)
½ fresh red chile pepper, seeded and finely chopped but not minced
⅓ cup coarsely chopped fresh cilantro
1 tablespoon freshly squeezed lime juice

Combine all the ingredients in a small bowl and toss to mix. Use right away or refrigerate, covered, for up to 3 days.

◇ ◇ ◇

◇ Chèvre Rosemary Popover Pudding

Popovers are a gem from my childhood. Not only were they an airy pleasure to eat, the hustle and bustle of taking them from the oven to the table before they "fell" was always good drama. Spurred by that memory, I devised a chèvre and rosemary–flavored version for the pressure cooker. It turned out more pudding than popover, but the flavor is similar.

Makes 4 to 6 servings

Butter for greasing the dish
1 tablespoon freshly grated parmesan cheese
2 large eggs
1 cup milk
2 tablespoons butter, melted
½ cup all-purpose flour
½ teaspoon salt
½ teaspoon chopped fresh rosemary, or scant ¼ teaspoon dried
¼ cup soft chèvre, at room temperature

1. Lightly grease a 1-quart soufflé dish or glass bowl that will fit inside the pressure cooker. Add the parmesan cheese and turn to coat the bottom and up the sides of the dish. Set a trivet in the pressure cooker and pour in 1 cup water.

2. Beat the eggs in a medium-size bowl. Whisk in the milk and melted butter. Add the flour, salt, and rosemary and whisk to smooth. Stir in the chèvre and pour into the prepared dish. Cover with foil, pinching around the edge to seal. Set in the pressure cooker. Lock on the lid and bring to pressure over high heat, about 3 minutes. Reduce the heat to medium-low and cook for 8 minutes. Remove from the heat and let sit for 5 minutes to finish cooking.

3. With the steam vent pointed away from your face, gently release any remaining pressure. Remove the lid and lift off the foil with kitchen tongs. Let sit another 5 minutes. Slice and serve warm.

◇ Savory Cornmeal Pudding with Tomato Concassé Sauce

Of the same ilk but a little different from spoonbread, cornmeal pudding has more egg in proportion to the cornmeal and no baking powder to facilitate its rising. As a savory concoction, it's a tasty alternative to polenta or cornbread, neither of which work in a pressure cooker. The Tomato Concassé Sauce makes it a bit fancy, but it's not very hard to do.

Makes 4 to 6 servings

Butter for greasing the dish
2 cups milk
1 teaspoon salt
1 teaspoon chopped fresh thyme, or ¼ teaspoon dried
½ cup fine yellow cornmeal
1 large egg
2 large egg yolks
2 tablespoons butter
¼ cup grated Monterey Jack or other melting cheese
1 cup Tomato Concassé Sauce (page 324), for serving

1. Lightly grease a 1-quart soufflé dish or glass bowl that will fit in the pressure cooker. Place a trivet in the pressure cooker and pour in 1 cup water.

2. Combine the milk, salt, and thyme in a medium-size saucepan. Heat just until beginning to boil, then whisk in the cornmeal. Stir over medium heat until thick, 1 minute. Remove from the heat and let cool for 5 minutes.

3. Stir in the egg, yolks, butter, and cheese. Spoon the mixture into the prepared dish. Cover with foil, pinching around the edges to seal. Set the dish in the pressure cooker. Lock on the lid and bring to pressure over high heat, about 3 minutes. Reduce the heat to medium-high and cook for 10 minutes. Remove from the heat and let sit for 10 minutes to finish cooking.

4. With the steam vent pointed away from your face, gently release any remaining pressure. Using 2 thick terry cloth kitchen towels, carefully lift the dish out of the pressure cooker. Dollop a bit of the tomato sauce over the top and serve right away, while still puffy like a soufflé, with the remaining sauce on the side.

Tomato Concassé Sauce

Makes 1 cup

2 juicy ripe tomatoes, peeled (see page 24), seeded,
    cut into ¼-inch dice, and juices strained and reserved
1 serrano chile pepper, minced (optional)
¼ cup shredded fresh basil
1 teaspoon balsamic vinegar
1 teaspoon extra virgin olive oil

Combine all the ingredients in a small bowl. Use right away or set aside at room temperature for several hours. May be stored in the refrigerator, covered, overnight.

Tomato Concassé and Its Possibilities

Sometimes a word alone can bring an extra bit of glamour to a preparation, as when the French word *concassé* replaces the more ordinary "peeled, seeded, and coarsely chopped" to describe the tomatoes. Either way, tossed with a splash of balsamic vinegar and a handful of fresh basil, the chopped tomatoes can top not only corn pudding but also many other vegetables, as well as chicken breasts or white fish fillets. And, there are numerous possibilities for varying the extras:

• Instead of the serrano chile pepper, use a pinch of cayenne

• Instead of basil, use fresh oregano, rosemary, thyme, tarragon, or cilantro for the herb

• Instead of balsamic vinegar, use red wine vinegar or lime juice

• Add a tablespoon of finely chopped shallot

◇ Double-Thrift Savory Bread Pudding with Lettuce, Onion, and Cheese

As a professional cook and backyard gardener, I have always sought ways to make good use of those not-so-pretty outside leaves of lettuce. My first introduction to that notion was from a French recipe for lettuce soup that called for a seeming ton of them; hooray, a way to use what might have been otherwise relegated to the compost pile. Much later, I ran across a Spanish recipe, one for a savory pudding of lettuce bolstered with a béchamel sauce and bread crumbs. For my pressure cooker custardy pudding, the crumbs have become cubes of stale bread and the béchamel is changed to a mix of just eggs and cheese. The outside leaves of lettuce remain. It's an elegant first course or side dish that appeals to the thrift in anyone's soul.

Makes 4 to 6 servings

2 tablespoons butter, plus extra for greasing the dish
½ small yellow or white onion, finely chopped
2 cups packed coarsely chopped outer romaine or Bibb lettuce leaves
½ cup milk
¾ cup ricotta cheese
½ cup crumbled feta cheese
¼ teaspoon chopped fresh sage, or ⅛ teaspoon dried
Pinch of ground nutmeg
¾ teaspoon kosher salt
3 large eggs
3½ to 4 cups 1-inch cubes stale bread
½ cup Tomato Concassé Sauce (optional, page 324), for serving

1. Lightly grease a 6-cup soufflé dish or glass bowl or five 6-ounce custard cups with butter.

2. Melt the 2 tablespoons butter in a sauté pan over medium heat. Add the onion and cook, stirring occasionally, until wilting, about 2 minutes. Stir in the lettuce and continue cooking until limp, about 1 minute. Set aside to cool.

3. Combine the milk, ricotta, feta, sage, nutmeg, and salt in a large bowl and whisk to smooth. Whisk in the eggs. Stir in the lettuce mixture, then the bread cubes. Ladle into the prepared dish or individual cups. Cover with foil, pinching around the edges to seal.

4. Place a trivet in the pressure cooker and pour in 2 cups water. Set the dish or stack the cups (see page 314) on the trivet. Lock on the lid and bring to pressure over high heat, 2 to 3 minutes. Reduce the heat to medium and cook for 20 minutes if using one dish or 10 minutes if using cups. Remove from the heat and let sit for 10 minutes to finish cooking.

5. With the steam vent pointed away from your face, gently release any remaining pressure. Remove the lid, lift off the foil with kitchen tongs, and let cool enough to handle.

6. While still warm, serve without unmolding if using one large dish, with the sauce, if using, on the side. If using custard cups, unmold onto individual plates and top with a dollop of the sauce, if using.

Sweet Finales

◇ ◇ ◇

At first I was dubious about creating recipes for the sweets chapter. The pressure cooker, after all, doesn't bake. So, no cookies, no flour cakes, no pies. But there are cheesecakes, including crust, that make you wonder why you ever baked one in the oven. There's a world of puddings and custards to delve into—indeed, some of the finest sweets to offer. There's also poached fruit, which doesn't need a thick sauce, and steamed fruit, like bananas napped in caramel sauce. And chocolate: There are some who think if there's no chocolate, it's not dessert. Ultimately, I wound up with a delightful assortment of sweets, plus many variations, that I think fit almost any desire for that "little taste of sweet" as meal finale.

Sweet Finales

Cheesecake with Mascarpone Cheese in Chocolate Cookie Crust

Mascarpone is a creamier cream cheese that's double right for a rich cheesecake. It is available in boutique delis and often in the cheese section in better supermarkets. The Nabisco chocolate wafers, the thin ones used to make icebox cookie cake with whipped cream, are available almost everywhere.

Makes one 7-inch cheesecake, or 8 to 10 servings

¼ cup (½ stick) unsalted butter, cut up

One-half 10-ounce box Nabisco Chocolate Wafer Cookies

8 ounces mascarpone cheese

4 ounces cream cheese

1 tablespoon freshly squeezed orange juice

1 tablespoon finely chopped orange zest

2 large eggs

¾ cup sugar

Cheesecake and Romance

You can make a half recipe of the cheesecake and turn it into a mini, 5-inch springform pan for a diminutive dessert just right for 4, or maybe 2 with leftovers if it's a romantic Valentine's evening. For that, I would definitely top it with Raspberry Sauce (page 339). Follow the instructions for the 7-inch cheesecake but cook for only 15 minutes and let sit for only 6 minutes.

1. Set a trivet in the pressure cooker and pour in 2 cups water.

2. Combine the butter and cookies in a food processor and pulse until mixed into a coarse crumble. Press the mixture across the bottom of a 7-inch springform pan, beveling a bit up the sides, to make a thick crust. Set aside.

3. Combine the mascarpone cheese, cream cheese, orange juice, zest, eggs, and sugar in a food processor or medium-size bowl. Mix until smooth.

4. Pour the mixture over the crust in the springform pan. Set the pan on a 30-inch length of aluminum foil. Cover the top with another piece of foil and pinch around the edges to seal. Scrunch up the ends of the length of foil and bring them together over the pan to create a handle. Twist together the 2 ends to make a secure handle.

5. Set the foil-wrapped pan in the pressure cooker and lock on the lid. Bring to pressure over high heat, 3 to 4 minutes. Reduce the heat to medium and cook for 20 minutes. Remove from the heat and let sit for 10 minutes to finish cooking.

6. With the steam vent pointed away from your face, gently release any remaining pressure. Remove the pan from the pressure cooker using the foil handle. Untwist the handle and lift off the foil top with kitchen tongs. Sop up any moisture in the middle of the cake with a paper towel. Cool completely, then cover with plastic wrap and refrigerate overnight, or up to 3 days.

7. When ready to serve, loosen the lever on the springform pan, remove the ring, and set the cake, still on its springform pan bottom, on a platter. Cut into individual slices and serve.

◈ Peanut Butter Swirl Cheesecake with Barnum's Animal Cracker Crust

The dividing line between kids and adults becomes quite blurry when serving up a cheesecake with peanut butter and an animal cracker crust. The only hard part of this delightful concoction is keeping hands off the peanut butter chips and crackers so you can have enough to make the cake.

Makes one 7-inch cheesecake, or 8 to 10 servings

¼ cup (½ stick) unsalted butter
Two 2⅛-ounce boxes Barnum's Animal Cracker Cookies
12 ounces cream cheese, at room temperature
½ cup sour cream
½ cup sugar
2 large eggs
1 cup Reese's Peanut Butter Chips
3 tablespoons water

1. Set a trivet in the pressure cooker and pour in 2 cups water.

2. Combine the butter and cookies in a food processor and pulse until mixed into a coarse crumble. Press the mixture across the bottom of a 7-inch springform pan, beveling a bit up the sides, to make a thick crust. Set aside.

3. Combine the cream cheese, sour cream, sugar, and eggs in a food processor or medium-size bowl. Mix until smooth. Pour the mixture over the crust in the springform pan.

4. Place the peanut butter chips in a microwave bowl or small saucepan. Sprinkle with the water and microwave on high or heat over medium-low heat on the stove top until halfway melted and beginning to collapse, about 2 minutes. Gently stir until smooth, then pour across the cheese mixture in the springform pan. With a wooden spoon, swirl the melted peanut butter through the cheese mixture without disturbing the crust on the bottom.

5. Set the pan on a 30-inch length of aluminum foil. Cover the top of the pan with another piece of foil and pinch around the edges to seal. Scrunch up the ends of the length of foil and bring them together over the pan to create a handle. Twist together the 2 ends make a secure handle.

6. Set the foil-wrapped pan in the pressure cooker, lock on the lid, and bring to pressure over high heat, 3 to 4 minutes. Reduce the heat to medium and cook for 20 minutes. Remove from the heat and let sit for 10 minutes to finish cooking.

7. With the steam vent pointed away from your face, gently release any remaining pressure. Remove the pan from the pressure cooker using the foil handle. Untwist the handle and lift off the foil top with kitchen tongs. Sop up any moisture in the middle of the cake with a paper towel. Cool completely, then cover with plastic wrap and refrigerate overnight, or up to 3 days.

8. When ready to serve, loosen the lever on the springform pan, remove the ring, and set the cheesecake, still on its springform pan bottom, on a serving platter. Cut into individual slices and serve.

◇ ◇ ◇

Arborio Rice Pudding with Rhubarb Strawberry Compote

Arborio rice is the best for a creamy, risotto-like pudding. For a slightly drier but nuttier and more perfumed version, use basmati or jasmine rice. Good-quality Texas or Carolina long grain rice is also excellent—the pudding won't be as creamy as with Arborio or as aromatic as with basmati or jasmine, but it will maintain the essence of what rice pudding is about. The cooking time is the same for any of them.

Makes 6 servings

1 cup rice, preferably Arborio
3½ cups milk
½ cup sugar
Pinch of ground nutmeg
2 large eggs, lightly beaten
1 teaspoon vanilla extract
2 cups Rhubarb Strawberry Compote (recipe follows), for topping

1. Combine the rice, milk, sugar, and nutmeg in the pressure cooker. Stir to mix and dissolve the sugar a bit. Lock on the lid and bring to pressure over high heat, about 6 minutes. Reduce the heat to low and cook for 5 minutes. Remove from the heat and let sit for 8 minutes to finish cooking.

2. With the steam vent pointed away from your face, gently release any remaining pressure. Remove the lid and let sit for 2 minutes, until the steam subsides. Stir in the eggs and vanilla. Spoon into individual bowls and top with the compote. Or refrigerate and reheat before serving. Will keep in the refrigerator, covered, for up to 4 days.

Rhubarb Strawberry Compote *Rhubarb strawberry doesn't fall so trippingly from the tongue as the more familiar order, strawberry rhubarb. But here the rhubarb prevails, so that's what I've titled this classic pairing in a compote for topping rice pudding, spreading on scones, or serving* *alongside pork roast. Cooked in the pressure cooker, the rhubarb becomes tender while the straw-berry halves remain recognizably whole.*   Makes about 2 cups

¾ pound rhubarb stalks, ends trimmed and cut into ¼-inch pieces
1¼ cups hulled and halved strawberries
¾ cup sugar
1 tablespoon water

1. Combine the ingredients in the pressure cooker. Stir to mix and dissolve the sugar a bit. Lock on the lid and bring to pressure over high heat, about 4 minutes. Reduce the heat to medium–high and cook for 2 minutes. Remove from the heat and let sit for 4 minutes to finish cooking.

2. With the steam vent pointed away from your face, gently release any remaining pressure. Remove the lid, stir, and let sit until com-pletely cool. Use right away or chilled. Will keep in the refrigerator, covered, for up to 4 weeks.

Other Toppings for Rice Pudding

In place of the Rhubarb Strawberry compote, top the pudding with:

• A sprinkle of ground cinnamon

• Several gratings of fresh nutmeg

• Fresh berries

• Sliced mango

• Lingonberry jam

• Maple syrup

• Cherries in Ouzo Syrup (page 312)

• Apricot Conserve with Slivered Almonds (page 308)

• Cranberry Sauce with Ginger and Tangerine (page 299)

• Toasted Coconut (page 218)

◈ Bread Pudding with Apples and Fennel Seeds *Warm cream and*

a whiff of cinnamon are all that's needed to complete the round of flavors in a classic dish made

new with fennel seeds. Spooned out soft and warm, the cream further soothes and makes a com-

pany-worthy dessert. Chilled and served the next day, the pudding alone is a snack with no further

embellishment required.   Makes 6 servings

¼ cup (½ stick) unsalted butter, plus extra for greasing the dish
2 medium-size Golden Delicious apples, quartered lengthwise,
    cored, and sliced ¼ inch thick
¼ teaspoon fennel seeds
3 large eggs
1 cup milk
½ cup sugar
1 teaspoon dark rum
½ loaf stale baguette, cut into ¼-inch slices (about 6 cups)
¾ cup heavy cream (optional), warmed at the last minute, for serving
Ground cinnamon (optional), for garnish

1. Lightly grease a 6-cup soufflé dish or heatproof glass bowl.

2. Melt the ¼ cup butter in a sauté pan over medium heat. Stir in the apple slices and fennel seeds and cook, stirring occasionally, until the apples soften, about 5 minutes. Set aside to cool.

3. Crack the eggs into a large bowl and beat lightly. Add the milk, sugar, rum, bread slices, and apple mixture and stir to mix. Ladle into the prepared dish and cover with aluminum foil, pinching around the edges to seal.

4. Set a trivet in the pressure cooker and pour in 2 cups water. Set the dish on top, lock on the lid, and bring to pressure over high heat, about 4 minutes. Reduce the heat to medium and cook for 20 minutes. Remove from the heat and let sit for 10 minutes to finish cooking.

5. With the steam vent pointed away from your face, gently release any remaining pressure. Remove the lid and puncture the foil to let steam escape. Lift off the foil with kitchen tongs and let the dish sit until cool enough to handle.

6. To serve, spoon the pudding onto individual plates. Pour the warm cream over the top and dust with a small amount of cinnamon. Or chill and serve the next day, without the warm cream.

◈ Sweet Cornmeal Pudding Cake with Rummy Corncob Syrup
Testing and tasting cornmeal puddings, from savory (see page 323) to sweet, is a culinary adventure in American cooking, as I found out in preparing this volume. And it's not only the taste variations but also the ways and means for turning out such a dish. A pressure cooker provides the means to have an old favorite in a short time, just as good as before.

Makes 4 to 6 servings

Unsalted butter, for greasing the dish
¼ cup sugar
2 cups milk
¼ teaspoon cardamom seeds, wrapped in cheesecloth or in a tea ball
½ cup fine yellow cornmeal
1 large egg
2 large egg yolks
2 tablespoons unsalted butter
2 tablespoons candied citrus peel or citrus marmalade
½ cup Rummy Corncob Syrup (page 336), for topping

1. Lightly grease a 1-quart soufflé dish or heatproof glass bowl. Set a trivet in the pressure cooker and pour in 1 cup water.

2. Place the sugar, milk, and cardamom in a medium-size saucepan. Heat until just beginning to boil, add the cornmeal, and simmer over medium heat, stirring, until thick, about 2 minutes. Remove from the heat and cool for a minute or two. Remove the cardamom.

3. Stir in the egg, egg yolks, butter, and candied citrus peel. Spoon the mixture into the soufflé dish and set it in the pressure cooker. Lock on the lid and bring to pressure over high heat, about 5 minutes. Reduce the heat to medium–high and cook for 10 minutes. Remove from the heat and let sit for 10 minutes to finish cooking.

4. With the steam vent pointed away from your face, gently release any remaining pressure. Remove the lid and, using 2 thick terry cloth kitchen towels, carefully lift the dish out of the pressure cooker. Pour the syrup over the top and serve.

Rummy Corncob Syrup   *As ever with American ingenuity and thriftiness, the cob of the corn is used, for something: Dried cobs carved into pipes became an artifact of the culture. Compost and pig feed is an enduring way to go for using the cobs. Then, there's corncob syrup; just cobs boiled up with sugar to make a syrup. A bit like maple syrup, only corny, it's a wonderful treat for top-ping any pancake, ice cream, or snow cone.*   Makes about ½ cup

3 to 4 corncobs, shaved of their kernels and cut into thirds
1 cup firmly packed dark brown sugar
3 cups water
1 tablespoon good-quality dark rum

1. Place the shaved corn cobs, brown sugar, and water in the pressure cooker. Lock on the lid and bring to pressure over high heat, 5 to 6 minutes. Reduce the heat to medium and cook for 6 minutes. Remove from the heat and let sit for 10 minutes to finish cooking.

2. With the steam vent pointed away from your face, gently release any remaining pressure. Remove and discard the cobs. Cook briskly over medium heat until the consistency of maple syrup, 10 to 15 minutes.

3. Stir in the rum and remove from the heat. Cool and use right away or store in the refrigerator, covered, for up to 6 months.

The Rave for Chocolate

As the seeds of the cacao tree pass from the hands of growers to the roasters to the processors and eventually to chefs and cooks, at each stage fortunes are made. The rave for chocolate is undeniable. One wonders how the culinary world got along before the age of exploration and importation of chocolate into Europe and points beyond. Getting in step, I offer two chocolate custards and two chocolate pudding cakes. They are easy chocolate delights, designed for the pressure cooker, that appease the lust for chocolate.

◇ Chocolate Almond Pudding Cake with Raspberry Sauce

This is as rich and dense as fudge, as gooey and moist as pudding, as light and springy as a cake. It's hard to pinpoint a single description, except maybe "intense chocolate dessert." The recipe is an adaptation of a dish Susanna Hoffman and I developed when we were writing The Well-Filled Microwave Cookbook. *It works for the pressure cooker for the same reasons it works in the microwave: almost no flour to toughen or weigh down the batter and steam cooking as the method of choice.*

Makes one 1-quart pudding cake, or 6 to 8 servings

Unsalted butter and granulated sugar, for preparing the dish

2 ounces bittersweet chocolate

2 ounces semisweet chocolate

6 tablespoons (¾ stick) unsalted butter

2 tablespoons Triple Sec or other orange liqueur

2 large eggs, separated

¼ cup granulated sugar

⅓ cup blanched almonds, pulverized in a food processor

2 tablespoons all-purpose flour

2 tablespoons confectioners' sugar, for topping

2 cups Raspberry Sauce (recipe follows), for topping

1. Lightly butter a 1-quart soufflé dish or heatproof glass bowl that will fit inside the pressure cooker. Sprinkle with sugar, turning the dish to coat the bottom and up the sides. Place a trivet in the pressure cooker and pour in 2 cups water.

2. Place the bittersweet and semisweet chocolate, butter, and Triple Sec in a medium-size microwave bowl or small saucepan. Microwave on high for 2 minutes or warm over medium heat until the butter melts and the chocolate softens. Stir, if necessary, to smooth the chocolate. Set aside.

3. Beat the egg yolks with the granulated sugar in a medium-size mixing bowl until pale yellow and thick. Blend in the chocolate mixture, almonds, and flour.

4. In a clean mixing bowl, beat the egg whites until soft peaks form. Fold them, one third at a time, into the chocolate and almond mixture. Spoon into the prepared dish and cover with aluminum foil, pinching around the edges to seal. Set the dish on the trivet in the pressure cooker, lock on the lid, and bring to pressure over high heat, about 4 minutes. Reduce the heat to medium and cook for 8 minutes. Remove from the heat and let sit for 5 minutes to finish cooking.

5. With the steam vent pointed away from your face, gently release any remaining pressure. Remove the lid and lift off the foil with kitchen tongs. Let sit, uncovered, for at least 20 minutes, or up to 4 hours.

6. When ready to serve, lift the dish out of the pressure cooker. Run a knife around the edge of the dish, set a plate over the top, and invert to unmold the pudding cake. Sift the confectioners' sugar through a fine-mesh sieve over the top of the pudding cake. Serve, accompanied by the raspberry sauce on the side.

Raspberry Sauce *At the height of the season, when raspberries are fragrant to the point of being heady, I take every opportunity to sauce desserts with them. With these, I never sieve out the seeds. Out of season, frozen, dry-pack raspberries make a fine sauce too, but then the seeds should be strained out because they are no longer supple and sweet.*   Makes about 2 cups

2 pints fresh raspberries or two 10- to 12-ounce packages
    frozen dry-pack raspberries
2 to 3 tablespoons confectioners' sugar, to your taste

Puree the raspberries in a food processor. If desired, press through a fine-mesh sieve to remove the seeds. Sift the sugar into the raspberries and stir to mix. Use right away or refrigerate for up to 3 days.

◇ Chocolate Ancho Chile Steamed Pudding Cake *Chocolate and chile pepper are a natural pair. In a pudding cake, they meld like old (actually ancient) boon companions who know exactly how to act together. Served warm, the pudding is more pudding-like. Later, at room temperature, it's more cake-like. I recommend Cherries in Ouzo Syrup (page 312) as extra profit, but a dollop of cream alone suffices.*

Makes one 1-quart pudding cake, or 6 to 8 servings

Unsalted butter, for greasing the dish
1 dried ancho chile pepper
3 ounces semisweet chocolate, broken up
6 tablespoons ($\frac{3}{4}$ stick) unsalted butter
$\frac{1}{4}$ teaspoon anise extract
1 tablespoon dry sherry
2 large eggs, separated
$\frac{1}{2}$ cup sugar
Pinch of ground cinnamon
2 tablespoons all-purpose flour
$\frac{1}{2}$ cup Crème Fraîche (page 282) or lightly whipped heavy cream, for garnish

1. Lightly grease a 1-quart soufflé dish or heatproof glass bowl. Set a trivet in the pressure cooker and pour in 2 cups water.

2. Tear open the ancho chile, remove the stem, and scrape away the seeds. Place the chile in a small saucepan with water barely to cover and bring to a boil. Simmer for 5 minutes, remove from the heat, and set aside for 30 to 45 minutes to soften. Scrape the pulp off the skin and discard the skin. Mash the pulp with 2 tablespoons of the soaking liquid. Set aside.

3. Combine the chocolate, butter, anise extract, and sherry in a small saucepan or microwave bowl. Heat on medium-low on the stove top or microwave on high until the chocolate is soft but still holds its shape, about 3 minutes either way. Set aside.

4. Beat together the egg yolks and sugar in a medium-size bowl until beginning to turn pale yellow. Whisk in the cinnamon, flour, ancho pulp, and chocolate mixture. In a clean bowl, beat the egg whites until soft peaks form and fold into the batter.

5. Pour the batter into the soufflé dish and cover with aluminum foil, pinching around the edges to seal. Set the dish on the trivet in the pressure cooker, lock on the lid, and bring to pressure over high heat, 3 to 4 minutes. Reduce the heat to low and cook for 25 minutes. Remove from the heat and let sit for 10 minutes to finish cooking.

6. With the steam vent pointed away from your face, gently release any remaining pressure. Remove the lid and lift off the foil with kitchen tongs. Let sit until cool enough to handle.

7. To serve, scoop the pudding cake onto individual plates and garnish with a dollop of Crème Fraîche. Or set aside at room temperature and leave out overnight without refrigerating. Serve the next day without reheating.

Chocolate Kirsch Custard with Whipped Cream and Shaved Chocolate

Not that chocolate doesn't go with more tastes than you could think of off the top of your head, but chocolate and cherries are a heavenly combination to sing about, and a cherry-flavored chocolate custard is a cloud-light delight from the pressure cooker. If fresh cherries are available, a bowl of them on the side would be a graceful touch.

Makes five 6-ounce ramekins

Unsalted butter, for greasing the ramekins

2 cups half-and-half

½ cup granulated sugar

4 ounces bittersweet chocolate

1 ounce unsweetened chocolate

2 tablespoons kirsch or other cherry liqueur

½ tablespoon water

4 large eggs

1 teaspoon vanilla extract

½ cup heavy cream

1 teaspoon confectioners' sugar

⅓ cup coarsely grated semisweet chocolate, for garnish

1. Lightly grease five 6-ounce ramekins. Set a trivet in the pressure cooker and pour in 1 cup water.

2. Stir together the half-and-half and granulated sugar in a microwave bowl or small saucepan. Microwave on high or warm over medium-high heat until steaming but not boiling, about 2 minutes. Set aside to cool.

3. Place the bittersweet and unsweetened chocolate, kirsch, and water in a microwave bowl or small saucepan. Microwave on high or warm over medium heat until the chocolate softens all the way through, about 2 minutes, stirring, if necessary, to smooth.

4. Beat the eggs in a medium-size bowl. Whisk in the half-and-half mixture. Add the chocolate mixture and then the vanilla, blending well.

5. Ladle into the prepared ramekins. Cover each with aluminum foil, pinching around the edges to seal. Place 3 of the ramekins on the trivet. Set another trivet over the top and set the remaining 2 ramekins on it. Lock on the lid and bring to pressure over high heat, 3 to 4 minutes. Reduce the heat to medium and cook for 10 minutes. Remove from the heat and let sit for 7 minutes to finish cooking.

6. With the steam vent pointed away from your face, gently release any remaining pressure. Remove the lid and puncture the foil covers to allow steam to escape. Let sit, uncovered, for 10 minutes more.

7. Meanwhile, beat together the cream and confectioners' sugar in a medium bowl until soft peaks form.

8. Using 2 thick terry cloth kitchen towels, carefully remove the ramekins from the pressure cooker. Garnish each custard with a large mound of the whipped cream, sprinkle grated chocolate over the top, and serve.

◇ Coconut Almond Custard with Sweet Azuki Beans and Blood Oranges

Warm or chilled, sweet custard with a side of sweet azuki beans is bound to be a topic for table talk. Garnished with rounds of flame-colored blood orange whose flavor is sweet enough to make you whimper, this dessert is a winner.

Makes five 6-ounce ramekins

Peanut oil, for greasing the ramekins
1⅔ cups unsweetened coconut milk
1½ teaspoons almond extract

⅓ cup fine granulated sugar (see Note)

4 large eggs, beaten

1½ cups Sweet Azuki Beans (page 344), for serving

1 blood orange, halved lengthwise, then sliced crosswise
¼ inch thick, for garnish

1. Lightly grease five 6-ounce ramekins with peanut oil. Set a trivet in the pressure cooker and pour in 1 cup water.

2. Whisk together the coconut milk, almond extract, and sugar until smooth and the sugar is dissolved. Whisk in the eggs. Ladle the mixture into the prepared ramekins. Cover each with aluminum foil and pinch around the edges to seal. Set 3 of the ramekins on the trivet. Place a second trivet over them and set the remaining 2 ramekins on it. Lock on the lid and bring to pressure over high heat, 3 to 4 minutes. Reduce the heat to medium-low and cook for 10 minutes. Remove from the heat and let sit for 5 minutes to finish cooking.

3. With the steam vent pointed away from your face, gently release any remaining pressure. Carefully remove the lid and puncture the foil covers to allow steam to escape. Let sit for 10 minutes more.

4. Using 2 thick terry cloth kitchen towels, carefully lift out the ramekins and set aside to cool for 10 minutes.

5. Run a knife around the edge of each custard and invert onto individual serving plates to unmold. Spoon some of the beans over the top and around the edges. Garnish with the blood orange slices and serve.

Note: Fine granulated sugar, also called baker's sugar, is available in specialty baking supply stores and better supermarkets. If you can't find it, substitute regular granulated sugar, not confectioners' sugar.

Sweet Azuki Beans *Not to be confused with small red beans, azukis are a special Old World bean considered in Japanese culture capable of beckoning good fortune and keeping away bad spirits when scattered around the house on New Year's. Most often they are cooked with sugar and mashed into a paste to fill sweet pastries. Here they are kept whole to tumble as they will around the plate and add textural interest to a smooth custard. Bulk or packaged azuki beans are available in Asian food stores and often in health food stores.* Makes 2 cups

Savory Azukis

Rarely are azuki beans served as a savory dish in Asian cooking, but I find them quite delicious spooned over steamed rice and topped with butter. For the unsweetened version, omit the sugar and the final 10 minutes of simmering in Step 2.

¾ cup azuki beans

2 cups water

¼ teaspoon salt

1½ cups sugar

1. Place the beans and water in the pressure cooker. Lock on the lid and bring to pressure over high heat, about 4 minutes. Reduce the heat to medium-low and cook for 10 minutes. Remove from the heat and let sit for 7 minutes to finish cooking.

2. With the steam vent pointed away from your face, gently release any remaining pressure. Carefully remove the lid. Stir in the salt and sugar and simmer, uncovered, for 10 minutes. Let cool, then use right away or refrigerate in the cooking liquid, covered, for up to 3 weeks.

◇ ◇ ◇

Coconut Almond Custard Variations

Instead of the almond extract, perfume the custard with:

• Lemongrass. Warm the coconut milk with a 6-inch length of lemongrass, cut into 3 or 4 pieces, over medium heat for 2 minutes. Strain out the lemongrass, cool, and proceed with the recipe.

• Ginger. Garnish with thin slivers of crystallized ginger.

• Lavender. Warm the coconut milk with 5 lavender blossoms over medium heat for 2 minutes. Strain out the lavender, cool, and proceed with the recipe. Garnish with fresh lavender blossoms.

Instead of the Sweet Azuki Beans and blood oranges, top the custard with:

• Toasted almond slices

• Toasted unsweetened coconut flakes

• Finely chopped mango tossed with fresh mint

• Lychee nuts

• Raspberries, only fresh, not frozen

• Filaments of crystallized orange peel

A particularly intriguing variation is a Thai dish of coconut custard steamed in a pumpkin shell. Scoop out the seeds from inside a small pumpkin or acorn squash, leaving the pulp intact. Fill the cavity with the coconut custard and steam in the pressure cooker over medium heat until the pumpkin is tender, 15 to 25 minutes, depending on the size.

Steamed Bananas in Rum Chocolate Caramel with Macadamia Nuts

Fresh banana rounds for topping cereal, banana halves for propping up an ice cream fudge sundae, a whole banana once a day for potassium. But cooked bananas are not a part of American cuisine, though they are popular elsewhere, in Caribbean, Chinese, Thai, and other Pacific Rim cuisines. In a homey dessert that's also enough of a surprise to serve guests at a casual dinner party, the pressure cooker brings sweet steamed bananas to the American table.

Makes 4 servings

Other Sprinkles for Steamed Bananas

Roasted peanuts
Toasted almonds
Toasted Coconut (page 218)
Raspberry Sauce (page 339)
Rummy Corncob Syrup
  (page 336)
Whipped cream
Crushed pineapple
Red hots
Candied ginger slices

¾ cup firmly packed dark brown sugar

¼ cup dark rum

⅓ cup heavy cream

2 bananas, halved crosswise

⅓ cup semisweet chocolate chips

¼ cup coarsely chopped dry-roasted macadamia nuts, for garnish

1. Combine the brown sugar, rum, and cream in the pressure cooker and whisk to mix. Add the bananas, lock on the lid, and bring to pressure over high heat, about 1 minute. Immediately remove from the heat and let sit for 3 minutes to finish cooking.

2. With the steam vent pointed away from your face, gently release any remaining pressure. Remove the lid and carefully transfer the bananas to a serving bowl or individual plates. Set aside.

3. Stir the chocolate chips into the sugar and cream mixture in the pressure cooker. Bring to a rapid boil, whisk to smooth, and pour over the bananas. Sprinkle with the macadamia nuts and serve right away.

Index
